COGNITIVE 2018

The Tenth International Conference on Advanced Cognitive Technologies and Applications

February 18 - 22, 2018

Barcelona, Spain

COGNITIVE 2018 Editors

Olga Chernavskaya, Lebeved Physical Institute, Moscow, Russia

Kazuhisa Miwa, Nagoya University, Japan

Printed from e-media with permission by:

Curran Associates, Inc.
57 Morehouse Lane
Red Hook, NY 12571

Some format issues inherent in the e-media version may also appear in this print version.

Printed by Curran Associates, Inc. (2018)

International Academy, Research, and Industry Association (IARIA)
412 Derby Way
Wilmington, DE 19810

Phone: (408) 893-6407
Fax: (408) 527-6351

petre@iaria.org

Additional copies of this publication are available from:

Curran Associates, Inc.
57 Morehouse Lane
Red Hook, NY 12571 USA
Phone: 845-758-0400
Fax: 845-758-2633
Email: curran@proceedings.com
Web: www.proceedings.com

COGNITIVE 2018

Forward

The Tenth International Conference on Advanced Cognitive Technologies and Applications (COGNITIVE 2018), held between February 18 - 22, 2018 - Barcelona, Spain, targeted advanced concepts, solutions and applications of artificial intelligence, knowledge processing, agents, as key-players, and autonomy as manifestation of self-organized entities and systems. The advances in applying ontology and semantics concepts, web-oriented agents, ambient intelligence, and coordination between autonomous entities led to different solutions on knowledge discovery, learning, and social solutions.

The conference had the following tracks:

- Brain information processing and informatics
- Artificial intelligence and cognition
- Agent-based adaptive systems
- Applications

Similar to the previous edition, this event attracted excellent contributions and active participation from all over the world. We were very pleased to receive top quality contributions.

We take here the opportunity to warmly thank all the members of the COGNITIVE 2018 technical program committee, as well as the numerous reviewers. The creation of such a high quality conference program would not have been possible without their involvement. We also kindly thank all the authors that dedicated much of their time and effort to contribute to COGNITIVE 2018. We truly believe that, thanks to all these efforts, the final conference program consisted of top quality contributions.

Also, this event could not have been a reality without the support of many individuals, organizations and sponsors. We also gratefully thank the members of the COGNITIVE 2018 organizing committee for their help in handling the logistics and for their work that made this professional meeting a success.

We hope COGNITIVE 2018 was a successful international forum for the exchange of ideas and results between academia and industry and to promote further progress in the area of cognitive technologies and applications. We also hope that Barcelona provided a pleasant environment during the conference and everyone saved some time for exploring this beautiful city.

COGNITIVE 2018 Chairs

COGNITIVE 2018 Steering Committee

Po-Hsun Cheng, National Kaohsiung Normal University, Taiwan
Jose Alfredo F. Costa, Federal University - UFRN, Brazil
Om Prakash Rishi, University of Kota, India
Kazuhisa Miwa, Nagoya University, Japan
Olga Chernavskaya, Lebeved Physical Institute, Moscow, Russia
Paul Smart, University of Southampton, UK
Ryotaro Kamimura, Tokai University, Japan
Olivier Chator, Ecole Nationale Supérieure de Cognitique, France

COGNITIVE 2018 Industry/Research Advisory Committee

Jayfus Tucker Doswell, The Juxtopia Group, Inc., USA
Tiago Thompsen Primo, Samsung Research Institute, Brazil
Galit Fuhrmann Alpert, computational neuroscientist, Israel

COGNITIVE 2018

Committee

COGNITIVE 2018 Steering Committee

Po-Hsun Cheng, National Kaohsiung Normal University, Taiwan
Jose Alfredo F. Costa, Federal University - UFRN, Brazil
Om Prakash Rishi, University of Kota, India
Kazuhisa Miwa, Nagoya University, Japan
Olga Chernavskaya, Lebeved Physical Institute, Moscow, Russia
Paul Smart, University of Southampton, UK
Ryotaro Kamimura, Tokai University, Japan
Olivier Chator, Ecole Nationale Supérieure de Cognitique, France

COGNITIVE 2018 Industry/Research Advisory Committee

Jayfus Tucker Doswell, The Juxtopia Group, Inc., USA
Tiago Thompsen Primo, Samsung Research Institute, Brazil
Galit Fuhrmann Alpert, computational neuroscientist, Israel

COGNITIVE 2018 Technical Program Committee

Mohammad Abido, King Fahd University of Petroleum & Minerals, Saudi Arabia
Witold Abramowicz, University of Economics and Business, Poland
Thomas Agotnes, University of Bergen, Norway
Jose Alfredo F. Costa, Federal University - UFRN, Brazil
Piotr Artiemjew, University of Warmia and Masuria, Poland
Petr Berka, University of Economics, Prague, Czech Republic
Gilberto Bernardes, INESC TEC, Portugal
Ateet Bhalla, Independent Consultant, India
Peter Brida, University of Zilina, Slovak Republic
Dilyana Budakova, Technical University of Sofia - Branch Plovdiv, Bulgaria
Albertas Caplinskas, Vilnius University, Lithuania
Facundo Carrillo, Laboratorio de Inteligencia Artificial Aplicada | ICC (UBA/CONICET), Buenos Aires, Argentina
Francesco Carlo Morabito, University Mediterranea of Reggio Calabria, Italy
Yaser Chaaban, Leibniz University of Hanover, Germany
Olivier Chator, Ecole Nationale Supérieure de Cognitique, France
Po-Hsun Cheng, National Kaohsiung Normal University, Taiwan
Olga Chernavskaya, Lebeved Physical Institute, Moscow, Russia
Sunil Choenni, Dutch Ministry of Security & Justice / Rotterdam University of Applied Sciences, Netherlands
Helder Coelho, Universidade de Lisboa, Portugal

Leonardo Dagui de Oliveira, University of São Paulo, Brazil
Darryl N. Davis, University of Hull, UK
Jayfus Tucker Doswell, The Juxtopia Group, Inc., USA
António Dourado, University of Coimbra, Portugal
Birgitta Dresp-Langley, Centre National de la Recherche Scientifique (CNRS) | ICube Lab, CNRS - University of Strasbourg, France
Wlodzislaw Duch, Nicolaus Copernicus University (UMK), Torun, Poland
Mounîm A. El Yacoubi, Telecom SudParis, France
Diego Fernandez Slezak, Universidad de Buenos Aires, Argentina
Galit Fuhrmann Alpert, computational neuroscientist, Israel
Mauro Gaggero, National Research Council of Italy, Italy
Franck Gechter, Université de Technologie de Belfort Montbéliard - UBFC, France
Alessandro Giuliani, University of Cagliari, Italy
Vincent Gripon, Institut Mines-Télécom, France
Foteini Grivokostopoulou, University of Patras, Greece
Fikret Gürgen, Bogazici University, Turkey
Jianye Hao, Tianjin University, China
Ioannis Hatzilygeroudis, University of Patras, Greece
Marion Hersh, University of Glasgow, UK
Koen Hindriks, Delft University of Technology, Netherlands
Tzung-Pei Hong, National University of Kaohsiung, Taiwan
Gongping Huang, Northwestern Polytechical University, China
Zhisheng Huang, Vrije University, Netherlands
Xinghua Jia, ULC Robotics, USA
Jianmin Jiang, Shenzhen University, China
Ryotaro Kamimura, Tokai University, Japan
Zhao Kang, University of Electronic Science and Technology, China
Jozef Kelemen, Institute of Computer Science - Silesian University, Opava, Czech Republic
Peter Kieseberg, SBA Research, Austria
Jonghwa Kim, University of Science & Technology (UST), Korea
Raşit Köker, Sakarya Üniversitesi, Turkey
Tom Krajnik, Artificial Intelligence Centre - Czech Technical University in Prague, Czech Republic
Miroslav Kulich, Czech Technical University in Prague, Czech Republic
Ruggero Donida Labati, Università degli Studi di Milano, Italy
Minho Lee, Kyungpook National University, Republic of Korea
Hai (Helen) Li, University of Pittsburgh, USA
Sheng Li, Northeastern University, Boston, USA
Yaliang Li, SUNY Buffalo, USA
Hakim Lounis, Universite du Quebec a Montreal (UQAM), Canada
Prabhat Mahanti, University of New Brunswick, Canada
Angel Alejandro Maldonado-Ramírez, CINVESTAV Campus Saltillo, Mexico
Giuseppe Mangioni, DIEEI - University of Catania, Italy
Francesco Marcelloni, University of Pisa, Italy
Franova Marta, CNRS, LRI & INRIA, France
Kathryn Merrick, University of New South Wales, Canberra, Australia
John-Jules Charles Meyer, Utrecht University, Netherlands
Toshiro Minami, KIIS, Japan
Kazuhisa Miwa, Nagoya University, Japan

Table of Contents

Copyright Information

Cartesian Systemic Emergence: Tackling Underspecified Notions in Incomplete Domains

Marta Franova, Yves Kodratoff
LRI, UMR8623 du CNRS & INRIA Saclay
Bât. 660, Orsay, France
e-mail: mf@lri.fr, yvekod@gmail.com

Abstract—**Pulsation is a model for a particular evolutive improvement that handles control and prevention in intelligent systems built following this 'pulsative' model in incomplete domains. Cartesian systemic emergence presented in this paper answers the question of strategic aspects of building such systems. The main problem to tackle here is working with informal specifications while aiming at their formalization in a way that is driven by the pulsation model.**

Keywords-Cartesian Systemic Emergence; pulsation; symbiosis of information; Symbiotic Recursive Pulsative Systems; practical completeness; human reasoning mechanisms; Computational Cognitive Science.

I. Introduction

In this paper, we present Cartesian systemic emergence (CSE) that describes how to handle what we call a pulsation ([6], redefined below in Section II.C), that is a particular evolutive improvement in incomplete domains. The desired improvements have to guarantee control and prevention in the built intelligent system. By lack of control is meant here an agreement to overlook some secondary effects of the improvements.

Our answer to the question of how to achieve this goal has several facets. Namely, tackling underspecified symbiosis of information, recursion, on-purpose solution invention instead of a search in a given search space and formulating fruitful experiments during this invention. All these facets are briefly described in order to allow us to present a self-containing coherent description of CSE. These facets are related to the topics of human reasoning mechanisms, cognitive and computation models, human cognitive functions and their relationship, and even to modelling human multi-perception mechanisms.

CSE is presented here on a non-trivial toy example. However, in the field of program synthesis from formal specifications via inductive theorem proving, an ongoing research takes place [5], productively using CSE's know-how.

The purpose of this paper is four-fold:

- Propose a general method - called Cartesian Systemic Emergence - implementing strategic aspects of pulsation.
- Illustrate this method (born from our work on automating program construction [5]) on a simpler example that does not concern program construction, though it deals with a problem that many researchers may be facing.
- Show that the main problem to handle in CSE is working with informal specifications for the purpose of their formalized delimitation in coherence with the pulsation model.
- Mention the main problems and challenges addressed by CSE to various fields of Cognitive Science.

The paper is organized as follows. In Section II, we present fundamental notions necessary for understanding CSE, such as symbiosis and pulsation. We present also a difference between deductive and formal systems. Section III presents CSE. Namely, in Section III.A, we first present the rigorous mechanism that inspired CSE. Then, in Sections III.B and III.C, we present CSE on a non-trivial toy example. In Section IV we say a few words about the relevance of CSE to (Computational) Cognitive Science.

II. Fundamental Notions

In this section we are going to present the notions that will be used in the description of CSE.

A. Symbiosis

By *symbiosis* we understand a composition of parts that is separation-sensitive. This means that a separation of one or several parts leads to extinction or irrecoverable mutilation of the whole and all the involved parts. The most available example of symbiosis is the well-known puzzle-like picture of 'two women in one' as given in [10]. Different overlapping features show either a young or an old woman. The important point is that the features necessary to see the young or the old woman are common to both visions, say for example their 'little chin versus big nose' or their 'necklace versus lips'. If we withdraw these common features of different interpretation, the women disappear, only leaving their common coat and a decorative feather in their hair. This defines a symbiotic occurrence of both women, that is, there exist a subset of features (here, almost all of them, but this is not necessary) such that deleting them from one occurrence induces an unrecoverable loss in both occurrences. As we show in [6], in some domains, a recursive representation may capture symbiosis of information. We explain there that non-primitive recursion (known mostly through Ackermann's function) captures prevention and control in handling symbiotic information. In CSE, *symbiotic feature of information* is one of the most important features.

In contrast to *symbiosis*, we understand by *synergy* a composition the parts of which are not separation-sensitive. Sometimes, synergy is called also modular composition.

B. *Deductive and Formal systems*

In our work, we introduce a difference between a deductive and a formal system. When a formal system is considered in science, its consistence is considered in terms of non existence of a proof for a formula as well as for its negation in this system. By deductive system we understand a system developed with a concrete real-world application as a model. This means that the consistence of deductive systems is proved by the existence of a concrete model. In fact, a deductive system is in our work viewed as a result of development of a relevant axiomatic system for a particular intended application. In the final stage of development, a deductive system can be viewed as a formal system, however, its completeness or incompleteness is not viewed from a theoretical point of view but from the point of view of a pragmatic evaluation. For instance, Gödel has shown the theoretical incompleteness of Natural Numbers (NAT) (i.e., the set 0, 1, 2, ...). However, when we consider natural numbers as a deductive theory the intended model of which are the numbers we all *use*, we can consider NAT as practically complete. In other words, for deductive systems, we introduce the notion of *practical completeness*. Practical completeness means that we all agree on the interpretation (i.e., the model) that is considered. Usually, this is allowed when there is no ambiguity as to the exact meaning of the notions in their practical manipulations. When there is a possibility of such an ambiguity, this indicates that the developed deductive system is incomplete. We say that the notions that are ambiguous are *informally specified* (or *defined*) notions. Selecting a concrete version of the intended model is only possible when the corresponding notions have been completed through a relevant completion of the developed deductive theory.

In order to illustrate the informal character of notions in incomplete theories, let us recall that, in a geometry obtained from Euclid's geometry by eliminating the postulate of parallels, a triangle can be defined. However, in this incomplete 'theory', the sum of the triangle angles may differ from 180°. This means that the notion of triangle is incompletely defined in this particular purged (or mutilated) Euclid's geometry. In practice, it means that an informal definition covers several possible different interpretations of each 'defined' object. It illustrates what we mean by an informal definition. This means also that the completion process of a definition (its emergence) needs to orient a choice – or rather, a construction – of an interpretation that is suitable for each particular problem to be solved. Such a choice, as well as the completion process, is guided by the formalization objectives oriented towards a convenient solution of the informally specified problem. This means in practice that, in any completion process, the goal is to formulate experiments oriented towards a construction of relevant constraints for the intended objective as well as the final delimitation of notions. This example illustrates also why we consider NAT as practically complete system. In order to illustrate the 'practical completeness' of natural numbers, think how all computer driven money exchanges in the world use the same intended model of the natural numbers.

In order to guarantee a rigorous development of deductive systems that corresponds to intended real-world technological applications, we have introduced the notion of pulsation [6]. We are going now to recall its main features.

C. *Pulsation*

Pulsation concerns incomplete or/and evolutive systems. The usual problem solving strategy can be represented formally by the formula

$$\forall \text{ Problem } \exists \text{ Idea Leads\_to\_a\_solution(Idea,Problem)}. \quad (1)$$

Another, more ambitious, goal can be represented by the formula

$$\exists \text{ Idea } \forall \text{ Problem Leads\_to\_a\_solution(Idea,Problem)}. \quad (2)$$

From implementation point of view, (2) can be written also as the specification

$$\exists\text{system } \forall\text{problem Solves(system,problem)}. \quad (3)$$

There are two main differences between these two paradigms. The first difference is that, in (1), each problem or a class of problems related to a system can have its own solution. However, in (2), a unique, universal solution is looked for. The first paradigm leads to a library of particular heuristics, while the second paradigm results in one universal method.

The second difference is that control and prevention are implicitly present in this second paradigm. This points out towards non-primitive recursion and its simple version, the well-known Ackermann's function. In [6], we show how Ackermann's function can be constructed so that the process of its construction illustrates the meaning of control and prevention of symbiotic information. This analogy is used to define the pulsation, i.e., evolutive improvement of incomplete systems in terms of an infinite sequence of constructed recursive systems - represented by axiomatic theories - such that each system in this sequence contains all the previously constructed systems and is more complex than all the previously constructed systems. So, we have

$$T_0 \subset T_1 \subset \ldots \subset T_n \subset \ldots \quad (4)$$

and

$$T_{i+1} = T_i + A_{i+1} \quad (5)$$

where A_{i+1} is a system of axioms that extends T_i. In terms of the paradigm (2), T_{i+1} allows to solve problems of considered primitive recursive system that had no solution in the previously constructed theories.

III. CARTESIAN SYSTEMIC EMERGENCE

As we said above, CSE is our answer to the following question: Knowing that we are working with informally specified systems represented by formalized theories, how the process of pulsation helps us to construct these systems?

This section is divided as follows. Firstly, in Section III.A, we shall present the mechanism of CM-formula construction that will introduce a vocabulary necessary for understanding the last two parts. Since this mechanism has been previously presented [4], our presentation here will be based on the suitability of drawing an analogy with CSE, in the same way as we perceive it while building our program synthesis system. We shall present it while insisting on parts that are the most important for working with incomplete theories. Secondly, in Section III.B, we shall present a specification of a concrete situation: A toy, though non-trivial, example. Thirdly, in Section III.C, we shall provide a description of CSE on this toy example.

A. *CM-formula construction for CSE*

In order to show that CSE is rigorous even without its formal description at the present state of our work, we shall present now its more formalized version in the context of inductive theorem proving (ITP). Indeed, ITP handles recursive notions. In other words, an illustration of ITP framework allows to mirror the emergence work also with informal specifications where the notions involved need to be recursively defined.

Let us proceed to this formalized version known as CM-formula construction and used in the framework of the development of a concrete Symbiotic Recursive Pulsative System (SRPS), as illustrated in [5].

For simplicity, let us suppose that, in an axiomatic theory A, F is a binary recursive predicate and t_1 and t_2 are two terms in A. We restrict here ourselves to primitive recursive theories only. CM-formula construction concerns either proving that $F(t_1,t_2)$ is true or finding conditions under which $F(t_1,t_2)$ might be true. In both cases, for simplicity, we shall speak of proving $F(t_1,t_2)$. CM-formula construction has been initially developed for program synthesis via inductive theorem proving. Thus, it is supposed that some existentially quantified variables may occur in $F(t_1,t_2)$. The mechanism works however also for the cases when there is no existentially quantified variable. In our description we shall point out the differences between these two cases.

Note that when the predicate F is defined in A, its definition expresses the relationship between (or constraints on) the variables x and y so that F(x,y) is true. Informally we may say that the definition of F expresses everything that is needed for F(x,y) to be true. CM-formula construction is based on this simple understanding. On the other hand, in program synthesis, usually $F(t_1,t_2)$ contains existentially quantified variables. This means that a simple unfolding of $F(t_1,t_2)$ using the definition of F and the functions involved in t_1 and t_2 does not lead to explicit values for these existentially quantified variables. The knack here consists in introducing a new type of arguments in the atomic formula to be proven. We call them *pivotal arguments*, since focusing on them enables to suitably handle existentially quantified variables and enables to decompose complex problems (such as strategic aspects of a proof) to conceptually simpler problems while remaining in the context of construction of possibly missing information (such as conditions or new axioms). Among the most usual problems generated is a transformation of a term into another, possibly finding sufficient conditions for this transformation. These pivotal arguments are denoted by ξ (or ξ' etc.) in the following.

Once a pivotal argument has been chosen (first step of the procedure), it replaces, in a purely syntactical way, one of the arguments of the given formula. In this presentation, let us suppose that we have chosen to work with $F(t_1,\xi)$, the second argument being chosen as the pivotal one. In an artificial, but custom-made manner, we state $C = \{\xi \mid F(t_1,\xi)$ is true$\}$. Implicitly, this can be viewed as a desire to find ξ such that $F(t_1,\xi)$ is true. Except the syntactical similarity with the formula to be proven, in this step, there is no semantic consideration postulating that $F(t_1,\xi)$ is true. It simply represents a 'quite-precise' purpose of trying to go from $F(t_1,\xi)$ to $F(t_1,t_2)$ while preserving the truth of $F(t_1,\xi)$.

In the second step, we unfold $F(t_1,\xi)$ using the definition of F and of the functions involved in the formulation of the term t_1. Given the axioms defining F and the functions occurring in t_1, we are thus able to obtain a set C_1 expressing the conditions on the set $\{ \xi \}$ for which $F(t_1,\xi)$ is true. In other words, calling 'cond' these conditions and C_1 the set of the ξ such that cond(ξ) is true, we define C_1 by $C_1 = \{\xi \mid \text{cond}(\xi)\}$. This implicitly means that C_1 is a constructed solution space in which we have to look for a solution of our initial desire to find ξ such that $F(t_1,\xi)$ is true.

We can also say that, with the help of the given axioms, we build a 'cond' such that the formula

$$\forall\xi \in C_1, F(t_1,\xi) \text{ is true.} \quad (6).$$

The third step relies on the fact that F is recursive and thus a recursive call in its definition suggests that an available induction hypothesis is available to prove (6).

In the third step, using the conditions in C_1 obtained in the second step, the induction hypothesis is applied. Thus, we build a form of ξ such that $F(t_1,\xi)$ is related to $F(t_1,t_2)$ by using the induction hypothesis. This simply means that ξ will be expressed in terms of involved operators. For the sake of clarity, let us call ξ_C the result of applying the induction hypothesis to C_1 resulting in its subset $C_2 = \{ \xi_C \mid \text{cond}_2(\xi_C)\}$. As we just said, ξ_C is expressed in terms of involved operators related to the given problem. Thus, it is no more as abstract as it was case in the first step. C_2 is thus such that $F(t_1,\xi_C)$ is true.

In the fourth step, we proceed to prove that t_2 belongs to C_2. If t_2 does not contain existential quantifiers, this is done by verifying $\text{cond}_2(t_2)$. If t_2 contains existentially quantified variables, this is achieved by a detour. We try to solve the problem $\text{cond}_2(\xi_C) \Rightarrow \exists\sigma\ (\xi_C = \sigma t_2)$, where σ has to provide a suitable instantiation for the existentially quantified variables in t_2. This solution may be recursive. With such an obtained σ we have then to prove $F(t_1,\sigma t_2)$. In other words, we have to prove that ξ_C and t_2 can be made identical (modulo substitution) when $\text{cond}_2(\xi_C)$ holds. If we succeed doing so, the proof is completed. If not, we need to start an additional step.

In this fifth step, a new lemma $cond_2(\xi_C) \Rightarrow \exists\sigma (\xi_C = \sigma t_2)$ with an appropriate quantification of the involved variables is generated. This lemma can be seen as a new experience to be performed. In some cases, this may lead to generating missing subroutines (as illustrated in [3]). An infinite sequence of 'failure formulas', i.e., lemmas or missing axioms, may be generated. It is therefore important that the generated sequence may be generalized either by using appropriate tools, some of which are still to be built, or relying on human ingenuity. The generalized formula logically covers the infinite sequence of lemmas or missing axioms and it thus fills the gap that cannot be overcome by a purely deductive formal approach to theorem proving or decision procedures. In the case of generation of missing axioms, the process of the initial theory completion is performed in coherence with the above described model of evolutive improvement of incomplete theories, i.e., pulsation. Be it achieved with or without human interaction, the resulting system is logically coherent by construction.

B. *Specification of a toy example*

In an ideal world, the transmission of information is a transitive relation. In other words, if x, y and z are variables for some conveyors of a given message, we can formally write

$$\text{conveys}(x,y) \ \& \ \text{conveys}(y,z) \Rightarrow \text{conveys}(x,z). \quad (7)$$

However, in the well-known children 'phone' play where a first child conveys a sentence to the second, and so on, the last child comes out usually with a sentence that has (almost) nothing to do with the initial message. In a more serious context, Francis Bacon has described several centuries ago how a bad transmission of work of Ancients not only mutilated their work, but also the original fertility (which may be seen as an intention for pulsation mentioned above) has been lost in such a transmission.

In our previous works, we have shown that symbiotic systems are very difficult to describe in the process of their construction. Indeed such a description goes back and forth connecting maybe yet non-existing parts together with already existing parts. This 'circular inductive' behavior has been properly described by Descartes in [2], p. 797. This is the reason why we speak of Cartesian systemic emergence. It concerns the development of symbiotic systems. In tribute to Descartes, who certainly faced this situation too, let us consider the following problem.

Let us suppose that René is a founder of a novel scientific field with a high pulsative potential. Referring back to the bad founders' experience in the past (mentioned by Bacon), he needs to ask himself: How to build some 'works' able to convey the full symbiotic complexity while protecting timelessly the pulsative potential of the field? In a more formal way, René must solve the problem

$$\exists \text{works} \ \forall \text{disciple conveys(René, works)} \ \& \ \text{conveys(works,disciple)} \Rightarrow \text{essential\_of(René)} = \text{essential\_of(disciple)} \quad (8)$$

Note that this problem has the same logical structure as the second paradigm presented in the form (3), i.e.

$$\exists \text{system} \ \forall \text{problem Solves(system,problem)}.$$

Description (8) requires some precisions. First of all, the notions that appear here are not defined in a rigorous way. They are only specified in an informal way in terms of some non-formal criteria. For instance, we know that 'to convey' in this description has to be transitive. However, at present, we do not know whether René, while trying to solve (8), is not forced to adopt some compromises concerning the final delimitation of this notion in this particular context aiming at conveying the full symbiotic complexity while protecting timelessly the pulsative potential of the field. In other words, a solution for (8) has to emerge simultaneously with suitable formalizations (thus, the final definitions) of notions that occur in (8). We shall say that all the notions in (8) are of *evolutive* and *flexible* character. In order to distinguish formal descriptions from descriptions containing evolutive and flexible notions, we call the latter *informal specifications*. CSE concerns thus informal specifications. It will become clear that emergence here cannot be seen as a sophisticated scanning through a given, in advance selected, search space. A solution for (8) does not result from a decision procedure. It is a result of formulating some significant relevant experiments aiming at obtaining simultaneously a concrete value for 'works' as well as a final delimitation of notions occurring in (8). This final delimitation will contain all the compromises adopted during the emergence. This means that solving (8) depends heavily on the ability of the developed mechanisms to create relevant experiments. We have shown in section III.A that CM-formula construction can be seen as a such relevant experiences activator.

C. *CSE through CM-formula construction*

Let us show now how CM-formula construction is applied to solving (8).

Since we look here for a concrete instance of 'works' that verifies (8), we replace 'works' by a pivotal argument ξ. We thus change the original status of 'works' from unknown variable to pivotal argument. This means underlining the importance of this pivotal argument for creating relevant experiences that may lead to the construction of a suitable solution for 'works'.

We thus obtain

$$\text{conveys(René},\xi) \ \& \ \text{conveys}(\xi,\text{disciple}) \Rightarrow \text{essential\_of(René)} = \text{essential\_of(disciple)} \quad (9)$$

Note that presently, in (9), the predicate 'conveys' as well as the function 'essential_of' are evolutive and flexible, as opposed to the formal operators handled in CM-formula construction. The two operators 'conveys' and 'essential_of' are here specified only informally by some set of sentences that represent the most general constraints that concern these notions. This set of sentences is not a set of formal definitions, as takes place with the formal operators handled in CM-formula construction. This means that instead of the evaluation of these operators, as we have seen in CM-formula construction, we shall replace these notions by their informal descriptions. We shall denote by $Descript_t$ the set of sentences specifying 'to convey' and by $Descript_e$ the set of sentences specifying 'essence_of'. Then, in a purely artificial way we shall write

$$Descript_t(René,\xi) \; \& \; Descript_t(\xi,disciple) \Rightarrow Descript_e(René) = Descript_e(disciple) \quad (10)$$

Note that we need now to start to 'move' things in a way similar to CM-formula construction. In other words, we have to start to create some relevant experiences that would enable the emergence of less informal descriptions of our operators and more concrete information about ξ. Since René is here a constant of the problem, we shall focus on the universally quantified variable 'disciple'. In order to create relevant experiences, we shall take a concrete example of 'disciple', say d_0, and try to find a particular informal solution for the problem

$$Descript_t(René,\xi) \; \& \; Descript_t(\xi, d0) \Rightarrow Descript_e(René) = Descript_e(d0) \quad (11)$$

The peculiarity of the informal solution we are looking for lies in the fact that we have to resolve the constraints expressed by this problem, while keeping in mind that the solution we are looking for must be applicable (thus relevant) to our general problem (8). This means that we consciously work here simultaneously on the above mentioned two paradigms (1) and (2). This is necessary to guarantee that we are working in the framework of a pulsation model. In other words, we try to find some refinement of the operators specified by their descriptors in (11) so that the resulting refinements can be, without loss of generality, applied also to other instances of 'disciple'. Our goal is thus to determine what are the basic problems (BP) that have to be solved while keeping our goal of solving (11) for d_0 as well as for other instances of 'disciple'. These basic problems will not only give more information about ξ that is looked for but also ξ will be expressed in terms of the solutions obtained for these BP. Thus, more concrete information about the final 'works' will be found. Note that it may happen, as it is the case in CM-formula construction, that new problems are discovered while solving BP.

The process described so far is however only a beginning. Since solutions for BP are still informal, we continue creating experiences for other instances of 'disciple'. Solving, even though incompletely, these BP in a coherent manner for many highly varied instances of 'disciple' is a good start for beginning an informal development of T_0 in pulsation sequence T_0, T_1, T_2, ...

For some instances of 'disciple' it may happen that new problems (NP) are recognized. Thus, a coherent solution with the solutions for BP has to be built. It may happen that the informal solutions found for BP are shown unsuitable for an extension with respect to NP. Thus, based on this constructive feedback, new solutions for BP ∪ NP need to be constructed. The flexibility of informal formulations of BP and NP allows, in general, to generate a new reformulation that covers a real possibility of coherently solving BP ∪ NP. Let us denote by ALLNP the set of all problems generated for all considered experimental instances of 'disciple'. The above process is thus repeated on many instances of 'disciple' so that the finalized solution for BP ∪ ALLNP represents the basis for an implementation of the solution expressed in the axiomatic framework of T_0. Of course, since we cannot examine all concrete instances of 'disciple', T_0 is potentially incomplete. This means that the notions constructed for T_0 are prone to a modification. However, with respect to the pulsative model of their development in the construction process, all these formalized notions are flexible for further improvement. In other words, the pulsative model of development, as defined here, guarantees the flexibility of the notions. The process is both flexible and rigorous.

Note that this process indeed illustrates how, during the construction process, we consider simultaneously the two above paradigms (1) and (2). In this emergence process, we simultaneously follow the general goal specified by the second paradigm (2) and we work with experiences in the framework of the first paradigm (1).

We call *oscillation* this particular feature of CSE in the pulsation model. Oscillation is thus considered at a local level for a particular T_i, while pulsation is a model that covers an infinite sequence of theories T_j verifying the above mentioned conditions ($i, j \in NAT$).

IV. CSE AND COMPUTATIONAL COGNITIVE SCIENCE

Cartesian systemic emergence seems to us heavily related to the topic of human reasoning mechanisms, cognitive and computation models, human cognitive functions and their relationship, and even to modeling human multi-perception mechanisms.

In [1], Bermúdez pointed out the influence of Computer Science on the development of Cognitive Science Paradigms. Cartesian Systemic Emergence, as an example of symbiotic thinking (i.e., simultaneously focusing mentally on several different topics), represents a way of thinking which, as far as we know, is not studied in Cognitive Science. One cause may be that symbiotic thinking is considered as not achievable in Cognitive Science. For instance, John Medina claims in [9] that our brain *is not conceived* to handle simultaneously several different topics. We may agree that it may be impossible for a non-trained person to perform two different physical challenging tasks. We believe, however, that this opinion, when generalized to mental processes, is born from existing brain synergic models (that are thus non symbiotic) as well as from some misinterpretations of external observations.

In particular, the observation of symbiotic modules in action may have problems with comprehending the emergence of a solution in an active performance. At least, its explication is bound to seem obscure and a clear (but inexact) presentation of its functioning tends to explain the modules roles once their interaction is completed, as if they were independent of each other, i.e., using a synergic model.

The problem of spotting symbiotic interaction, in itself, is therefore hard to tackle. This difficulty becomes obvious when psychoanalysis describes harmful relationships of the sick person with his/her self. A solution to the problems seems to become possible when, as suggested by famous psychoanalyst C. G. Jung, a symbiotic solution starts to be built following the rule that: "... it is as much a vital necessity for the unconscious to be joined to the conscious as it is for the latter not to lose contact with the unconscious." ([8], section 457, p. 298). We could use a similar way of speech to express the fact that two modules of an emerging system should not 'lose contact' one with the other.

It follows that Cartesian systemic emergence might well be part of a challenge for Cognitive Science. This will be achieved by developing Cognitive Science models that capture all the essential characteristics of CSE, by finding methods and tools to study the emergence process in an active performance and developing on-purpose computational models for this particular way of thinking. Even though the topic is challenging, we are convinced that a strong desire or need to solve problems that CSE suggests to Cognitive Science will lead soon or later to a fruitful empowerment of Cognitive Science. We hope that the models presented in the present paper might be of help in such a difficult task.

V. Conclusion

In this paper we have introduced and exemplified a general method called Cartesian Systemic Emergence (CSE) that implements strategic aspects of pulsation (introduced previously in [6]). We have shown that the main problem to handle in CSE is working with informal specifications for the purpose of their formalized delimitation in coherence with the pulsation model. We have illustrated that, in this delimitation context, CSE is very convenient as an experiences activator. We have also mentioned the main problems and challenges addressed by CSE to various fields of Cognitive Science.

We have been led to CSE in two complementary ways. Firstly, CSE is a by-product of our research on Program Synthesis from their formal specifications as presented by Manna and Waldinger in [11]. Secondly, our efforts in this domain, so to say, 'forced' us to handle the problem of automating recursive programs synthesis in incomplete domains [4], which, in turn, led us to recognize the necessity of CSE. In other words, this paper is a result of our formalization of the method that guided, from the start, our program synthesis research. However, we have also recognized the great potential of this method to model and solve other real-world problems. CSE thus seems a know-how that might show its importance in all incomplete domains where solving problems requires rigor, as well as pragmatic considerations and experimentations.

Cognitive Science already interacted with computer science in a topic that somewhat 'looks like' ours, namely the so called Emergent Computing that was defined in the beginning of the nineties by Stephanie Forrest [12] by "Emergent computation is proposed in the study of self-organization, collective and cooperative behavior." The comprehensive review of Xiao, Zhang and Huang [13] provides different views on how to define it. None of these definitions alludes to any symbiosis imposed on Emergent Computing systems, a theme central to our research. It is still an open problem, and an interesting research field, to decide whether human brain does or not use symbiotic modules for thinking, at least for deep thinking, such as the one of a mathematician trying to prove a still unproved theorem, where the proof the theorem demands completion of some currently available incomplete specification of what is to be proven. At any rate, the views presented in this paper constitute a challenge for Cognitive Science, and we cannot presently do more than hoping it will be a fruitful challenge.

Acknowledgment

We thank to Michèle Sebag and Yannis Manoussakis for a moral support. Anonymous referees of the submitted version provided a very useful feedback.

References

[1] J. L. Bermúdez, Cognitive Science: An Introduction to the Science of the Mind, Cambridge University Press, 2014.

[2] R. Descartes, Complete Works (Oeuvres philosophiques), Édition de F. Alquié, Vol. 1, Bordas, 1988.

[3] M. Franova, "A Construction of Several Definitions Recursive over the Variable under the Exponent for the Exponent function," Rapport de Recherche No.1519, L.R.I., Université de Paris-Sud, Orsay, France, June, 2009.

[4] M. Franova, "Cartesian versus Newtonian Paradigms for Recursive Program Synthesis," International Journal on Advances in Systems and Measurements, vol. 7, no 3&4, pp. 209-222, 2014.

[5] M. Franova and Y. Kodratoff, "Cartesian Handling Informal Specifications in Incomplete Frameworks," Proc. INTELLI 2016, The Fifth International Conference on Intelligent Systems and Applications, pp. 100-107, 2016.

[6] M. Franova and Y. Kodratoff, "A Model of Pulsation for Evolutive Formalizing Incomplete Intelligent Systems," Proc INTELLI 2017, The Sixth International Conference on Intelligent Systems and Applications, pp. 1 - 6, 2017.

[7] K. Gödel, "Some metamathematical results on completeness and consistency" in J. van Heijenoort: From Frege to Godel, A source book in mathematical logic, 1879-1931, Harvard University Press, Cambridge, Massachusets, 592-618, 1967.

[8] C. G. Jung, Symbols of transformation, Princeton University Press, 1956.

[9] J. Medina, Brain Rules, Pear Press, 2008.

[10] E. W. Weisstein, Young Girl-Old Woman Illusion; From MathWorld - A Wolfram Web Resource. http://mathworld.wolfram.com/YoungGirl-OldWomanIllusion.html . (accessed January 2, 2018)

[11] Z. Manna and R.Waldinger, "A Deductive Approach to Program Synthesis", ACM Transactions on Programming Languages and Systems, Vol. 2., No.1, January, 1980, 90-121.

[12] Stephanie Forrest, "Emergent Computation: Self-Organizing, Collective, and Cooperative Phenomena in Natural and Artificial Computing Networks" 1991, Physica D, Vol. 42, Nos. 1–3, pp.1–11.

[13] Xiao R., Zhang Y. and Huang Z., "Emergent computation of complex systems: a comprehensive review", Int. J. Bio-Inspired Computation, Vol. 7, No. 2, 2015, pp.126–139.

Feature Extraction Process with an Adaptive Filter on Brain Signals Motion Intention Classification

Luis F. Marín-Urías, J. Alejandro Vásquez-Santacruz, Rogelio de J. Portillo-Vélez, Félix O. Rivera-Hernández
Facultad de Ingeniería
Universidad Veracruzana
Boca del Río, Ver. Mexico
e-mail: luismarin@uv.mx

Mario Castelán
Robótica y Manufactura Avanzada
CINVESTAV - IPN
Ramos Arispe, 25900, Mexico
e-mail: mario.mcastelan@cinvestav.mx

Abstract—**Identifying motor imagery from an electroencephalogram (EEG) has been researched from different perspectives and methods of classification. Translating a brain signal into a language understandable for machines relies on feature extraction techniques, which vary from working on the frequency domain to dealing with raw data. Using statistical information to classify motor imagery has shown encouraging results. In this paper we benefit from statistical approaches and propose a different perspective to boost results obtained through brain signals provided by a low cost EEG. Our motivation is based on the natural separability of classes exhibited by statistical indicators such as the mean and standard deviation. A special emphasis in our method is made on filtering data to subject readings in an adaptive manner, leading to a successful classification rate of 97%, outperforming Hjorth's mobility and complexity measure, a state-of the art technique used in EEG signal classification.**

Keywords: BCI; EEG; Motion Intention Classification; Motor Imagery; KNN.

I. INTRODUCTION

In order to improve self-sufficiency in people with reduced motion capabilities, it is necessary to create assistive technologies that not only are governed by a specific control strategy for a desired task, but that also allow the interpretation of motion intentions.

Giving this self-sufficiency has been partially addressed from different perspectives. For instance, an autonomous service robot may facilitate users with objects they desire [1][2], easing quality of life but lacking in providing a sensation of independency. Another approach has been to provide robots with a tele-operation based control [3] or even using exoskeletons with muscular signal activation [14]. These are significant approaches that offer a greater sensation of self-sufficiency to users. Still, patients that have suffered motion disorder diseases like sclerosis and Parkinson are not able to steadily control robots or exoskeletons, neither by using hands or extremities nor by using signals provided by muscular nervous terminals. Identifying brain motion intentions is therefore an open problem as stated in [4], where a review of motion command identification is developed.

Most of the work done on classifying brain signals uses a fixed band pass filter based on the work in Yuan et al. [4] where fixed frequencies are established for each type of data describing a mental state for a specific activity. Nevertheless, the brain is a labile organ, i.e., neural signals change through time while performing activities, which is known as neuroplasticity.

In order to identify and decode elements of information, non-stationary models are required. For this reason, some signal treatment strategy is needed to identify neural activities, as in the work of Wang et al. [5], where a method to modulate brain signals through a mathematical model was proposed.

From the efforts of Hazarika et al. [11], authors have used the discrete wavelet transform to obtain features and classify epileptic seizures by means of artificial neural networks (ANNs) as in [12] or Support Vector Machines (SVM) as in the work of [10]. Other classification approaches can be found in [9]. As statistical features obtained from wavelets are more susceptible to time-frequency localization than Fourier Transform, which is band limited, the latter assumes a more feasible approach for analysis.

Using statistical data to classify elements from brain signals has been analyzed in [6][18] in order to obtain human emotions from different statistical methods, such as the mean and standard deviation analysis. The results of their work indicated that these two features are not effective enough compared to other approaches. Nevertheless, since their analysis is developed directly from raw data, a lack of pre-processing operations may be a cause for the modest success exhibited by the mean and STD statistical analysis. Another feature extraction method based on statistical data is used in [19], where three features are obtained from the Fisher ratio of the Hjorth's *activity*, *complexity* and *mobility* in order to classify motor imagery. These statistical methods include time rather than only frequency domain as in STFT, increasing the flexibility of data.

Brainwaves of motor imagery classification have also been used to control either virtual [15][16] or real [3] objects that respond to motion commands in two or three dimensions. This has been achieved by using a 64-channel

EEG cap to describe thoughts, supported by a specific control technique.

The main objective of our paper is to gather and classify motion intention commands from brainwaves by using a low cost EEG. Non-invasive EEG brain-computer interface systems have gained interest inside the research community. On one hand, they represent a harmless solution for humans; on the other hand, it is possible to obtain reliable enough information from brain signals after some processing of the data.

This paper is structured as follows: in Section II, the general structure of the motion intention classification is introduced. Additionally, it is explained how pre-processing data through an adaptive filter is useful for achieving feature vector separability. In Section III, results are presented. Finally, in Section IV, we discuss the concluding remarks about the proposed approach.

II. DATA ACQUISITION AND FILTERING

The Motion Intention Classificator (MIC) system is basically done throughout three phases: 1) pre-processing raw information from brainwaves, 2) extraction of dominant features and 3) classification of the resulting features. These phases normally act sequentially and are interdependent. Figure 1 shows the inner work of a general architecture to interpret raw brainwaves into commands for tele-operation.

The output features depend on the extraction methodology, which in this paper is addressed with a statistical mean-STD approach and with the Hjorth's Mobility and Complexity technique.

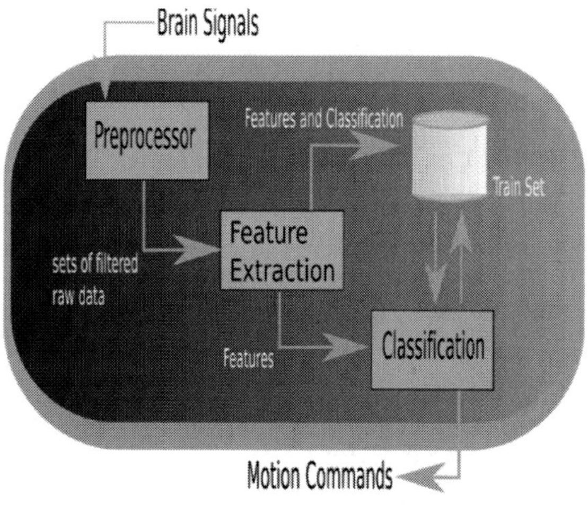

Figure 1. General Architecture of the MIC.

A. Preprocessing data

In order to obtain features from brainwave signals, it is required to set information that will serve as training data to be filtered from the noise induced by sensor readings.

For setting the training data it is necessary to split raw data into sections according to a defined task that a test subject should execute. Once this has been carried out, synchronization with the training system is developed by parsing corresponding sections labeled with the task.

In particular, the test subject is guided by computer images indicating a command of motion intention. The image is basically a geometric form that suggests the subject to concentrate on a particular mental task during 18 seconds with a specific intermittent signal (2 seconds of a displaying task and 2 seconds of a neutral activity). This pattern is periodically repeated with a different command after T seconds for resting between tasks, as depicted in Figure 2. Four different active tasks of motion intention (here referred to as activities) are intended to be extracted: Right (R), Left (L), Up (U) and Down (D), while one more for no intention activity is considered as Neutral (N). The data acquisition process is an important part of this approach and it is illustrated in Figure 2, showing the alternation of the N activity (marked as checkerboard patterns) on each of the tasks. The total process lasted 97s for each test subject. We have set T to 5s between tasks to avoid interference.

We asked 14 naive subjects to sit in front of a monitor giving instructions to them, the subjects must be focused on thinking the action indicated while avoiding body motions during the 97s experiment. After some experiments, we could notice that the neutral activity was correlated with its precedent mental activity, i.e., the N activity had some remaining "inertia" from previous R, L, U and D tasks. In other words, while the training of the N activity was expected to occur during the 2s pause between each trial, in reality there was a presence of neutrality preceded by a non-neutral emotion. This led to different Neutral Activities (NR, NL, NU, ND), which we used for classification.

B. Filtering Data

One key element proposed in our approach is the implementation of an adaptive filter, which is based on statistical information.

Raw data, as used in the work of [6], is usually contaminated with noise that makes it difficult to perform the appropriate classification of different activities. This effect can be seen in Figure 3, where features from each class (represented as geometric figures), which have been obtained from raw data, appear not only close to each other but also mixed, i.e., they are hardly separable and their classification is harder. For this reason, applying a filter becomes necessary to reduce the noise coming from sensor signals.

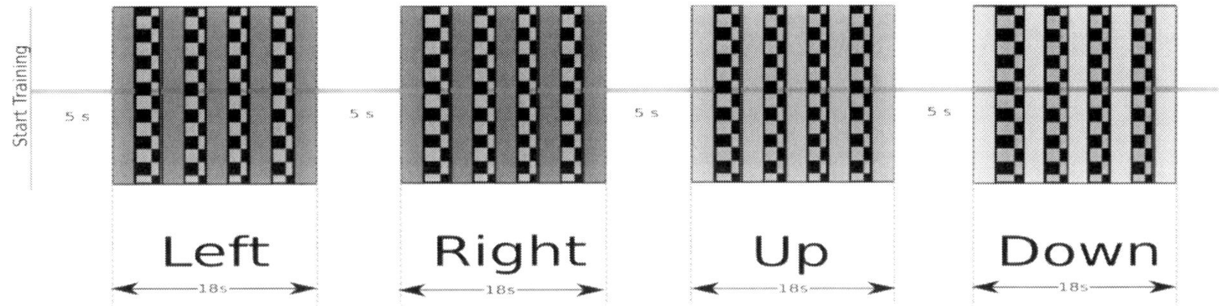

Figure 2. Training session schema, task mental activities are in colors (duration 2s), while neutral activities are in grey between each training task.

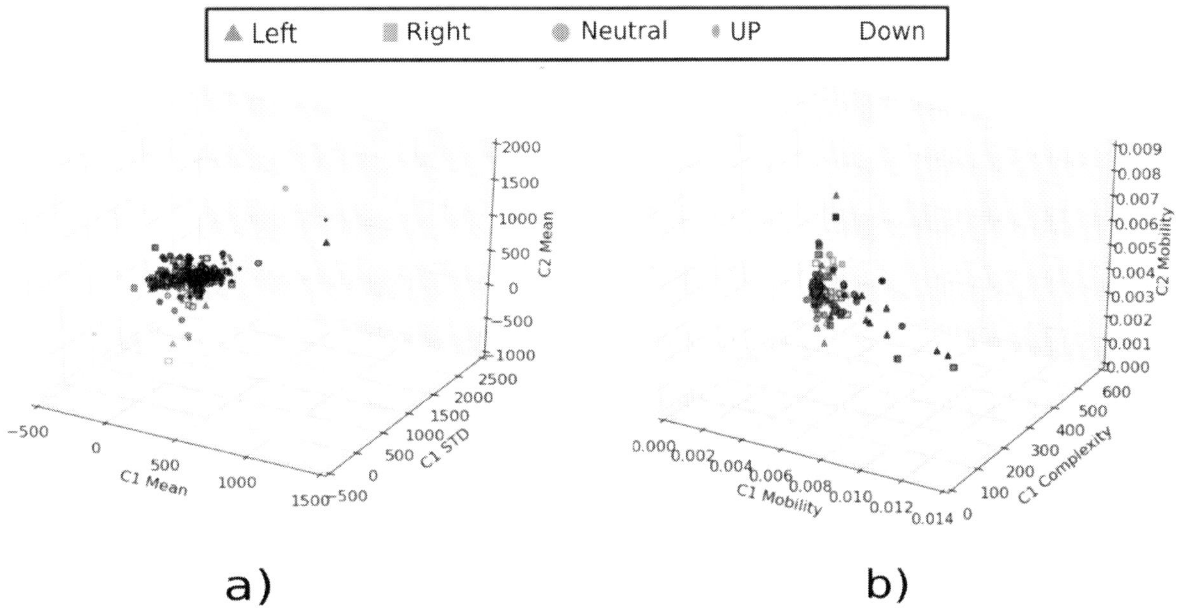

Figure 3. Features extracted without pre-procesing data with two different feature extraction methods. Note how it is difficult to separate features due to their proximity between each activity class..

It is common to use a band pass filter based on fixed frequencies as in [18] for each brain region or for different kinds of mental activities. As mentioned above, the filter used in our approach is based on statistical information from raw data for each sensor, each set and each subject. It is worth noticing that our filter is not based on channels, but in information from activities (L, R, U, D and N).

Let us define the high ($\mu_{\max}$) and low ($\mu_{\min}$) thresholds from data as:

$$\mu_{max}(x_{kj}) = \overline{S}(x_{kj}) + \sigma(x_{kj}) \quad (1)$$

$$\mu_{min}(x_{kj}) = \overline{S}(x_{kj}) - \sigma(x_{kj}) \quad (2)$$

with:

$$\overline{S}(x_{kj}) = \frac{1}{m}\sum_{i=0}^{m} w_{x_{kj}}(t_i) \quad (3)$$

$$\sigma(x_{kj}) = \sqrt{\frac{1}{m}\sum_{i=0}^{m}(w_{x_{kj}}(t_i) - \overline{S}(x_{kj}))^2} \quad (4)$$

where x_{kj} is the training set with the elements of a mental action k from sensor j, and w is the amplitude of the brainwave at the sample time t_i in a total of m discrete readings from sensor.

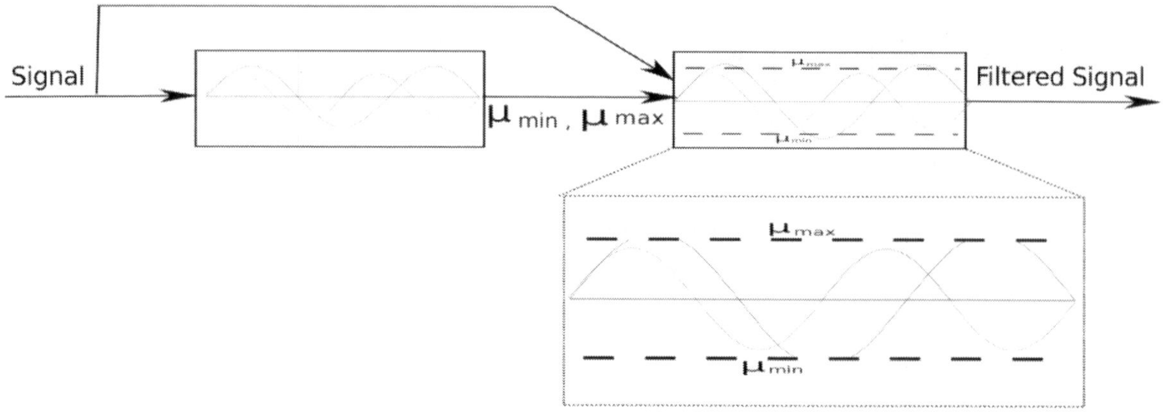

Figure 4. Illustrating thresholds high μ_{max} and low μ_{min} used on each brain wave. Data above or below these thresholds are dismissed.

Setting thresholds in this way (as depicted in Figure 4) provides flexibility to the filter band so that the filter adapts to each subject and to the wave characteristics. This makes feature vectors belonging to one activity be closer to those from the same activity, and makes them more separated from those belonging to another class. The effects of the filter are more noticeable when comparing Figure 3a with Figure 5 and Figure 3b with Figure 6. Similar filters have been used in [17] to classify frog call sounds (from different frogs), and are also commonly used in data transmission.

C. Feature Extraction.

After separating wave sections corresponding to mental activities and afer having filtered noise, it is necessary to reduce dimensionality by obtaining characteristics from waves, which facilitates classification.

Due to the nature of the Emotiv Epoc device, there are 14 analyzed individual signals (AF3, F7, F3, FC5, T7, P7, O1, O2, P8, T8, FC6, F4, F8, AF4). Additionally, a couple of features for each signal are required to extract corresponding activities, which are represented by a classification feature vector in the training set. In total, 28 features for each mental activity, period and subject are acquired and stored as features.

We present two statistical methods for comparison: M1) taking mean and standard deviation as shown in Fig. 5, a close approach to what has been done in [6] and [18], but applied to motor imagery instead of emotions, and compare it with another statistical feature extraction method called M2) the Hjorth's mobility and complexity, a similar approach to what has been developed in [19]. Note that we do not take into account the Fisher ratio because in [19] they use it to find the dominant frequency to adapt in the training phase. This action is solved in our filter phase. Furthermore, we do not take into account Hjorth's Activity as a feature, which is highly correlated with Complexity and Mobility, so as to avoid redundant information. The behavior of M2 can be observed in Figure 6. Note how, while Figure 5 reveals a more noticeable separability between classes, Figure 6 shows how some features are highly separated although classes are still mixing.

III. CLASSIFICATION RESULTS

For experiments, 14 subjects were selected to generate the knowledge base; each subject participated at different times of the day (3 times per day for each subject) and in some subjects different "head/hair conditions" (wet/dry, with/without hair products). The knowledge base is formed leaving one subject out to test the classification results. The sensor used in the experiments is the Emotive Epoc one, which is a non-invasive sensor that provides 14 signals from each user; this is a low cost sensor that naturally induces noise through the wireless communication with the computer (RF). Nevertheless, the approach presented here is a generic approach that can be used with any sensor model, also improving classification rate in the presence of noise.

Even when extracted features are filtered to increase the distance between them in the plot, as depicted in Figures 5 and 6, those features are not linearly separable, so it is necessary to implement a different method to identify each mental activity from brainwaves.

We propose using a *k*NN (*k* Nearest Neighbors) algorithm, where different values of *k* are analyzed (the number of neighbors from all activities) to identify which of them fits the best results. This algorithm has been widely used in many classification problems for its simplicity of training. As we had the hypothesis that features obtained in this way would generate equidistant clusters, *k*NN appeared to fit the best and helped us prove that a good outcome could be achieved.

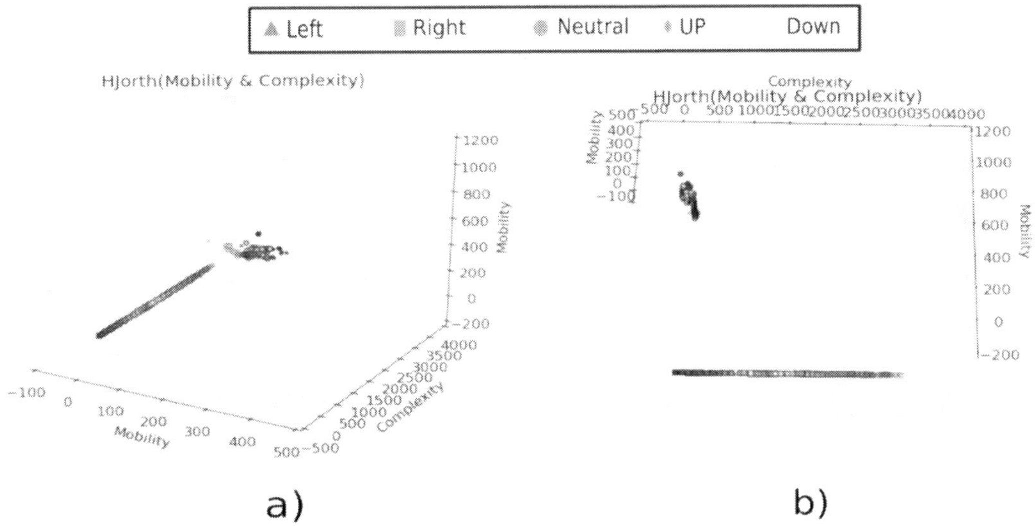

Figure 5. 4D plot showing features after filtering distances on two signals (FC5 and FC6), with Mean FC5 vs Mean FC6 represented by the X and Y axis, while STD FC5 vs STD FC6 are represented by Z. Colors (from blue to red) refer to distances.

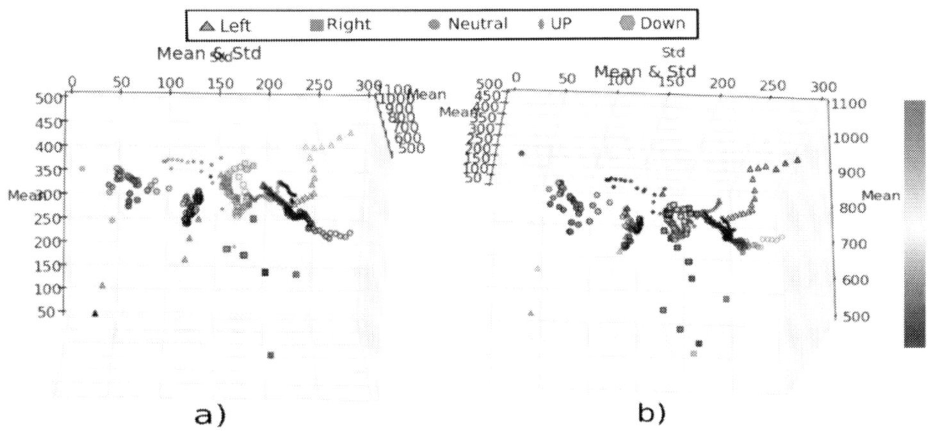

Figure 6. 4D plot showing two perspectives of the distance on two signals (FC5 and FC6) using Hjorth's mobility and complexity features after filtering, axes and colors (from blue to red) refer to distances.

The results from the classification algorithms over Mean and STD are presented in Table I, where it can be noticed that it is best to only consider three neighbors for effectiveness, training and search times. This can be caused by the structure of the class, which seems to be arranged more along lines (as seen in Figures 5 and 6) than along equidistant clusters.

Figure 7 and Table II present the difference between both methods M1 and M2. From the figure, it is noticeable how using an STD-mean strategy provides better results than Hjorth's Mobility and Complexity in all cases of classification, since the overall percentage of effectiveness is higher. Even though the method M2 has a lower accuracy rate than M1, it shows better results in motor imagery classification than in [19] (79.1%) where the same features are used. In Figure 7 and 8, the dashed line represents M1 while the continuous line represents M2; the X-axis refers to neighbor number.

TABLE I. KNN K-VALUES, EFFECTIVENESS, TRAINING TIME AND SEARCH TIME OVER MEAN AND STD

K	Avg. Performance		
	Effectiveness (%)	*Training(s)*	*Search(s)*
3	97.23	0.000641731	0.0006567
5	96.27	0.000661157	0.00066496
9	94.67	0.000644846	0.00068063
13	94.00	0.000644687	0.00068448
17	89.20	0.000647488	0.00070822
25	82.80	0.000638758	0.00073605
30	78.40	0.000653181	0.000760

TABLE II. KNN AVG. OF EFFECTIVENESS COMPARISSON BETWEEN M1 AND M2

K	Avg. Effectivenes (%)	
	M1	*M2*
3	97.23 ± 3.7	94.27 ± 4.39
5	96.27 ± 3.1	91.87 ± 7.2
9	94.67 ± 3.91	83.2 ± 8.37
13	94.00 ± 4.57	79.33 ± 8.24
17	89.20 ± 10.05	78.93 ± 7.95
25	82.80 ± 17.92	75.20 ± 6.66
30	78.40 ± 18.99	74.93 ± 12.15

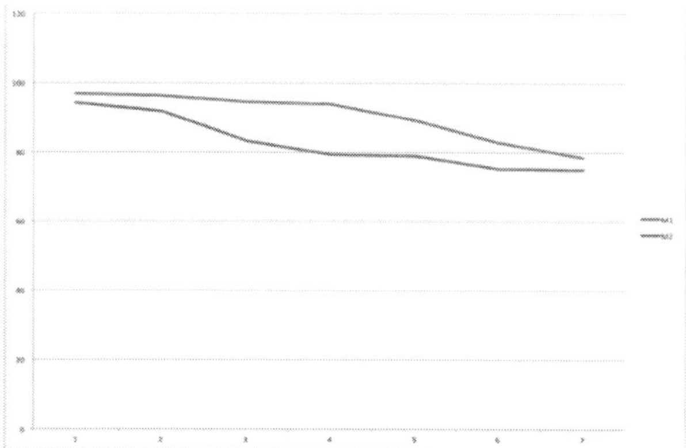

Figure 7. Effectiveness rates of classification between the two feature extraction methods M1 (blue) and M2 (red).

In Table III, we show 250 classification tests done with 50 cases of each class (the same 14 subjects with different conditions in cross-validation) for *k=3* while leaving one subject out and validating with the rest. From the table it can be inferred that the errors in classification are mainly related with the Left activity. This can be related with the structure of the training process, where Left activity is the first in the training set.

TABLE III. CLASSIFICATION

Intention	Confusion Matrix for k=3 using only mean and standard deviation				
	Left	*Right*	*Neutral*	*Front*	*Back*
Left	50	0	0	0	0
Right	3	47	0	0	0
Neutral	1	1	48	0	0
Front	0	0	0	50	0
Back	2	0	0	0	48

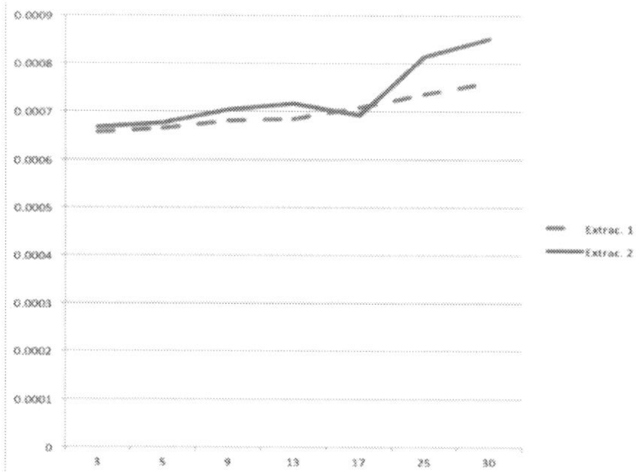

Figure 8. Searching time between methods M1 and M2.

IV. CONCLUSION AND FUTURE WORK

We have presented a statistical-based approach to train, filter and classify motion intentions from brain signals. Our method was motivated by the good separability of classes provided by the mean and standard deviations of the gathered data. Filtering and performing data acquisition in this manner allow us to report satisfactory results, reaching above 97% of accuracy on our test data and with a "lazy" classifier such as *k*NN, allowing the brain signals to become suitable not only for tele-operation purposes, but also for the purposes of emotion recognition. As an additional result, brain inertia could be observed from the experiments. We found that this brain behavior depended on the previous immediate motion intention of the subject, pushing the neutral intention to be closely related with previous brain activities, deeper experiments in this subject will be needed in order to obtain more quantitative results. This inertia helped us re-organize the training process by inserting neutral actions between each activity, thus redefining the usual methodology in literature where "pause" is not taken into account as a part of the knowledge base.

As an extension to this work, we will seek for obtaining a bigger sample of subjects in order to avoid biasing our results. Also, it is recommendable to use some other classification techniques (e.g., Artificial Neural Networks) to obtain more stable results. Furthermore, we plan to implement our methodology on a real-time tele-operation system, which could be used to identify emotions and mental states that are relevant in tele-operation issues. For this, it may be necessary to induce emotions while acquiring at the same time the mental states.

REFERENCES

[1] E. A. Sisbot, L. F. Marin-Urias, R. Alami, and T. Simeon, "A human Aware Robot Motion Planner", IEEE Transactions on Robotics, Vol 25, Issue: 5, pp. 874-883 Oct. 2007.

[2] E. A. Sisbot, L. F. Marin-Urias, X. Broker, D. Sidobre, and R. Alami "Synthesizing robot motions Adapted to human presence", Intl. J. of Social Robotics, Vol. 2 Issue 3, pp. 329-343, Sep. 2010.

[3] K. LaFleur, "Quadcopter control in three-dimensional space using a noninvasive motor imagery-based braincomputer interface". Journal of Neural Engineering, Vol. 10. (2013)

[4] H. Yuan, and B. He, "Brain-Computer Interfaces Using Sensorimotor Rythms: Current State and Future Perspectives", IEEE Transactions On Biomedical Engineering, Vol. 61 NO. 5, pp 1425-1435, May, 2014.

[5] Y. Wang et al., "Tracking Neural Modulation Depth by Dual Sequential Monte Carlo Estimation Point Process for Brain-Machine Interfaces.", IEEE Transactions On Biomedical Engineering, Vol. 63 NO. 8,p.p 1728- 1741, May, 2016.

[6] T. Y. Chai, S. S. Woo, M Rizon and C.S. Tan, "Classification of human emotions from EEG signals using statistical features and neural network", International Journal of Integrated Engineering, 1 (3), 71-79, 2010.

[7] I. Juarez-Moreno, L.F Marin-Urias, J.A. Vasquez-Santacruz, M. Vigueras-Zuñiga "Interface de comunicación remota entre un sistema clasificador de ondas cerebrales y un robot móvil", Revista de aplicaciones de ingeniera, Volumen 3 No. 9 Pg. 109-116 2016

[8] E. A. Sisbot, L. F. Marin-Urias, X. Broquere, D. Sidobre, R Alami Synthe- sizing robot motions adapted to human presence International Journal of Social Robotics 2 (3), 329-343 2010

[9] A. Subasi, "EEG Signal Clasification using wavelet feature estraction and a mixture of expert model, Expert Systems with Applications", vol. 32 , 1084-1093, 2007.

[10] A. Subasi, and M. I. Gursoy, "EEG Signal Classification using PCA, ICA, LDA and support vector machines", Expert Systems with Applications, vol. 37, 8659-8666, 2010.

[11] N. Hazarika, J. Z. Chen, A.C. Tsoi, and A. Sergejew, "Classification of EEG signals Using the wavelet transform", Journal of Signal Procesing, Vol.59, 61-72. 1997

[12] H. Adeli, Z. Zhou and N. Dadmehr, "Analysis of EEG records in an epileptic patient using wavelet transform". Journal of Neuroscience Methods, vol. 123, 69-87, 2003

[13] N. Kwak, N. Muller, and S. Lee, "A lower limb exoskeleton control system based on visual evoked potentials", Journal of Neural Engineering, Vol. 12, No. 15, 2015.

[14] K. Kiguchi, T. Tanaka and T. Fukuda, "Neuro-Fuzzy control of a robotic exoskeleton with EMG signals". IEEE Transactions on Fuzzy Systems, Vol 12, No. 14. 2004.

[15] D. J. McFarland, W. A. Sarnacki, and J. R. Wolpaw, "Electroencephalographic (EEG) control of three dimensional movement" Journal of Neural Engineering, vol.7 No. 3 036007, 2010.

[16] A. S. Roye, A. J. Doud, M. L. Rose and B. He, "EEG control of a virtual helicopter in 3 dimensional space using intelligent control strategies", IEEE Transactions Neural Systems Rehabilitation Engineering, Vol. 18. No. 6, pp 581-589, Dec. 2010.

[17] J. Xie, M. Towsey, L. Zhang, J. Zhang and P. Roe, "Feature Extraction Based on Bandpass Filtering for Frog Call Classification", International Conference on Image and Signal Processing ICISP 2016: Image and Signal Processing pp 231-239, Trois- Rivires, QC, Canada, May 30 - June 1, 2016.

[18] K. Takahashi "Remarks on SVM-Based Emotion Recognition from Multi-Modal Bio-Potential Signals", IEEE International Workshop on Robot and Human Interactive Communication Proceedings of the, Kurashiki, Okoyama Japan, September 20-22 2004.

[19] S. Oh, Y. Lee, and H. Kim, "A Novel EEG Feature Extraction Method Using Hjorth Parameter", International Jour- nal of Electronics and Electrical Engineering Vol. 2, No. 2, June, 2014

The Impact of Human Factors on Digitization: An Eye-tracking Study of OCR Proofreading Strategies

Flavia De Simone, Barbara Balbi, Vincenzo Broscritto, Simona Collina, Roberto Montanari
Università Suor Orsola Benincasa
Centro Scienza Nuova
Naples, Italy
e-mail: flavia.desimone@centroscienzanuova.it
barbara.balbi@centroscienzanuova.it
vincenzo.broscritto@studenti.unisob.na.it
simona.collina@unisob.na.it
roberto.montanari@unisob.na.it

Federico Boschetti, Anas Fahad Kahn
Consiglio Nazionale delle Ricerche
Istituto di Linguistica Computazionale "A. Zampolli"
Pisa, Italy

e-mail: federico.boschetti@ilc.cnr.it
fahad.kahn@ilc.cnr.it

Abstract— **An Optical Character Recognition (OCR) System is a piece of software that can scan a printed text and translate it into a digital format that can be subsequently edited with a computer. Often the output from OCR software does not correspond closely enough to the original text and a manual correction phase is needed in order to improve accuracy. The aim of the study presented in this paper is to test human strategies in proof correction by means of an eye-tracker. The experiment, which we designed to investigate these strategies consisted in a proofreading task. Participants were divided into two groups: a target group that was trained in how to carry out the task and a control group that had not been so trained. The performances of each group were evaluated in terms of accuracy and time of execution. Results highlighted an effect of learning, an optimization strategy of the target group resulting in higher accuracy and lower time of execution of the task. The practical implications of these results will be discussed.**

Keywords - Optical Character Recognition; Eye-tracking; Reading; Cognitive processe.

I. Introduction

Of all the processes that impact on the production of resources in the Digital Humanities, the digitization of texts by means of an Optical Character Recognition (OCR) system, and in particular the correction phase, is one of the most complex. This is due both to how resource and time consuming it can be, and also because of the role that human factor issues play in ensuring the accuracy of the final output [1]. On the other hand, the accuracy of digitized corpora is a fundamental requirement for any further phases of analysis and treatment of texts, such as for instance linguistic annotation. To improve the effectiveness of OCR systems, we believe that it is important to study the role of human factors in proofreading activities and to use this information to develop strategies in order to make systems more adaptive to users' needs [2]. The adaptivity of a system, or a machine, is its ability to adapt to its human operator and to thereby reduce his or her cognitive workload [3]. The background to the present study is in human factor psychology, a branch of psychology dedicated to the study of human-machine interaction with a strong connection with cognitive theories [4].

In the following, we present related work needed to place our research and experimental efforts in Section II. We delve into the details of our experimental procedure in Section III.. Finally, we conclude and introduce future work in Section IV.

II. Theories and Models

Reading is the complex outcome of a learning process which permits the conversion of a visual representation into a phonological form. The success of the process implies that there is access to a background store of memories containing not only morphological and phonological information but also semantic and syntactic knowledge. Nevertheless, the process is rapid, taking only a matter of milliseconds, it is error free most of the time, and partially unconscious as proved by the Stroop effect [5]. The Stroop paradigm is one of the most commonly used technologies for studying lexical production. The task is very simple: participants are asked to name the color of the ink used to write a word without reading the word. The dependent variable is the time to response. Participants are found to perform the task significantly faster when the color of the ink corresponds to the meaning of the word, despite the fact that they are instructed to ignore the content of the words themselves.

One of the most well-known models for explaining the reading process is the Dual Route Cascaded Model [6], which hypothesizes that two different mechanisms are involved in reading aloud. One mechanism, the lexical route, assumes that an expert reader has a mental representation for every learned word and the visual recognition of the written word directly activates the internal representation thus speeding up the reading process. The other mechanism, the non-lexical route, is applicable to non-words or new words for which a mental representation is not available. In this case, the reader decomposes the words into constituents (graphemes) and then applies graphemes/phonemes conversion rules.

The first step of the reading process in both routes is a visual recognition phase. This is well explained by the model of word perception developed by McClelland and Rummelhart [7] in which the first level of processing corresponds to visual features that differentiate letters (e.g., the letter E is formed by one vertical and three horizontal tracts). Starting from this theory we decided to work on this visual level to introduce errors into the OCR output, as explained below in Section III-B.

So far, we have described models which have been developed to explain chronometric data and error corpora, but research on reading processes enjoyed a significant boost in the 70s with the introduction of eye-tracking technology into the sciences. Eye-tracking technology has made it possible to study eye movements and to infer underlying cognitive processes, in particular selective attention, that is, the ability to elaborate a stimulus by ignoring all competing stimuli [8]. Although attention can be oriented regardless of eye movement it is more often eye-driven. To better understand this process it is necessary to introduce some additional concepts [9]:

- foveal vision: the fovea is a small region in the retina with a diameter of 1,55 millimeters where visual acuity is at its highest;
- smooth pursuit movements: slow eye movements that follow an object moving in the visual field, keeping it into the fovea;
- saccades: rapid movements of the eyes that change the fixation point;
- fixations: the maintaining of the eyes on a portion of the visual field for a time longer than 250 milliseconds; fixations have two main attributes: location and duration.

Previous studies have used eye-tracking technology in OCR domain. In particular, Rello and Baeza-Yates [10] use the eye-tracker to evaluate the readability of digital texts that contain OCR errors (among other types of errors). Ishiguro et al. [11] apply eye-tracking to study the achievement of multiple tasks at the same time, such as face recognition, object detection and text reading. In order to monitor these activities, each region of interest is processed by the suitable recognizer, which is OCR in the case of text. Buscher et al. [12] use the eye-tracker on OCR documents, in order to annotate which areas are read and which areas are skimmed.

Starting from this scientific background, we developed an eye-tracking study with the specific aim to investigate reading strategies in proofreading task.

III. EXPERIMENT

In the study presented below, we tested for two different aspects:

1- the first related to a question of methodology: the possibility of studying the visual strategies adopted by OCR proofreaders by means of eye-tracking technology;

2- a learning effect: the influence of learning on proofreading strategies.

Towards this aim we compared performances in proofreading tasks of two groups of participants, a group trained for the task and an untrained group, using eye-tracking instruments. We expected that the group trained to the task to be more rapid and accurate in the execution of the task.

A. *Participants*

Thirty subjects volunteered in the experiment. The age range was between 20 and 45 years old. They all were Italian mother-tongue speakers. They had normal or corrected to normal vision. None of the participants received any money or course credits for participation. In addition, none of them had any previous experience in proofreading. They were equally distributed into two groups: a target group (TG) undergoing a learning phase for the proofreading task before the proper experiment and a control group (CG) that received no training for the task.

B. *Materials*

The text used for the experiment was an OCR scan extracted from the book "Gomorra" written by Roberto Saviano. We opted for a contemporary Italian text for reasons of ease and familiarity of semantic and syntax.

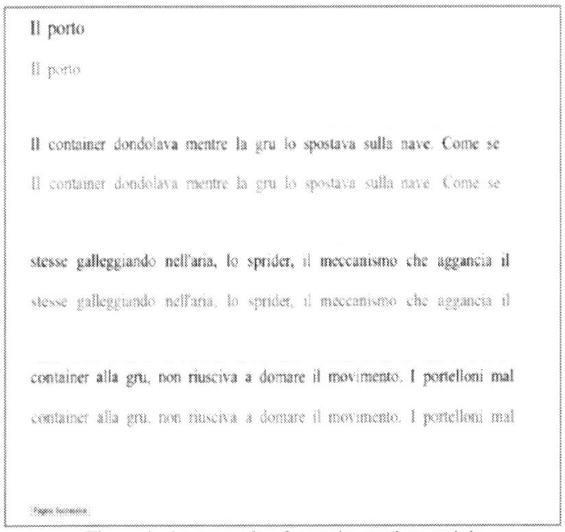

Figure 1: An example of experimental materials

The text was integrated into a web platform and divided in thirty screens: each screen was composed of four sessions and each session was made up of two parts, an image obtained by a high-resolution scan (600 DPI) and a line containing the output of the OCR software, an editable text, where the errors to be corrected by participants could be presented (Figure 1). Orthographical errors were manually inserted in the OCR output by the experimenter. Errors were letters substitutions of two types: "rn" instead of "m" and vice versa, "O" instead of "o" and vice versa[13;14].

C. *Equipment*

To control visual behavior of participants and acquire eye movement data an eye-tracker was used. We opted for a remote, non-contact system, FaceLab (Figure 2), as it was suitable for use in a controlled environment, a laboratory, with a task presented via computer desktop. The system consists of an infrared pod and two cameras posed on the desk at the base of the computer monitor. Before data acquisition, the eye-tracker is calibrated and cameras position is adjusted for each participant to increase data accuracy.

One great advantage of this system, compared to a wearable system, is the stability and accuracy of the resulting data due to the upright and stable position of participants. This favors calibration and avoids the kind of data loss that might result from wireless connection issues.

Figure 2. FaceLab 5.0

D. *Procedure*

The experiment was carried out in a quiet ad-hoc prepared room. Participants were seated in front of a 17" computer monitor with a maximum resolution of 1280x1024 at 60 Hz. The two groups of participants received different instructions. Participants in the TG were familiarized with the task in a learning phase in which they could correct thirty screens of text before starting with the experiment proper. They were informed that in the experiment they would find the same errors as in the learning phase. The entire procedure lasted about one hour. Participants in the CT were asked to pass directly to the experimental phase without any specific training. This experiment lasted about half an hour.

E. *Results*

To evaluate the accuracy of performances the number of detected errors has been acquired and analyzed. A statistical test on frequencies (chi-squared) revealed a significant effect of learning (Figure 3): participants inserted in the TG corrected a significant major number of errors respect to CG ($p<.004$).

To compare the strategies adopted by the two groups we focused on three metrics: the time to complete the task, the mean number of fixations and the mean fixation duration [15]. To extract metrics about fixations we designed two Areas of Interest (AOIs) for each of the sessions into which the text is divided, the image and the OCR editable text (see Section III-B). Statistical tests on the means (t-test) highlighted that the two groups adopted two different visual strategies: TG tended to be more rapid in executing the task compared to CG ($p<.06$) because the participants mostly focused their attention on the OCR output as can be inferred by an higher number of fixations ($p<.02$; Figure 4) and a longer fixation duration ($p<.0003$; Figure 5).

IV. CONCLUSION

Taken together the data confirm the two hypotheses: the suitability of the adopted methodology to study human-factor issues in digital era and the learning effect, an advantage in terms of accuracy and time of execution, on proofreading strategies. Our next step will consist in the application of the same methodology to study the strategies adopted by expert proofreaders; in addition, we are also looking into the possibility of verifying the strategies adopted by proofreaders to correct different types of errors (syntactic, semantic). The main aim of this direction of study is to use the knowledge acquired to design and develop OCR systems that are ever more adaptive to human users' needs.

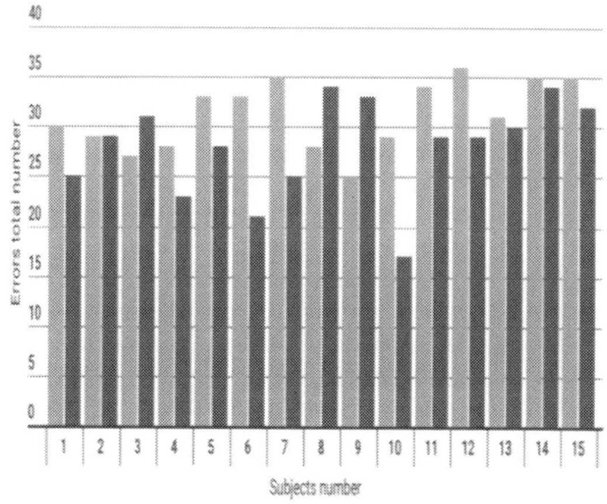

Figure 3. Number of detected errors for each subject.

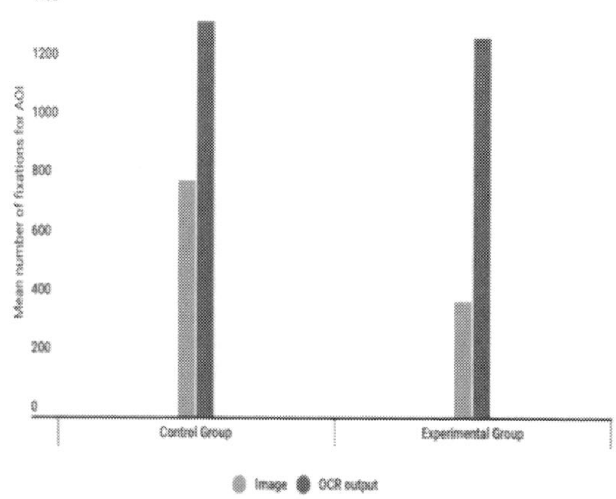

Figure 4. Mean number of fixations per AOIs (image: green bar; OCR output: red bar) for each group

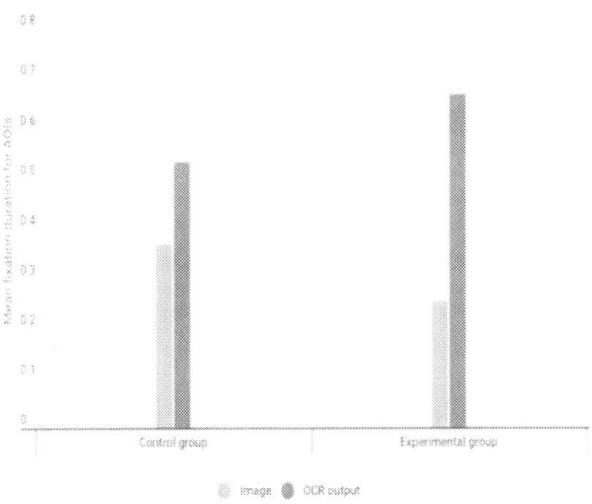

Figure 5. Mean fixation duration per AOIs (image: green bar; OCR output: red bar) for each group

REFERENCES

[1] G. Nagy, "At the frontiers of OCR". Proceedings of IEEE, 80 (7), pp. 1093-1100, 1992.

[2] H. Lieberman, F. Paternò, M. Klann and V. Wulf, "End-user development: An emerging paradigm". In End user development. Springer Netherlands, pp.1-8, 2006.

[3] L. A. Zadeh, "On the definition of adaptivity". Proceedings of the IEEE, 51(3), pp. 469-470, 1963.

[4] C. D. Wickens, J. G. Hollands, S. Banbury and R. Parasuraman, Engineering psychology & human performance. Psychology Press, 2015.

[5] J. Stroop, "Studies of interference in serial verbal reactions". Journal of Experimental Psychology, 18 (6), pp. 643-662, 1935.

[6] M. Coltheart, K. Rastle, C. Perry, R. Langdon and J. Ziegler, "DRC: A dual route cascaded model of visual word recognition and reading aloud". Psychological Review, 108 (1), pp. 204-256, 2001.

[7] J. L. McClelland and D. E. Rumelhart, . "An interactive activation model of context effects in letter perception: Part 1. An account of basic findings". Psychological Review, 88, pp. 375-407, 1981.

[8] L. Pei – Lin, "Using eye tracking to understand learners' reading process through the concept-mapping learning strategy". Computers & Education, 78, pp. 237-249, 2014.

[9] K. Rayner, "Eye movements in reading and information processing: 20 years of research". Psychological Bulletin, 124(3), pp. 372-422, 1998.

[10] L. Rello and R. Baeza-Yates, "Lexical quality as a proxy for web text understandability". Proceedings of the 21st International Conference on World Wide Web (WWW '12 Companion). ACM, New York, NY, USA, pp. 591-592, 2012.

[11] Y. Ishiguro, A. Mujibiya, T. Miyaki and J. Rekimoto, "Aided eyes: eye activity sensing for daily life". Proceedings of the 1st Augmented Human International Conference (AH '10). ACM, New York, NY, USA, Article 25, pp. 7, 2010.

[12] G. Buscher, A. Dengel, L. van Elst and F. Mittag, 2008. "Generating and using gaze-based document annotations". In CHI '08 Extended Abstracts on Human Factors in Computing Systems (CHI EA '08). ACM, New York, NY, USA, pp. 3045-3050, 2008.

[13] D. Fiset et al., "Features for identification of Uppercase and lowercase letters". Psychological Science, 19 (11), pp. 1161-1168, 2008.

[14] F. Peressotti and J. Grangier, "The role of letter identity and letter position in orthographic priming". Perception & Psychophysics, 61 (4), pp. 691-706, 1999.

[15] M. Just and P. Carpenter, "Eye Fixations and Cognitive Processes". Cognitive Psychology, 8, pp. 441-480, 1976.

Strategies for Learning Lexemes Efficiently: A Graph-Based Approach

Jean-Marie Poulin, Alexandre Blondin Massé and Alexsandro Fonseca

Département d'informatique
Université du Québec à Montréal
Montréal, QC, Canada H3C 3P8
Email: poulin.jean_marie@courrier.uqam.ca

Abstract—**Given a particular lexicon, what would be the best strategy to learn all of its lexemes? By using elementary graph theory, we propose a simple formal model that answers this question. We also study several learning strategies by comparing their efficiency on eight digital English dictionaries. It turns out that a simple strategy based purely on the degree of the vertices associated with the lexemes could improve significantly the learning process with respect to other psycholinguistical strategies.**

Keywords–Lexicons; Learning; Strategies; Graph theory.

I. INTRODUCTION

When learning a new language, the effort to develop a sufficient vocabulary basis plays an important role. Notwithstanding the fact that various cognitive skills are required, being able to associate a word with its meaning, its definition, is an essential part of the learning process. According to Schmitt [1], the "form-meaning link is the first and most essential lexical aspect which must be acquired". But as Gu and Johnson [2] mention, vocabulary acquisition is an intricate task. Joyce identifies and compares two such strategies, aimed at vocabulary improvement [3]: L_1 traduction, from the speaker's native language, and L_2 definition, in the language being learned. Traduction is in itself a very different problem, which we do not address here. As for the "L_2 definition" approach, it can be seen as the action of consulting a dictionary to acquaint oneself with the definition of a word in the new language, thus establishing this crucial "form-meaning link".

But what if this definition contains unknown words? Shall the reader examine in turn the definition of these unknown words in the lexicon? And then the unknown words in the definition of the unknown words, and so on? As discussed by Blondin Massé et al. in [4], this can lead to an infinite regression, the symbol grounding problem [5]. At some point in time, it is necessary to learn some words in ways other than dictionary perusal: either by sensorimotor experience, or through some other external contribution. In particular, it seems interesting to design a learning strategy to alleviate the burden of these potentially expensive forms of learning.

Dansereau characterizes a learning strategy as a sequence of "processes or steps that can facilitate the acquisition, storage and/or utilization of information" [6]. And in the more specific context of second language pedagogy, Bialystok defines it as "activities in which the learner may engage for the purpose of improving target language competence" [7]. One compelling alternative to the expensive direct learning approach is to identify a sequence of words, as small as possible, and ordered so as to minimize the overall learning effort: an "efficient learning strategy".

There is a large amount of related work aiming to identify small subsets of words from which one can learn all remaining words of a given language. It has been for a long time of great interest from psycholinguistic, pedagogical and computational points of view. For instance, in 1936, Ogden proposed a reduced list of 850 English words which would suffice to express virtually any complex words or thought [8]. In 1953, West [9] published the "General Service List" (GSL). Based on a corpus of 5 million words and containing about 2000 words, it is oriented toward the needs of students learning english as a second language. Despite having been criticized numerous times for its shortcomings and its incompleteness, it was considered until very recently as irreplaceable [10]. In the last few years, two principal contenders have been vying with one another to replace West's GSL. At about the same time in 2013, Brezina and Gablasova [11], and Browne [12] both presented what they call their New General Service List (NGSL), whose purpose is to restrict the attention to the most basic English words that should be understood first by non native speakers. A question remains open though: What is the optimal way to establish those word lists in an automated way?

All the word lists discussed above were built using large corpora. In a recent work, Nation [13] even describes a detailed corpus-based appoach to word list building. Our main contribution in this paper is to present a different, lexicon-based technique. To our knowledge, there has never been a fully computational, graph-based approach for identifying efficient learning strategies of a complete lexicon. Although in real life the process of learning words is clearly more intricate than the method we present here, our results suggest that an hybrid strategy, based both on cognitive observations and on formal tools such as graphs, could enhance significantly the way people improve their L_2 vocabulary.

The manuscript is divided as follows. In Section II, we introduce definitions and notation about lexicons, graphs and grounding sets. In Section III, we discuss different lexicon-based learning strategies. Section IV describes the data sets used in our analyses. Section V is devoted to the comparison of the efficiency of those different strategies. Finally, we briefly conclude in Section VI.

II. LEXICONS, GRAPHS AND GROUNDING SETS

We now propose formal definitions and notation about lexicons, when viewed as directed graphs. We believe that this rather formal representation simplifies the discussion when comparing the efficiency of several lexicon learning strategies.

Roughly speaking, a *lexicon* can be defined as a set of lexical units, called *lexemes* enriched with definitions and arbitrary additional information [14]. For our purposes, we consider the following simplified representation of a lexicon.

Definition 1. A *lexicon* is a quadruple $X = (\mathcal{A}, \mathcal{P}, \mathcal{L}, \mathcal{D})$, where

(*i*) $\mathcal{A}$ is a finite *alphabet*, whose elements are called *letters*.

(*ii*) $\mathcal{P}$ is a nonempty finite set whose elements are syntactic categories, called *parts-of-speech* (POS). In particular, it contains a special element denoted by STOP, which identifies lexemes whose semantic value is ignored.

(*iii*) $\mathcal{L}$ is a finite set of triples $\ell = (w, i, p)$ called *lexemes*, denoted by $\ell = w_p^i$, where $w \in \mathcal{A}^*$ is a word form or simply word, $i \geq 1$ is an integer and $p \in \mathcal{P}$. If $p = \text{STOP}$, then ℓ is called a *stop lexeme*. We say that (w, i, p) is the *i-th sense of the pos-tagged word* (w, p). To make the numbering consistent, we also assume that if $(w, i, p) \in \mathcal{L}$ and $i > 1$, then $(w, i-1, p) \in \mathcal{L}$ as well. Whenever there exists $(w, i, p) \in \mathcal{L}$ with $i > 1$, we say that (w, p) and $\mathcal{L}$ are *polysemic*.

(*iv*) $\mathcal{D}$ is a map associating, with each lexeme $\ell \in L$, a finite sequence $D(\ell) = (d_1, d_2, \ldots, d_k)$, where $d_i \in \mathcal{A}^*$ for $i = 1, 2, \ldots, k$, called the definition of ℓ.

If we replace the condition $d_i \in \mathcal{A}^*$ by $d_i \in \mathcal{A}^* \times \mathcal{P}$ in (*iv*), then $D(\ell)$ is called a *POS-tagged definition* of ℓ and we say that X is a *POS-tagged lexicon*. It is also convenient to consider only the lemmatized, canonical form of words. If we replace in (*iv*) the condition by $d_i \in \mathcal{L}$, then $D(\ell)$ is called a *disambiguated definition* and we say that X is a *disambiguated lexicon*. Finally, if $D(\ell)$ is non empty whenever ℓ is a non-stop lexeme, then we say that X is *complete*.

Example 1. Let $X_1 = (\mathcal{A}, \mathcal{P}, \mathcal{L}, \mathcal{D})$ be the lexicon such that

$$\mathcal{A} = \{a, b, \ldots, z\},$$
$$\mathcal{P} = \{\text{N}, \text{V}, \text{A}, \text{R}, \text{S}\},$$

where N, V, A, R, S stand for *noun*, *verb*, *adjective*, *adverb*, STOP respectively, and $\mathcal{L}$ and $\mathcal{D}$ are both defined by Table I. Then X_1 is polysemic, lemmatized and disambiguated. Moreover, assuming that all words used in at least one definition are defined as well, X_1 is complete.

TABLE I. A DISAMBIGUATED LEXICON

Lexeme ℓ	$D(\ell)$
$fruit_N^1$	$(plant_N^1, part_N^1, that_S^1, have_V^1, seed_N^1, and_S^1, edible_A^1, flesh_N^1)$
$fruit_N^2$	$(the_S^1, result_N^1, of_S^1, work_N^1, or_S^1, action_N^1)$
$flesh_N^1$	$(the_S^1, edible_A^1, part_N^1, of_S^1, a_S^1, fruit_N^1, or_S^1, vegetable_N^1)$
$flesh_N^2$	$(the_S^1, part_N^1, of_S^1, an_S^1, animal_N^1, use_V^1, as_S^1, food_N^1)$
$seed_N^1$	$(the_S^1, small_A^1, part_N^1, of_S^1, a_S^1, plant_N^1, from_S^1, which_S^1, a_S^1, new_A^1, plant_N^1, can_S^1, develop_V^1)$
$plant_N^1$	...
etc.	...

Lexicons are naturally converted to directed graphs. For a complete introduction to graph theory, the reader is referred to the classical book by Bondy and Murty [15], but for sake of self-consistency, we briefly recall some definitions and notation. The formal representation of lexicons is inspired from the definition of dictionaries found in [4].

A *directed graph* is an ordered pair $G = (V, A)$, where V is a finite set whose elements are called *vertices* and $A \subseteq V \times V$ is a finite set whose elements are called *arcs*. Directed graphs are useful for representing the relation "lexeme ℓ *defines* lexeme ℓ'": Given a disambiguated lexicon $X = (\mathcal{A}, \mathcal{P}, \mathcal{L}, \mathcal{D})$, we define the *graph* $G(X)$ of X as the directed graph whose set of vertices is $V = \mathcal{L}$ and whose set of arcs A satisfies $(\ell, \ell') \in A$ if and only if $\ell \in D(\ell')$. In other words, the lexemes are the vertices, and there is an arrow from ℓ to ℓ' if and only if ℓ appears in the definition of ℓ'. Figure 1 depicts a subgraph of the graph $G(X_1)$ (see Example 1).

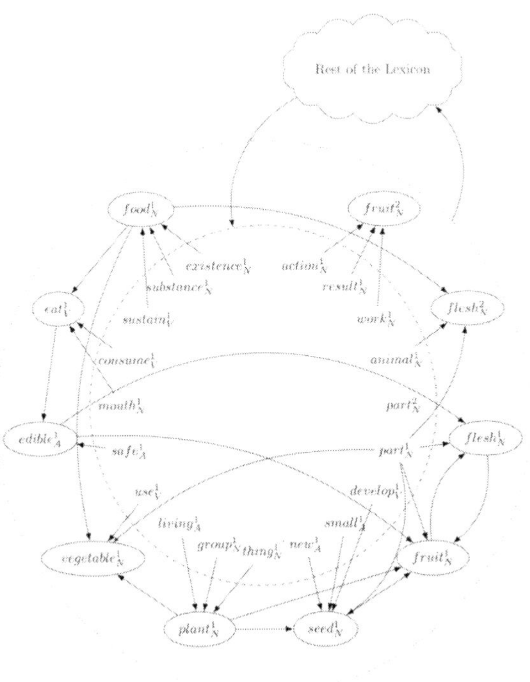

Figure 1. Graph of a polysemic, lemmatized, disambiguated, complete lexicon

Let $G = (V, A)$ be a directed graph. Given $u, v \in V$, we say that u is a *predecessor of* v if $(u, v) \in A$. The set of predecessors of v is denoted by $N^-(v)$ and the number of predecessors of v is called its *in-degree*, denoted by $\deg^-(v)$. Similarly, we say that v is a *successor of* u if $(u, v) \in A$, we denote by $N^+(u)$ the set of successors of u and we defined the *out-degree* by $\deg^+(u) = |N^+(u)|$. We define a map L on the subsets U of V by

$$L(U) = U \cup \{v \in V \mid N^-(v) \subseteq U\}.$$

From a linguistic point of view, $L(U)$ can be interpreted as the set of lexemes that can be *learned* from U, assuming that we can learn a new lexeme if and only if we already know it or if we know all lexemes appearing in its definition. In other words, L is a map associating with each set of lexemes U the set of lexemes $L(U)$ that can be learned directly from U. The set U is called a *grounding set* of G if there exists a positive integer k such that $L^k(U) = V$, i.e., knowing U is sufficient to learn all remaining lexemes by definition alone in a finite number of steps.

We say that $p = (v_1, v_2, \ldots, v_k) \in V^k$ is a *path* of G if $(v_i, v_{i+1}) \in A$ for $i = 1, 2, \ldots, k-1$. If $v_1 = v_k$, then p is called a *circuit*. A *feedback vertex set of* G is a subset $U \subseteq V$ of vertices such that for every circuit c of G, the set $U \cap c$ is nonempty, i.e., U covers every circuit of G. It was proved in [4] that grounding sets are the same as *feedback vertex sets*, a well-known concept of graph theory. Unfortunately, the problem of computing feedback vertex sets is NP-hard for general graph, i.e., it is unlikely that one will ever find a general polynomial time algorithm solving the problem, as it has been shown by Karp [16]. Nevertheless, we were able to compute at least one minimum grounding set for most of our digital lexicons or find close approximations. According to Vincent-Lamarre et al,. it turns out that these minimum grounding sets present distinctive characteristics in comparison with other words: they are learned earlier, are more frequent and are slightly more concrete [17].

III. Learning Strategies

For sake of simplicity, we assume that there are essentially two complementary approaches for learning a new lexeme (see Harnad [5]): *(1) Directly*, i.e., by seeing, hearing, smelling, tasting, touching, or interacting in any other way with the object referenced by the lexeme; (2) *By definition*, i.e., by reading its definition or by having someone explain, describe, characterize the object with other lexemes.

We also make the following, quite strong assumptions in order to streamline the model: (*i*) Whenever the meaning of a lexeme is learned, it is learned permanently, i.e., it will never be forgotten; (*ii*) If we already know the meaning of all the lexemes occurring in the definition of some lexeme ℓ, then we can learn the meaning of ℓ simply by reading its definition; (*iii*) The effort of learning a lexeme *directly*, is more significant than the one of learning a lexeme *by definition*. (*iv*) Learning a lexicon efficiently amounts to learn its complete set of lexemes at a minimal cost. Taking into account the preceding assumptions, we define a learning strategy as follows.

Definition 2. Let $X = (\mathcal{A}, \mathcal{P}, \mathcal{L}, \mathcal{D})$ a disambiguated lexicon. A *learning strategy of* X is any ordered sequence S whose elements are in $\mathcal{L}$. If X is a grounding set of X, then we say that S is *exhaustive*, otherwise we say that it is *partial*.

Simply stated, a learning strategy is a list of lexemes, ordered by decreasing priority. It is exhaustive if and only if it allows one to learn the complete lexicon. Intuitively, taking into account Assumption (*iii*), a learning strategy is efficient if its associated cost is as low as possible, which is realized exactly when the number of lexemes learned directly is minimal. Therefore, without loss of generality, we assume from now on that lexemes learned directly have cost 1, while lexemes learned by verbal instruction (definition) have cost 0.

The cost of a learning strategy can be handily computed. It is also easy to check if S is complete. In Algorithm 1, $\textsc{Cost}(S, X)$ returns an ordered pair $(cost, X')$, where *cost* is the cost of the learning strategy S for the lexicon X, and X' is the remaining part of the lexicon that could not be learned. Hence, S is complete if and only if X' is empty.

More precisely, Algorithm 1 proceeds as follows. First, it selects the next available lexeme in the strategy S and "learns it" with cost 1. Then, it learns all lexemes with no predecessor, i.e., lexemes whose definition contains only references to known lexemes, each at cost 0. This last step is repeated as long as there are available lexemes that can be learned at cost 0. Finally, it selects the next lexeme available in S and repeats the same process, until S is exhausted. The cost of using the strategy S is thus simply computed as the sum of the learning cost of all the lexemes in the lexicon.

Algorithm 1 Cost of a learning strategy

1: **function** $\textsc{Cost}(S : \text{strategy}, X : \text{lexicon}) : (\text{cost}, \text{lexicon})$
2: $\quad cost \leftarrow 0$
3: $\quad$ **while** $S \neq \emptyset$ **and** $X \neq \emptyset$ **do**
4: $\quad\quad \ell \leftarrow S.\textsc{pop}()$ $\quad \triangleright$ We extract the next lexeme
5: $\quad\quad$ Remove ℓ from X $\quad \triangleright$ ℓ is learned at cost 1
6: $\quad\quad cost \leftarrow cost + 1$
7: $\quad\quad$ **while** there exists $\ell \in X$ with $\deg^-(\ell) = 0$ **do**
8: $\quad\quad\quad$ Remove ℓ from X $\quad \triangleright$ ℓ is learned at cost 0
9: $\quad\quad$ **end while**
10: $\quad$ **end while**
11: $\quad$ **return** $(cost, X)$
12: **end function**

Any partial strategy S can easily be extended into a complete strategy S' by choosing a fallback strategy as soon as the list S of lexemes is exhausted. For instance, we could simply choose any random lexeme or choose a lexeme having a particular property, and repeat this process as long as there remain lexemes in the lexicon. Algorithm 2 presents such an extension by choosing, at each step, a lexeme whose number of occurrences in definitions is maximum.

Algorithm 2 Cost of a complete learning strategy

1: **function** $\textsc{CompleteCost}(S : \text{strategy}, X : \text{lexicon}) : \text{cost}$
2: $\quad (cost, X') \leftarrow \textsc{Cost}(S, X)$
3: $\quad$ **while** $X' \neq \emptyset$ **do**
4: $\quad\quad \ell \leftarrow$ a lexeme of X' such that $\deg^+(\ell)$ is maximal
5: $\quad\quad$ Remove ℓ from X $\quad \triangleright$ ℓ is learned at cost 1
6: $\quad\quad cost \leftarrow cost + 1$
7: $\quad\quad$ **while** there exists $\ell \in X$ with $\deg^-(\ell) = 0$ **do**
8: $\quad\quad\quad$ Remove ℓ from X $\quad \triangleright$ ℓ is learned at cost 0
9: $\quad\quad$ **end while**
10: $\quad$ **end while**
11: $\quad$ **return** *cost*
12: **end function**

Both Algorithms 1 and 2 are efficient and easy to implement. More precisely, let n and m be respectively the number of vertices and arcs in the graph of the lexicon X. On one hand, Algorithm 1 has $\mathcal{O}(n+m)$ time complexity and $\mathcal{O}(n)$ space complexity, assuming that the removal of a single vertex is done in $\mathcal{O}(1)$, and by considering only *neighbors* of removed vertices when checking the condition in Line 7. On the other hand, Algorithm 2 runs in $\mathcal{O}(m \log n)$ time and $\mathcal{O}(n)$ space, with the same assumptions as for Algorithm 1, and by storing the candidate vertices in a priority queue. Indeed, in that case, Line 4 is done in $\mathcal{O}(\log n)$ time, and the time cost of all priority updates is $\mathcal{O}(m \log n)$, since each vertex v is updated in $\mathcal{O}(n)$ at most $\mathcal{O}(\deg(v))$ times.

It is obvious that some learning strategies are more efficient than other ones, given that the cost of a strategy depends strongly on the order in which the lexemes are organized.

IV. Data Sets

We now briefly describe the digital dictionaries and the psycholinguistic material for building the different learning strategies compared later in Section V.

Digital dictionaries. In our research, we construct and analyze 8 different digital lexicons, using dictionaries coming from 5 different sources. Two of the dictionaries, the *Longman's Dictionary of Contemporary English* (LDOCE) [18], and the *Cambridge International Dictionary of English* (CIDE) [19], are described by their authors as being built using a controlled vocabulary, using as few distinct words as possible in the definitions. The LDOCE is an advanced learner's dictionary, originally published in 1978. The CIDE is a dictionary originally developped in 1995 for advanced learners of English using the Cambridge Corpus. The 11th edition of the *Merriam-Webster's Collegiate Dictionary* (MWC) was published in 2003 [20]. With over 250 000 entries, it is by far the largest lexicon analyzed. *Wordsmyth* [21] is a linguistical educational project. It provides four different dictionaries: the *Wordsmyth Educational Dictionary-Thesaurus* (WEDT) was first developed in 1980, followed later by the *Wordsmyth Learner's Dictionary-Thesaurus* (WLDT), the *Wordsmyth Children's Dictionary-Thesaurus* (WCDT) and the *Wordsmyth Illustrated Learner's Dictionary* (WILD). The first two are targetted at adults, WEDT being for advanced learners and WLDT for beginners, while the last two are aimed at children. Finally, *WordNet* (WN) [22] is a well-known lexical network, whose purpose is not only to provide definitions of words, but also semantical relations between them, quasi-synonymy, antonymy and hypernymy being the most important. Table II presents statistics for the lexicons after preprocessing and removal of stop lexemes:

- The number of lexemes in each dictionary (#Lexemes);
- The number of POS-tagged lemmas (#Lemmas);
- The average number of senses by lemma (Polysemy);
- The number of lemmas actually used in definitions (#Lemmas used);
- The ratio of lemmas used over the total number of lemmas (#Usage ratio).

TABLE II. BASIC STATISTICS.

Lexicon	#Lexemes	#Lemmas	Polysemy	#Lemmas Used	Usage ratio
WILD	4 244	3 081	1.377	2 995	0.972
WLDT	6 036	3 433	1.758	2 212	0.644
WCDT	20 128	9 303	2.164	6 597	0.709
CIDE	47 092	18 694	2.519	8 773	0.469
LDOCE	69 204	22 511	3.074	10 074	0.448
WEDT	73 091	28 986	2.522	18 197	0.628
WN	132 547	57 243	2.316	29 600	0.517
MWC	249 137	68 181	3.654	33 533	0.492

The eight lexicons were then converted to disambiguated, graph-based lexicons, by using the Stanford's POS-tagger [23] and the "most frequent sense" heuristics, i.e., by choosing the most frequent sense each time it appears in some given definition. Graph structural statistics for the digital lexicons are shown in Table III:

- The number of nodes in the directed graph (#Nodes);
- The number of arcs in the directed graph (#Arcs);
- The number of strongly connected components (#SCCs);
- The size of the largest SCC (<SCC);
- The diameter of the largest strongly connected component (Diam.);
- The density of the graph (Density);
- The characteristic path length (CPL).

TABLE III. GRAPH STRUCTURAL STATISTICS.

Lexicon	#Nodes	#Arcs	#SCCs	<SCC	Diam.	Density	CPL
WILD	4 244	45 789	2 750	1 446	17	10.79	1.75
WLDT	6 036	28 623	5 088	858	25	4.74	1.10
WCDT	20 128	102 657	17 551	2 341	22	5.10	0.87
CIDE	47 092	334 888	45 306	1 702	16	7.11	0.21
LDOCE	69 204	415 052	67 224	1 770	16	6.00	0.16
WEDT	73 091	362 569	67 318	5 056	29	4.96	0.61
WN	132 547	694 067	124 589	7 079	30	5.24	0.50
MWC	249 137	1 155 085	239 478	8 842	29	4.64	0.31

Psycholinguistic variables. In order to build our learning strategies, we considered three different psycholinguistic variables: the *age of acquisition* (AOA), the *concreteness* (Conc) and the written and oral *frequency* (Freq). The *age of acquisition* variable indicates the age at which a word is first learned, on average. As references, we used two different sources. The first one is a database made available by Brysbaert, with words learned between the ages 1 and 21, with their surface forms and lemmas [24]. The second one comes from the *Child Language Data Exchange System* (CHILDES) project [25]. It contains transcripts of children's conversations with words learned between the ages 1 and 11. The *concreteness* variable indicates the level of materiality of a word, which varies from 1 (the less concrete/most abstract) to 5 (the most concrete). It was collected by asking participants to classify words into these categories [26]. For example: *banana*, *apple* and *baby* are level 5, *belief* is level 1.19 and *although* is level 1.07. Finally, the *frequency* variable corresponds to the rate of occurrence of words in a given corpus, normalized to one million. Brysbaert et al. used the SUBTLEX_{US} corpus, as described in [27].

Derivated learning strategies. The number of learning strategies that one can design is huge. For a given dictionary containing n distinct senses, there are as many as $n!$, which is the number of permutations of the set $\{1, 2, \ldots, n\}$. We can distinguish two high-level categories:

1) *Graph-based* strategies are lists of lexemes built by exploiting the graph structure of a given lexicon. For instance, we could choose the next lexeme to learn by always picking the one whose out-degree is maximal (i.e., it appears in many definitions). It is worth mentioning that graph-based strategies are lexicon-dependent, i.e., they are adapted to the data.
2) *Psycholinguistic* strategies are obtained by choosing a lexeme according to its value with respect to a psycholinguistic variable. An example would be to pick first the lexemes that have been learned younger on average, up to the lexemes that have been learned later. Note that in that case, the strategies are lexicon-independent and are often incomplete, since psycholinguistic databases do not list all possible lexemes. Therefore, we need to complete the strategies by using a graph-based fallback strategy.

We focus our attention on 11 learning strategies that we now describe in more details. In the *minimum grouding set* strategy, the sequence of lexemes is built by picking minimum feedback vertex sets for each dictionary (see Section II). Although the problem is NP-complete in general, we were able to compute at least one optimal solution for 6 out of 8 dictionaries, and close approximations for the 2 remaining dictionaries. For the *dynamic degree* strategy, the list of lexemes is merely obtained by picking, at each step, the lexeme whose out-degree is maximal (since lexemes are "removed" at each step, the vertices degrees are indeed dynamic). From an algorithmic point of view, it corresponds to calling COMPLETECOST with S being the empty list. Concerning the *static degree* strategy, the list of lexemes is built beforehand in descending order of the vertices out-degree. This corresponds exactly to ordering the lexeme from the most frequently used in definitions to the less frequently used. The *Brysbaert/AOA*, *Brysbaert/Concreteness*, *Brysbaert/Frequency* and *Childes/AOA* are all "psycholinguistic strategies" built from [24]-[27]. A last strategy that we considered, called *NGSL/Frequency*, is obtained from the NGSL, designed precisely to help students learning English as a second language [12]. For the purpose of our analyses, this last list was enriched with 3 other lists provided by the same authors: the New Academic Word List (NAWL), the Business Service List (BSL), and the Technical Service List (TSL). In this last case, we also considered all the possible lemmas combinations as part of the strategy. For example, all the lemmas $something_{\text{NOUN}}$, $something_{\text{VERB}}$, $something_{\text{ADJ}}$, $something_{\text{ADV}}$ of the word *something* are included in the strategy. Finally, the strategies labelled *mixed* (*Grounding Set/Mixed*, *Dynamic Degree/Mixed* and *Static Degree/Mixed*) are described in Section V, as they are mostly used for comparing graph-based strategies with psycholinguistic strategies.

V. RESULTS AND DISCUSSION

Table IV compares the efficiency of the learning strategies against each one of the 8 digital dictionaries. The following measures are shown:

- The total number of lexemes learned directly (Cost);
- The efficiency, which is the ratio of the total number of lexemes learned over the number of lexemes learned through direct learning (Effect). More precisely, if the efficiency of a strategy S for a lexicon X is e, then, on average, it costs 1 to learn e lexemes from X using strategy S.
- In a few cases, we also include the coverage (Cover), which is the percentage of lexemes that are learned before resorting to the fallback strategy (see Algorithm 2). Only those cases where the coverage is below 90% are shown.

The efficiency of the 8 English dictionaries is plotted in Figure 2. Note that, in both figures, the strategies are ordered in decreasing order of efficiency.

From Table IV and Figure 2, one can distinguish three groups, which are characterized by the speed with which they break "definition cycles". The first group consists only of the *minimum grounding set* strategy. Naturally, it is the most efficient, since it has been optimized in this regard. We include it mostly as a baseline for comparison with other strategies. The second group is composed of the *dynamic and static degree* strategies, plus the three mixed ones, are all graph-based, the

TABLE IV. LEARNING STRATEGIES EFFICIENCY. MGS: MINIMUM GROUNDING SET, DD: DYNAMIC DEGREE, SD: STATIC DEGREE, MGM: MINIMUM GROUNDING SET/MIXED, DDM: DYNAMIC DEGREE/MIXED, SDM: STATIC DEGREE/MIXED, NF: NGSL/FREQ., BF: BRYSBAERT/FREQ., CA: CHILDES/AOA, BA: BRYSBAERT/AOA, BC: BRYSBAERT/CONCRETENESS

Strat.	Meas.	CIDE	LDOCE	MWC	WN	WEDT	WCDT	WLDT	WILD
	Lexemes	47 092	69 204	249 137	132 547	73 091	20 128	6 036	4 244
MGS	Cost	349	484	1 544	1 251	1 365	570	231	340
	Effic	134.93	142.98	161.36	105.95	53.55	35.31	26.13	12.48
DD	Cost	684	843	3 095	2 566	2 389	897	394	574
	Effic	68.85	82.09	80.50	51.66	30.59	22.44	15.32	7.39
SD	Cost	687	838	3 081	2 558	2 386	899	394	577
	Effic	68.55	82.58	80.86	51.82	30.63	22.39	15.32	7.36
MGM	Cost	704	966	3 077	2 835	2 348	957	398	612
	Effic	66.85	71.64	80.96	46.75	31.13	21.03	15.17	6.93
DDM	Cost	768	963	3 466	3 002	2 574	987	448	645
	Effic	61.32	71.82	71.88	44.15	28.39	20.39	13.47	6.57
SDM	Cost	793	988	3 776	3 021	2 721	1 024	454	678
	Effic	59.32	70.00	65.98	43.87	26.86	19.65	13.30	6.25
NF	Cost	2 813	1 954	5 010	4 126	3 236	1 354	712	1 260
	Effic	16.74	35.42	49.73	32.12	22.59	14.87	8.48	3.37
	Cover.			**71.3%**	**73.4%**	**67.6%**	**82.9%**		
BF	Cost	6 751	2 170	8 217	7 204	6 555	1 999	960	1 193
	Effic	6.98	31.89	30.32	18.40	11.15	10.07	6.29	3.56
CA	Cost	4 971	5 010	7 729	7 284	5 586	3 409	1 585	2 016
	Effic	9.47	13.81	32.23	18.20	13.08	5.90	3.81	2.11
	Cover.			**82.9%**	**86.3%**	**84.3%**			
BA	Cost	7 105	4 851	10 119	10 340	8 278	2 950	1 284	1 430
	Effic	6.63	14.27	24.62	12.82	8.83	6.82	4.70	2.97
BC	Cost	8 900	11 669	16 580	17 037	12 792	6 042	2 373	2 477
	Effic	5.29	5.93	15.03	7.78	5.71	3.33	2.54	1.71

dynamic degree strategy being slightly better on average. In contrast, all strategies of the third group (*NGSL/Frequency*, *Brysbaert/Frequency*, *Childes/AOA*, *Brysbaert/AOA* and *Brysbaert/Concreteness*) can be qualified as "noisy". Indeed, they contain lexemes chosen and ordered based on some external criteria or psycholinguistic variables. Because of this specific ordering, many lexemes that could otherwise have been learned by definition are learned through direct learning and therefore increase the total cost. Hence, these strategies are not as efficient for definition cycle breaking.

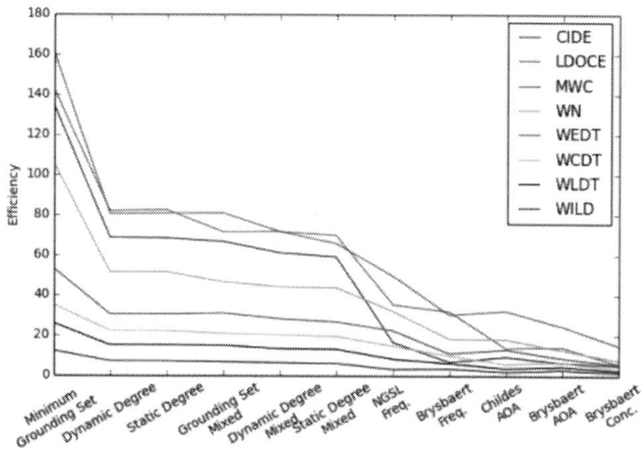

Figure 2. Dictionaries's efficiency

If we focus on the psycholinguistic strategies in the third group, it is worth mentioning that *NGSL/Frequency* turns out to be quite efficient, followed by *Brysbaert/Frequency*, both AOA-based strategies and, finally, *Brysbaert/Concreteness*. The fact that *Brysbaert/Concreteness* performs poorly is not very surprising. It seems quite natural to assume that one cannot learn a complete lexicon using only concrete lexemes: it is the combination of both concrete and abstract lexeme that conveys a complete understanding of a lexicon. Although the AOA-based strategies do not perform well in comparison with other strategies, it still shows that knowing less than 10% of the lexemes is sufficient to learn all remaining ones by definition alone. A plausible explanation for this observation is that learning new lexemes cannot be done only by reading definitions. In other words, our model does not capture the whole learning process, which is not surprising. Another possibility is that the databases are not sufficiently complete and may contain errors which impact significantly the efficiency of the strategy.

Since the best strategies seem to be lexicon-dependent, one might wonder if an efficient lexicon-independent strategy could be designed or if the *NGSL/Frequency* strategy is optimal. This is not the case, as illustrated by three additional strategies called *Mixed MFVS*, *Mixed Dynamic* and *Mixed Static*. These lists have been obtained by merging strategies from the eight dictionaries, which implies that the *same list* is used for each dictionary. Although the performance decreases slightly when the lists are mixed in comparison with the nonmixed versions, they still all perform better than *NGSL/Frequency*.

VI. Concluding Remarks

In this paper, we introduced a new automated method for the construction of lexeme learning strategies. Instead of using a corpus or psycholinguistic variable, our approach is based on the internal structure of lexicons related to the domain of interest. We also described a formal model for representing lexicons and learning strategies, as well as related algorithms and metrics. These tools allowed us to quantitatively compare the overall performance of various strategies for learning complete lexicons.

In our experimentation with English language lexicons, we discovered that the most efficient strategies are those that quickly break definition circularity. In this regard, a simple strategy ordering the words according to the number of times they appear in other words definition turned out to be very efficient. Although we do not pretend that the value of word lists resides solely in their efficiency, we believe our approach is of interest, especially in situations where neither public word lists or large corpora in the domain of interest are available. In this case, the use of a digital lexicon or specialized dictionary would allow one to easily build a list of words or concepts pertinent to that domain, and above all, the order in which one should learn them.

We have many ideas to extend further our observations. For instance, we would like to study other lexemes learning strategies, either based on the graph structure of the lexicon or from psycholinguistic variables. It would also be interesting to apply our model to lexicons specialized for a particular field, such as mathematics, medical care, computer sciences, etc. Finally, it seems reasonable to expect that our observations are language independent. However, this is harder to verify since the databases available in languages other than English are often less complete.

References

[1] N. Schmitt, "Instructed second language vocabulary learning," *Language teaching research*, vol. 12, no. 3, pp. 329–363, 2008.

[2] Y. Gu and R. K. Johnson, "Vocabulary learning strategies and language learning outcomes," *Language Learning*, vol. 46, no. 4, pp. 643–679, 1996.

[3] P. Joyce, "L2 vocabulary learning and testing: The use of l1 translation versus l2 definition," *The Language Learning Journal*, pp. 1–12, 2015.

[4] A. Blondin Massé, G. Chicoisne, Y. Gargouri, S. Harnad, O. Picard, and O. Marcotte, "How is meaning grounded in dictionary definitions?" in *TextGraphs-3*. Morristown, NJ, USA: Association for Computational Linguistics, 2008, pp. 17–24.

[5] S. Harnad, "The symbol grounding problem," *Physica D: Nonlinear Phenomena*, vol. 42, no. 1-3, pp. 335–346, 1990.

[6] D. F. Dansereau, "Learning strategy research," *Thinking and learning skills*, vol. 1, pp. 209–239, 1985.

[7] E. Bialystok, "Some factors in the selection and implementation of communication strategies," *Strategies in interlanguage communication*, pp. 100–118, 1983.

[8] C. K. Ogden, *Basic English: A general introduction with rules and grammar*. K. Paul, Trench, Trubner, 1944, vol. 29.

[9] M. West and M. P. West, *A general service list of English words: with semantic frequencies and a supplementary word-list for the writing of popular science and technology*. Addison-Wesley Longman Ltd, 1953.

[10] A. Coxhead, "A new academic word list," *TESOL Quarterly*, vol. 34, no. 2, pp. 213–238, July 2000.

[11] V. Brezina and D. Gablasova, "Is there a core general vocabulary? introducing the new general service list," *Applied Linguistics*, vol. 36, no. 1, pp. 1–22, 2013.

[12] C. Browne, "A new general service list: The better mousetrap we've been looking for," *Vocabulary Learning and Instruction*, vol. 3, no. 2, pp. 1–10, 2014.

[13] I. S. Nation, *Making and using word lists for language learning and testing*. John Benjamins Publishing Company, 2016.

[14] M. Aronoff and J. Rees-Miller, *The handbook of linguistics*, 1st ed. John Wiley & Sons, 2002.

[15] J. A. Bondy and U. S. R. Murty, *Graph Theory with Applications*. New York: Elsevier, 1976.

[16] R. M. Karp, *Reducibility among Combinatorial Problems*. Boston, MA: Springer US, 1972, pp. 85–103.

[17] P. Vincent-Lamarre, A. Blondin Massé, M. Lopes, M. Lord, O. Marcotte, and S. Harnad, "The latent structure of dictionaries," *TopiCS: Discovering principles of cognition by mining large, real-world data sets*, 2016.

[18] P. Procter, *Longman Dictionary of Contemporary English (LDOCE)*. Essex, UK: Longman Group Ltd., 1978.

[19] ——, *Cambridge International Dictionary of English (CIDE)*. Cambridge University Press, 1995.

[20] *Merriam-Webster's Collegiate Dictionary*, 11th ed., 2003.

[21] Wordsmyth, [Retrieved: January 2018]. [Online]. Available: https://www.wordsmyth.net

[22] C. Fellbaum, Ed., *WordNet An Electronic Lexical Database*. Cambridge, MA ; London: The MIT Press, 1998.

[23] K. Toutanova, D. Klein, C. D. Manning, and Y. Singer, "Feature-rich part-of-speech tagging with a cyclic dependency network," in *NAACL 2003*. Stroudsburg, PA, USA: Association for Computational Linguistics, 2003, pp. 173–180.

[24] V. Kuperman, H. Stadthagen-Gonzalez, and M. Brysbaert, "Age-of-acquisition ratings for 30,000 english words," *Behavior Research Methods*, vol. 44, no. 4, pp. 978–990, 2012.

[25] B. MacWhinney, *The CHILDES Project: Tools for Analyzing Talk*. Mahwah, NJ: Lawrence Erlbaum Associates, third edition, 2000.

[26] M. Brysbaert, A. B. Warriner, and V. Kuperman, "Concreteness ratings for 40 thousand generally known english word lemmas," *Behavior research methods*, vol. 46, no. 3, pp. 904–911, 2014.

[27] M. Brysbaert and B. New, "Moving beyond kučera and francis: A critical evaluation of current word frequency norms and the introduction of a new and improved word frequency measure for american english," *Behavior research methods*, vol. 41, no. 4, pp. 977–990, 2009.

Problems of the System Approach to the Study of Psychophysiology of Aesthetic Emotions Concerning an Architecture

Olga Chebereva
Federal State Budgetary Educational Institution of Higher Education "Nizhny Novgorod State University of Architecture and Civil Engineering"
Nizhny Novgorod, Russia
e-mail: chebereva_on@nngasu.ru, chebereva@mail.ru, chebereva02@gmail.com

***Abstract*— The forming in architectural creativity is the process of generation of architectural forms, the morphogenesis of "structural information". The search for principles, methods, and regularities of the forming process, i.e., the semiotic basis of the theory should be carried out as the search for cognitive principles and objective psycho-physiological foudation for creation and perception of the spatial environment by humans. This paper is aimed to reveal the essence of the interrelation between psychophysiology and geometric semantics of architectural form as a lingosemyotic structure. This interrelation represents the affective and reflexogenic basis of the spatial imagination and the corresponding dominant activity of the neural network. It turns out to be the basis of the theoretical concept of the study of psychophysiology of aesthetic emotions in the perception of form. The main subject of the paper is discussion of proper theoretical base for revealing the directions of experemental work providing objective results in neiroscience and for developing the architecture education methods. A list of necessary expepiments on personal emotional reactions on architecture objects is proposed.**

Keywords - architecture; structural information, cognitive; spatial imagination; neural network; emotional perception; experimental aesthetics.

I. Introduction

Neuropsychology of perception of the architectural form and artificial spatial environments by humans is an actual scientific problem. The study of it has become a special subject of the American Academy of Neuroscience for Architecture. There is a whole direction of "healing architecture" in European projects for healthcare. While studying the influence of three-dimensional visual stimuli on the brain, Russian and European scientists may potentially need a multidisciplinary study of the processes related to cognition and perception.

The paper is organized as follows. Section II differentiates streams of aesthetic rating and cognition of recognizable pattern vs archetype of perception [1]-[5]. Section III presents theoretical basis for the separation psychophysiologically conditioned modes of spatial imagination according to Duran [6] and some visual geometric representations of those modes [7]-[9]. In Section IV, it is given a brief comparison of the concepts discussed by Duran [6] and Ukhtomsky [10]. In Section V, it is proposed a list of necessary experiments. The conclusion outlines future effects and unresolved problems of investigating the connection between formal characteristics of an architectural form as a visual stimulus and psycho-physiological responses.

II. Cognition of Recognizable Pattern vs Perception of Archiptype

From the variety of conceptions [2], we see that cognitive and perception processes (see Table 1) are the interaction of two informative horizons, i.e., the language of concepts and the visual language representing a three-dimensional lattice for sliding the composite design. The experimental aesthetics of Fechner (Table 1) discerns associative and direct factors of the aesthetic impact of the form, similar to the concept of Shapoval [3] (see Fig. 1).

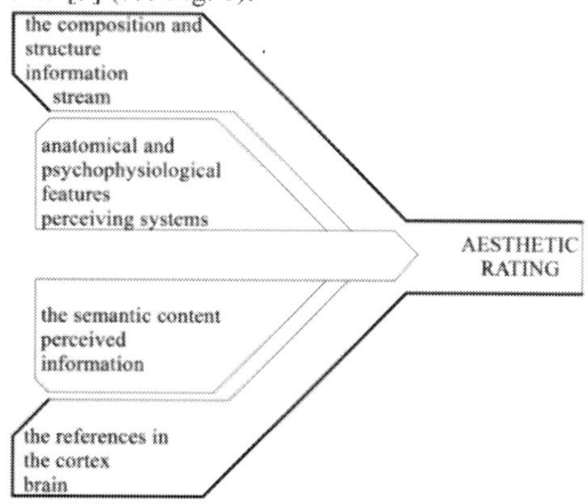

Figure 1. Two streams of aesthetic evaluation.

There is a wide connection between the streams of aesthetic impact and combinatoric levels of architectural form. The structure of architectural form is a kind of two-level grammatics (see Table 1).

TABLE I. COMBINATORIC LEVELS OF ARCHITECTURAL FORM

Researcher	Combinatorial level of architectural form	
	Signs, symbols, Pattern associations	***formal geometric (archetypes)and Absrtract assotiations***
Fechner [1]	associative factor	formal factor
Jenks [4]	signifier	signifying
Alekxander[5]	pattern language	-
general	recognizable types of forming	geometry archetypes

Primary geometrical elements give abstract associations because of connection with genetic archetypes of artificial perception. The problems of genetic archetypes (primary instruments of forming the architectural object), rhythm, meter, space, metaphor, etc. equally (if not more) belong to the problem area of architecture, which is usually defined as the theory of architecture. The rhythm archetype has no clear foundation in the theory of architecture: there is a lack of general theory of composition at the formal and subject levels [1]. The fundamental archetypes of architectural forming are determined as geometrical manifestations of revealed anthropological structures of the imagination [6]. This implies the reflexes based on archetypal groups of the spatial-imagination basic patterns [6]. Stable morphological artifacts of the architecture could be called "ARCHItypes" by analogy with recognizable types in other fields of culture. The neuropsychological studies of the archaeologist and anthropologist David Lewis Williams [7] are interesting in this regard. His experimental work shows that the motor skills of the modern subjects at drawing geometric primitives are completely analogous to the cave ones [7]: metric linear grid, ornamental concentric and rhythmic motives, spiral forms, etc (see Fig. 2).

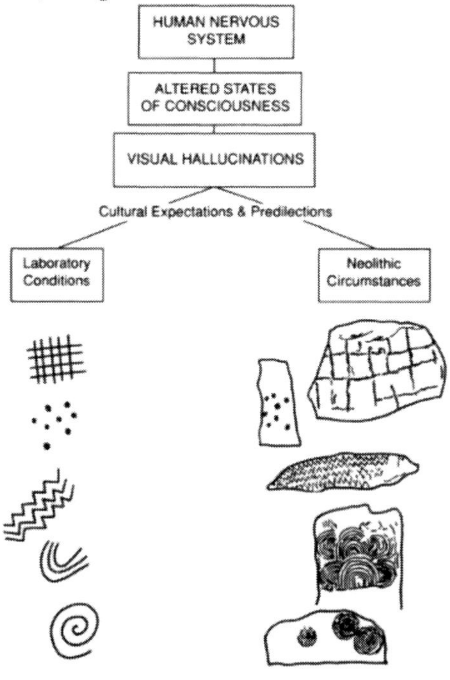

Figure 2. Comparison of the entoptic forms depicted under laboratory conditions (after Siegel 1977) and in Neolithic art [7].

All this is currently used by the formal contemporary art and architecture. That is why ARCHItypes should be considered as stable and typologically recognizable elements of architectural forms and composite structures composed of them, bearing certain symbolic meanings and correlated with the epoch and style. Archetypes are geometrized manifestations of the spatial-imagination modes having a reflexogenic nature, as it was shown in Williams's experiments and Picasso drawings (see Fig. 2 and Fig. 3). Let us recall that the primary art examples are more ancient than languages and architecture for more than 40 800 years BC [8]. From this viewpoint, the imagination mechanisms for the mass, space, and metro-rhythmic ratio represent the "archetypes" of architectural form [1]. The primary elements of architecture and the rules for their connection are still the main problem in the theory of architectural composition, being not its specific subject.

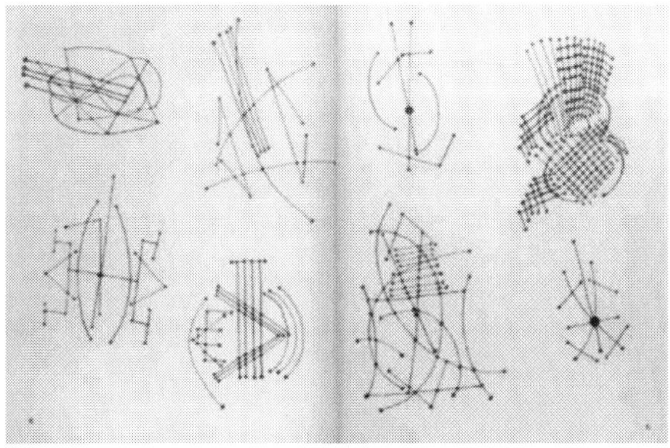

Figure 3. Drawings of Picasso (extracted from [9]).

Figure 3 represents the drawing of Picasso (1924) included in the illustrated edition "Unknown Masterpiece" [9].

III. Durand's Cognition Concept

A. *Durand's concept about archetypes of spatial imagination*

An interesting research of the archetype revealing in art structures has been performed by Durand (1921-2012) in the middle of the XXth century [6]. This research was based on the reflexology of Bekhterev, Jung's psychotherapy statistics, and the seminars "Eranos" (see [6] and refs. therein). The Durand's concept is completely compatible with the system-active approach [2] currently used in researches on the theory of architecture. It refers to the triad of the thinking and modalities as the base for the superstructure. This triad involves the imagination, the subject, and the object of imagination. Within the Durand's concept, this triad confronts the absolutely opposite (with respect to imagination) concept, i.e., "the time is death" [6]. An analysis of imagination modes leads to the inference that they are based on both, psychological as well as physiological mechanisms of perception and interpreting the physical laws and phenomena of the material world. From the viewpoint of Durand, anthropological structures of imagination, i.e., the process of forming appears to be essentially the result of the mode geometrization.

Since we are talking about very ancient archetypes of spatial imagination, only psychophysiological basis of Durand's concept is employed. It consists of three basic imagination modes. The first one is the postulated imagination mode corresponding to a social thinking [6]. The main psychophysiological mechanisms of the postulated correspond to the instinct "toward the goal", the extrapolation instinct, etc. Spatial geometrization of postulated mode is based on biomechanical functions of the skeletal musculature and vestibular apparatus, and on the peculiarities of interaction with other individuals. In the triad of Vitruvius [11], the postulated corresponds to the "benefit", as well as to the "function" (see Fig. 4). The form depends on its purpose. This concept includes the aggregate of social meanings of the form and its ideology as indirect function providing the social certainty of the form.

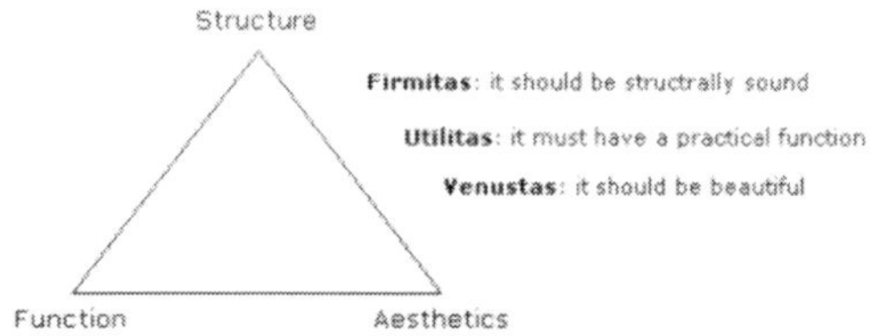

Figure 4. Vitruvian triad.

The scheme for geometrization of postulated imagination in architectural form becomes to be a structural frame for the dynamic and static axes. This mode is based on the geometrization of the uprightness instinct and the resistance to gravity (tectonics, in analogy to "gravitational forming"). Postulated basis underlies the parametric descriptions of the boundaries of objects and spaces, as a subject of social agreement. The same refers as well to movement representation in general, including the spatial element connection scheme, functional routes, etc.

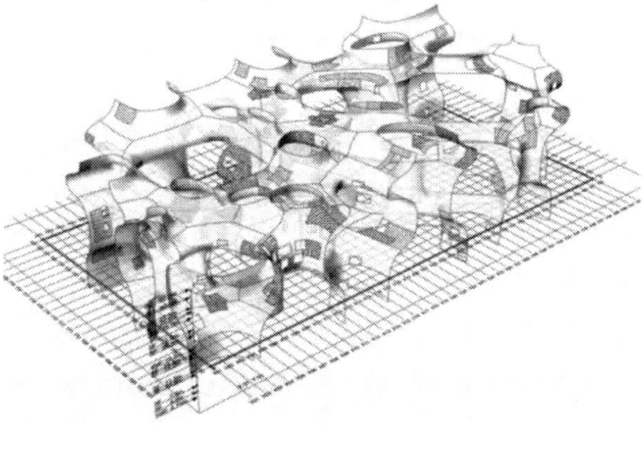

Figure 5. The Toyo Ito project of the National Taichung Theater [12].

The formal and semantic bases of the postulated mode of spatial imagination are linked with geometric metaphors of physical phenomena, such as configuration of force fields, momentums, trajectories, lines of forces, directions, points of force application, etc. Visual representation of these metaphors is very close to mathematical concepts in a symbolic graphic form used in natural sciences since Euclid's "Elements". So, postulated elements of the spatial imagination are inspired by anatomic proprioceptive signals (receptors in the muscles, tendons, joints) and corresponding excitation in the neuron ensemble. This statement could be illustrated by the project of Toyo Ito [12] with the plan based on a math concept (Voronoi diagram, see Fig. 5).

Implementation of the postulated imagination in the architectural form occurs mainly in the structure static and dynamic (tonic) axes, but also manifests itself in a gradient distribution of visual masses along these axes.

The digestive mode of imagination corresponds to the ontogenetic modality of thinking. The digestive mode is based on the physiological food instinct, i.e., the need for potential energy for building systems. This is similar to individual growth of a particular organism (the ontogenesis process). The digestive metaphor in the architecture could be associated with the mass. In the triad of Vitruvius «Utilitas, Firmitas, Venustas» [11], it actually corresponds to the «structure»; the same is the "strength". The digestive mode represents the constructive definiteness of the form. The basis of the mental representations of the "mass" is a material body or, in a broader sense, matter in a condensed state. Anatomically, the digestive mode is controlled by the interoceptive signals (from receptors of internal organs) to the Central Nervous System (CNS). Implementation of the digestive imagination mode is realized in the mass-to-space ratio in the architecture forms.

The copulative imagination mode should be interpreted more broadly as a regime of change, organizing rhythms, divisions, intervals, and fluctuations in the proportions of mass and space. Durand's copulative mode implies that an imagination is inherent to the human physiological processes of higher nervous activity, biophysics, phylogenetics, i.e., anthropogenic modality of thinking. The semantic subtext of rhythm is a manifestation of the most important property of life, i.e., the changes. The copulative mode highlights the difference between psychological states (joy, sorrow) as functional transition from one process to another one, from one mode to the next one, and affects the psychophysiology. General physical sense and the archetype of the copulative imagination mode is the wave, i.e., the oscillatory nature of the matter in general, including biological and physiological processes (the electrogenesis in CNS). In the triad of Vitruvius, the manifestation of copulative imagination mode is expressed by the term "Aesthetics"; aesthetic certainty of the form. Physiologically, this mode is based on the signals from exteroceptive receptors (cutaneous, visual, auditory, olfactory ones), subconscious internal perception of electrogenesis (alternating currents) of the brain and CNS, and low energy electromagnetic fields of the body cells.

The thesis "primary characteristic of architectural masterpiece is the space" [1] corresponds to the antithesis of the imagination triad as an objective source "the time is death". The time (under the relativity) and the death (biological or cultural memory termination) exist in the physical sense only where any substance is presented, i.e., the substance in a condensed state, or the biological life. The imagination modes control the space as objective (i.e., existing regardless of imagination) reality. An artistic extreme metaphor "time as death" is opposite to the notion of "mass" as emptiness or vacuum, i.e., the something that is opposite to the human beings.

A single natural-scientific source of discoveries and "white spots" of the theory of composition is called by the term "physiomimetics". It was introduced by Soar and Andreen [13] for modeling the spatial structures for buildings by analogy with the molecular lattices. But this

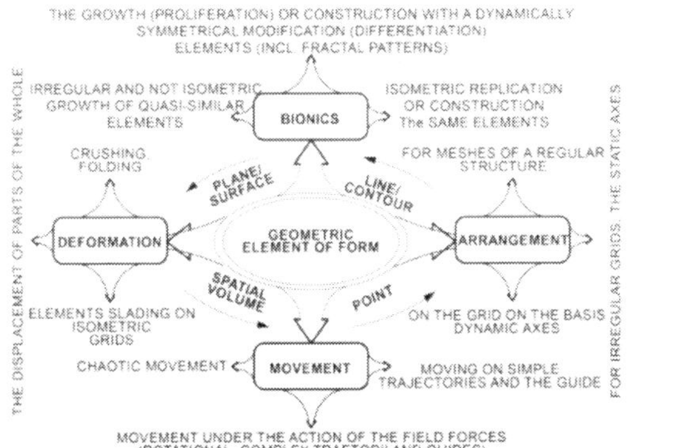

Figure 6. Interrelation and integration between phisiomimetical methods and the principles of architeture forming.

term reflects the core of all methodological techniques of architectural forming, in line with the fundamental and applied physics (in math models), not only bionics (Fig.6).

B. Durand's concept and Anokhin's "cognitom"

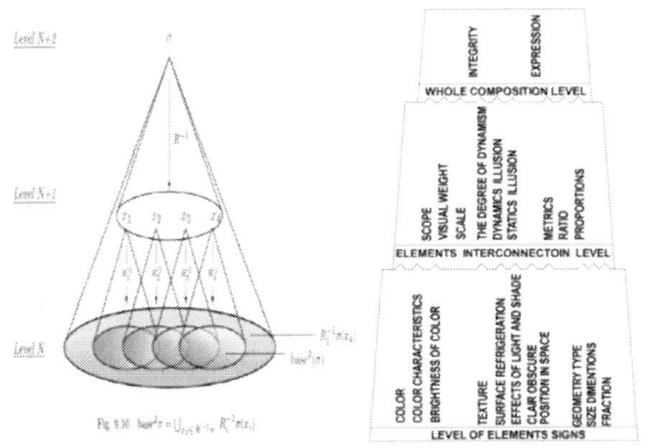

Figure 7. Comparison of the "cognitom" formalization accoding to Anokhin [11] and the hierarchy of formal compisition properties.

Architectural forms represent the systemic encoded visual "information" in stereo-metric elements of the form/space, reflecting the multidimensional data from the highest physiological functions. At the same time, the functions work as filters and are included into the conversion mechanisms (see Figs. 6, 7, 8). The triad of imagination (according to Durand: imagining-imagination-fantastic) is a three-step statement, which corresponds to the graphs structure of "cognitom", i.e. a hypennetwork brain model proposed by Anokhin [14]. Similar interconnection exist between the "cognitom" formalization of the architecture of mind and the hierarchy of formal composition properties [15] (see Fig. 6). The highest level usually represents typical patterns, compositions (ARCHItypes), the lowest collects plimary visual elements (extraception stimulus and arhetypes), the middle one includes instruments of interconnection of elements (intraception archetypes).

IV. Durand's Concept and Ukhtomsky's Dominance

Interesting results come from the consideration of architecture history as the homological sets of various forms. The architectural form itself becomes a derivative of the four spatial operators, which are geometrical representations of abstract psychophysiological associations (see Fig. 9). The system of higher mental functions is controlled by a dynamic dominance. According to Ukhtomsky [10], the principle of dominance is applicable to the strategies of visual perception, which were studied by Arnheim [14]. The dominance might serve as the most determining factor integrating feelings in the process of visual perception into the whole picture-«gestalt». The linguistic approach [5] to architecture is unable to explain, how a suite of primary geometric elements transform into the «enigmatic signifier» [4]. The way of transmission of multidimensional data of elements into the symbolic form of architecture is the actual problem of the architectural theory.

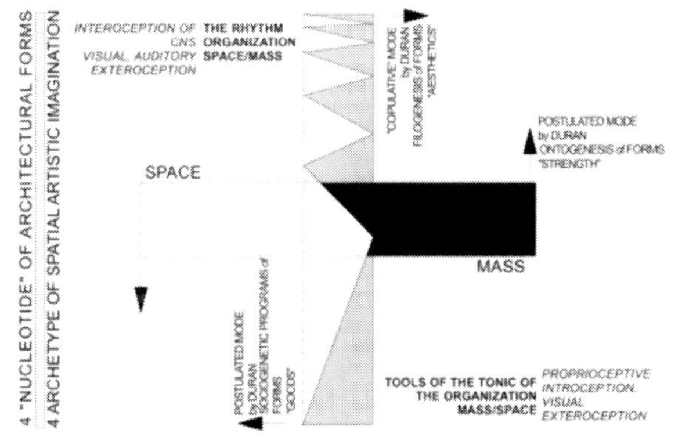

Figure 8. Four «nucleatides» of architecture form have complementary pairs crossing each other.

Any architectural form can be represented as a vector field model. The model's complexity depends on the forming paradigm. The change of paradigms is connected with revolutions of scientific knowledge, which implies that the science changes the ideology of art [16]. Consideration of the archetypical imagination modes in the light of physiology and the hypothesis on bi-similar basis of spatial imagination (see Fig. 1, Table 1) leads to a natural-science concept of the geometrical imagination. This implies that there is mutual reflection of the conscious- (ARCHItypes) and subconscious-level (archetypes) regularities, phenomena, principles of matter organization in living and nonliving nature (see Fig. 6). This concept explains the hypothesis of supra-modality of visual art and music according to Korsakova-Kreyn [17].

The dominance is also controlled by the experiences and beliefs, as well as by the physiology. According to Maslow [18], the pyramid of self-censorship reflects the "upward" sequence of dominances from the lowest to the highest level. Durand repeated Ukhtomsky regarding the concept of an art.

Three functional modes of imagination, i.e., digestive, copulative, and postulated ones, could be called as the mass mode; the metro-rhythmic mode; and the tonic-axis mode of the architectural structure. The concept "the time is death" transforms into the mode of space-time. The proof of interrelation between the dominance principle and the geometry forming could be provided by representation of the ontological categories of architecture (i.e., function, design, style, etc.) as a set of connected parameters. Ancient Egyptian architecture describes the mass prevalence. The Gothic and Baroque architecture actualizes the vertical elements (prevalence of the postulated mode). The analysis of actual for each style set of formal parameters gives the sequence of imagination modes in the history of architecture, which is equal to the structure of pyramid of self-censorship according to Maslow (see Fig. 9).

The projection of this concept onto the forming process gives an understanding of the form scale as a consequence of interaction of copulative and digestive imagination modes (see Figs. 8, 9). The archetypes and manifestations of the anthropomorphic scale vs socio scale (Neolithic community had about 30-40 people) emerged in the Neolithic period.

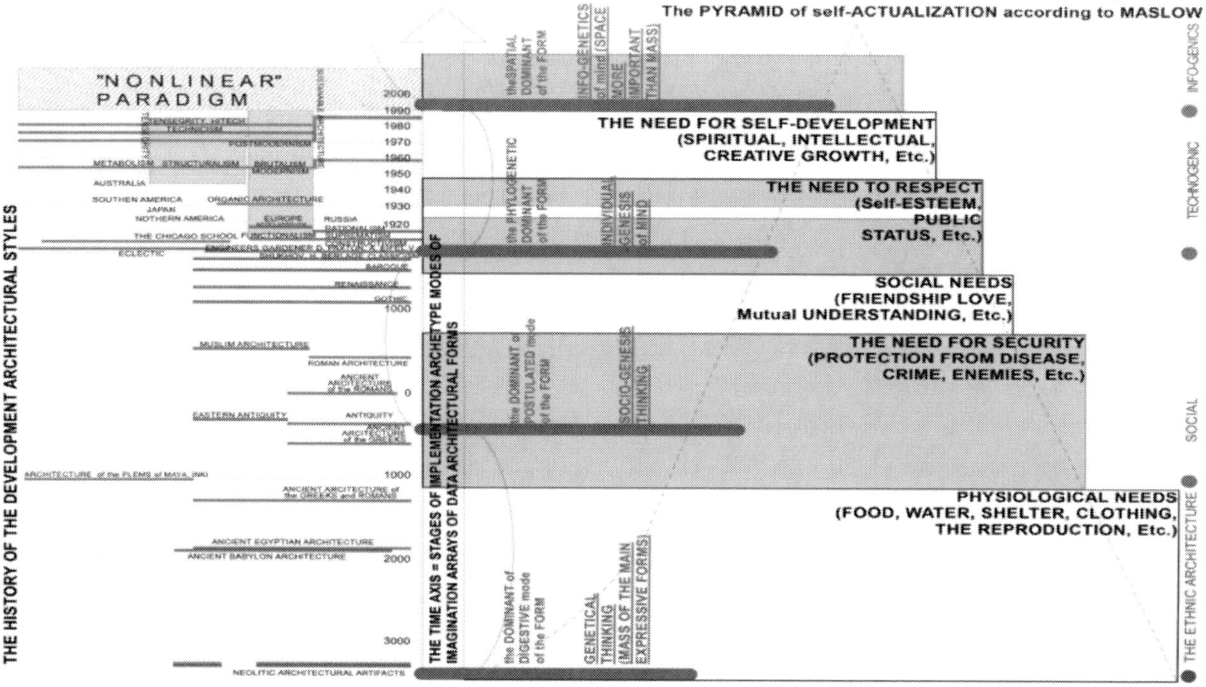

Figure 9. Comparison Preliminary graphical analysis of the actualization of imagination modes in the history of architecture.

V. CONSEQUENCES FOR FUTURE EXPERIMENTS

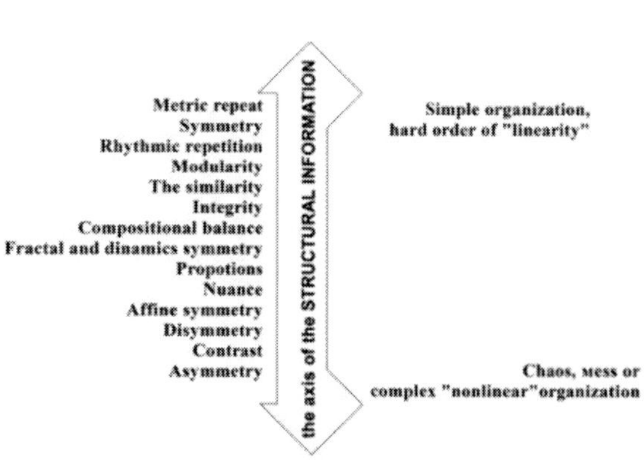

Figure 10. Structural information from the forming processes.

So, the architecture form appears at the intersection of four imagination modes (see Fig. 8), namely the material of architecture (mass/space), composition tools (and the metro-rhythmic frames of axes). They could be treated as "operators" of the three-dimensional form related to "structural information" (see Fig. 10) and semantic features. Analysis of the form as a set of parameters of archetype modes opened the way for researching dominances of emotional perception (Fig.7). It is reasonable to combine the tracking of physiological processes (the frequency of respiration, palpitation, EEG parameters, etc.) with purely cognitive tasks associated with individual perception and spatial thinking of the subjects. This includes the following groups of studies with the fixation of the physiological systems work and the objects of the subject's concentration:

1. Experiments on the mental rotation of figures (spatial and impossible) without changing the proportions. In this

case, the analysis of the results should take into account the different character of the silhouette, the discrete or specific configuration of the forms.

Experiments on the mental rotation of figures (spatial and impossible) with changed the proportions, color, texture, etc.

2. Testing the physiological changes when displaying video with different scenarios of perception of the same architectural form, as well as groups of architectural forms of different styles, groups of architectural objects that are topologically equivalent (homologous series of architectural forms).

3. Video rotation of models of architectural forms with the study of fixation of attention on their structure, comparison of little changes of the similar structures.

4. The study of the role of the part, the relationship between details and the whole, a group of experiments on the perception of generalized models of known architectural objects.

5. Perception of monotonous visual media and architectural fields (short and long surfaces, facades).

6. Cognitive tasks before and after the experiment.

7. The comparison of the perception of artificial three-dimensional objects with the perception of natural prototypes.

It is necessary also to account for the possibility of cognitive dissonance and other stress factors in the subjects' reaction, comparison of results for different age and other categories of subjects. For diagnostics of the physiological reactions, not so expensive equipment is needed, such as fMRI, the thermal imager, ECG, EEG, and the eye-tracker (to account for the attention-fixing points of the testing subjects).

VI. Conclusions

It is necessary to mark that a structure of an architectural form can be taken as a system of psychophysiologicaly encoded visual stimulus information. The systemic relationship between psychophysiological concepts and the theory of formal composition promises an effective experimental study. The list of experimental study proposed in this paper is not completed because it should be supplemented by wide graphic and video series of visual stimuli. A convincing chain of relations between the formal characteristics of the architectural form as visual stimuli and neural responses is not complete. However, the developed theoretical base guarantees not only the right direction of the experimental strategy, but also its reliability. The main aim of this study is to find clear interrelations between the geometry of architectural form and the way of emotional perception. The second aim is to establish an interrelation between emotional reactions and phisiomimetic patterns of forming to reveal possible new ways in architecture forming. The third goal is to clarify possible new directions in architectural education, namely — methods, strategies, necessary new disciplines, etc. However, the greatest difficulty of the forthcoming work will be precisely the analysis of the experimental data.

References

[1] L. Azizyan, I. Dobritsyna, G. Lebedeva. Theory of composition as a poetics of architecture. Moscow: Progress-Tradition, 2002.

[2] Y. Yankovskaya, "The architectural composition and semiotics are the genesis of ideas", Architecton: news from universities, vol. 7, 2004. Availble from http://archvuz.ru/2004_2/3. Retrieved 2018.01.06

[3] A. Shapoval. The Theory of Formal Composition: A Textbook for Universities. Kazan: "Design quarter", 2016.

[4] Cr. Alexander. A pattern language.Towns.Buildings.Construction. Oxford University Press, 1977.

[5] Ch. A. Jencks. The New Paradigm in Architecture. Yale University Press, 2002.

[6] G. Durand. Les structures antropologiques de l'imaginaire. Paris:Dunod, 1992.

[7] J. D. Lewis-Williams, "Discussion and Criticism. on Vision and Power in the Neolitic: Evidence from the Decorated Monuments", Current Antropology, vol. 34(1), pp. 55-56, 1993.

[8] "Paleolithic paintings in El Castillo cave in Northern Spain. Uranium-series dating reveals Iberian paintings are Europe's oldest cave art", University of Bristol news, vol. 14, 2012. Available from http://www.bris.ac.uk/news/2012/8560.html. Retrieved 2018.01.06

[9] "Pablo Picasso Asemic line drawing". Available from: http://seks-ua.blogspot.ru/2013/10/pablo-picasso-asemic-line-drawing.htm Retrieved 2018.01.06

[10] E.Y.Zueva and K.B. Zueva. The Concept of Dominance by A.A. Ukhtomsky and Anticipation. Springer International Publishing Switzerland, 2015.

[11] V. Mako. Architecture and Ideology. Cambridge Scholars Publishing, 2014.

[12] Toyo Ito& Associates: Architects, Projects. Available from http://toyo-ito.co.jp/WWW/Project_Descript/2015-/2015-p_04/2015-p_04_en.html Retrieved 2018.01.06

[13] R. Soar and D. Andreen, "The Role of Additive Manufacturing and Physiomimetic Computational Design for Digital Construction", Architectural Design, Vol. 82(2), pp. 126–135, 2012.

[14] K. Anokhin, "Cognitom is a hyper-network model of a dump", Lecture given in Kurchatov Institute. Available from: http://neuroinfo.ru/conf/Content/Presentations/Anokhin2015.pdf. Retrieved 2018.01.06

[15] R. Anheim. Art and visisual perception: A phichology of the creative eye. University of California press. Berkeley and Los Andgeles, California, 1997.

[16] L. Shlain. Art and phisics:parallel visions in space, time, and light. New York: W. Morrow & Company, Inc.,1991

[17] M. Korsakova-Kreyn and W. J. Dowling, "Emotional Processing Music: Study in Affective Responses to Tonal Modulationin Controlled Harmonic Progressions and Real Music", Psychomusicology: Music, Mind and Brain, vol. 24(1), pp. 4/20, 2014.

[18] Abraham H. and Maslow. Motivation and Personality (2nd ed.) N.Y.: Harper & Row, 1970.

[19] S.Parin, S.Polevaya, A.Polavaya, "A Neirochemical Framework to Stress and the Role of the Endogenous Opioid System in the Control of Healf Rate Variability for Cognitive Load" Proc. of COGNITIVE 2017: The Ninth International Conference on Advanced Cognitive Tecnologies and Applications, pp. 16-20, Copyright ©IARIA, 2017.,2017

Image Transformations in a Cognitive System

Tunnel transition and combining ensembles

Ekaterina D. Kazimirova
Kaspersky Lab
Moscow, Russia
e-mail: Ekaterina.Kazimirova@kaspersky.com

***Abstract* — The nature of creativity and its hidden mechanisms are areas that researchers have only recently begun to approach. In this paper, within the symbol-image cognitive architecture paradigm, we consider some operations on graphs that can be compared to the process of image synthesis and transformation in a cognitive system. We address such phenomena as the combination of neural ensembles and tunnel (sub-barrier) transition in a cognitive system. We also consider degree of fusibility of a cognitive system that characterizes its creative ability.**

Keywords- graph; symbol; attribute; cognitive architecture; creativity.

I. Introduction

In the era of the rapidly developing ecosystem of living things (the Internet of Things) and human-friendly anthropomorphic robots [1][2][3], the issues related to developing artificial intelligence systems that are not only rational, but also creative, take on a special significance. The ability of cognitive systems to generate new thoughts and new images will turn machine into man's equal partner in addressing important issues of the 21st century, in solving its challenges, such as overcoming disease and resolving complicated economic problems.

In this paper, we discuss some of the mechanisms that could be employed in artificial cognitive systems to generate new information. Such ability is treated as a synonym for creativity.

The paper is organized as follows. A description of the model is provided in Section II. An example of the model's application is provided in Section III. The summary and conclusions are in Section IV.

II. Description of the Model

We consider the following organization of a cognitive system. Each image encoded in the system is represented by its attributes and the corresponding symbol. The attributes are linked together by the image's symbol [4][5]. The main role of symbolization is compressing information, but we believe it is equally important that it prevents images with the same attributes from being mixed together. This idea was briefly described in [6].

For the sake of brevity, we consider a two-layer system (graph), where the first layer encodes image attributes and the second layer encodes image symbols.

A. Basic Relationships

In our model, the following relationships are formed between a symbol and its attributes. When two or more attributes are activated, the symbol is also activated. Conversely, when a symbol is activated, the attributes of its image are also activated.

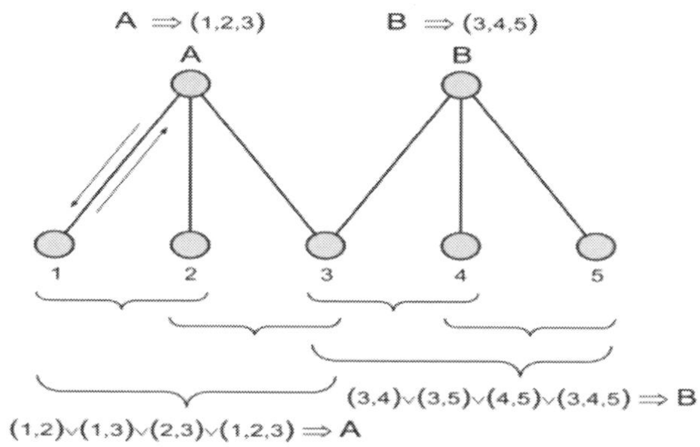

Figure 1. The basic model represented by a two-layer graph. The markers "A" and "B" correspond to symbols, 1, 2, 3, 4, 5 correspond to their attributes.

In Figure 1, the basic two-layer model is presented. The symbol "A" is activated when there are signals from particular attributes (nodes 1, 2, or 3) in different combinations, (provided that more than one node is involved). The symbol "B" is activated when there are signals from nodes 3, 4, or 5 in different combinations (also provided that more than one attribute is involved). When the symbol "A" is activated, this leads to the activation of an image consisting of a set of attributes (1, 2, 3). Activation of the symbol "B" leads to the activation of an image consisting of a different set of attributes (3, 4, 5).

Let us consider the following example. The relations between attributes and symbols in our model of a cognitive system work similarly to children's riddles. Something that is round, striped, and sweet (nodes: attributes) is a watermelon (node: symbol); something that is striped and orange, with sharp claws and teeth, is a tiger.

Concerning the problem of the possibility of images being mixed together, note that a cat and a dog have many attributes in common. According to our model, it is symbols that enable the cognitive system to tell them apart.

Let us illustrate the "more than one attribute" rule. Given the attributes "striped" and "round", we can guess "watermelon" and given the attributes "striped" and "with sharp teeth", we can guess "tiger". However, given only one attribute (e.g., "striped"), we cannot guess what the object is. And conversely, specifying a symbol (e.g., watermelon), brings its attributes to mind ("striped", "round", "sweet", "with seeds", etc.).

In a real-world system, the number of layers is obviously much greater. For example, there is the integrative symbol "carnivores" (Lat. Carnivora) above the symbols "cat" and "dog", etc.

B. Attribute and Attention

We assume that a cognitive process starts when one of the cognitive system's elements appears in the field of attention. The development of a thought involves revealing connections between that element and its neighbors, as well as forming its new relationships and connections with other elements of the cognitive system.

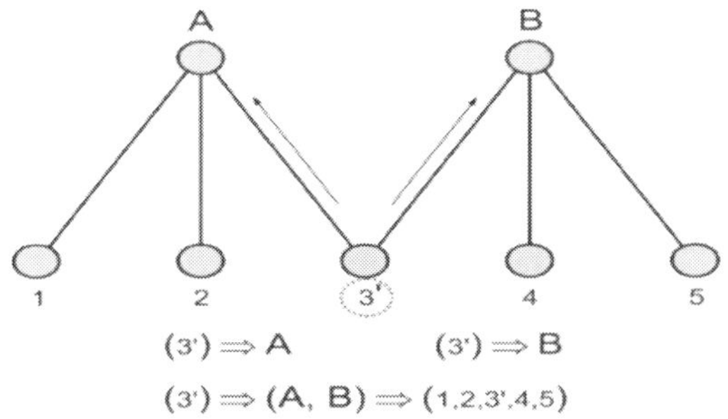

Figure 2. Activation of two symbols by one attribute.

According to our concept, prolonged activation of one attribute (for a time interval $t > t_{att}$) increases its influence. As a result, that attribute, even if it is alone, can activate the associated symbols. In Figure 2, the attribute "3" is activated by attention and, in turn, activates the symbols "A" and "B".

For example, thinking about speed, we can recall a car, a cheetah, and an airplane.

Below we look at the ways in which a system based on these rules can generate new information by transforming images – that is, creating new images out of existing ones.

C. Combining ensembles

The symbols associated with a certain attribute can be activated by activating the attribute for a time interval $t > t_{att}$. These symbols, in turn, activate the rest of their attributes. As a result, a new ensemble combining the elements of two images (symbols and attributes) is formed.

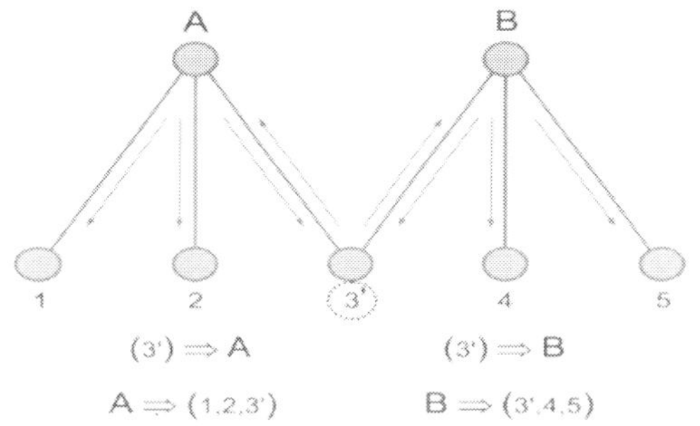

Figure 3. The activation of symbols A and B leads to the activation of all their attributes. This gives rise to an ensemble ("A + B").

In Figure 3, the attribute "3" is enhanced by attention or emotion, i.e., it receives additional activation from "neurons" (represented by nodes in our model) that are external relative to the ensembles A and B. Due to enduring activation, it activates both neuron-symbols "A" and "B" simultaneously. These two images, i.e., symbols "A" and "B" plus all their attributes, are temporarily united into an ensemble. Starting from that moment, the attributes of image "B" also belong to the symbol "A", and vice versa (for a certain time interval). This mechanism could serve as the basis for metaphorical thinking (feature transfer). We briefly described this problem in [7]. Issues related to the integration of information in the cognitive system are also discussed in [8].

Let us consider the following example of metaphorical thinking. In [9], the general metaphor "argument is war" is presented. G. Lakoff and M. Johnsen write, "We see the person we are arguing with as an opponent. We attack his positions and we defend our own. We gain and lose ground. We plan and use strategies. If we find a position indefensible, we can abandon it and take a new line of attack." What they describe in this passage is attribute transfer between the concepts "war" and "argument".

It is important to realize that the transfer process starts after the common attribute of two concepts is found. In the case of the metaphor "argument is war", the term "confrontation" represents the common attribute, while the transfer process follows the mechanism described above.

G. Lakoff and M. Johnsen write, "The most important claim we have made so far is that metaphor is not just a matter of language, that is, of mere words. We shall argue that, on the contrary, human thought processes are largely metaphorical."

D. Tunnel transition

Under certain conditions, the activation of attributes can lead to transitions on the same (attribute) level (activation of attributes through attributes) rather than the activation of symbols. Suppose that there is a neurotransmitter acting at the network's attribute level, dynamically strengthening the connections and thus facilitating the transition from one attribute to another. Under such conditions, attributes (neuron attributes) can activate each other without the activation of symbols (see Figure 4). We called this effect "tunnel (sub-barrier) transition". In this case, the activation wave can "dive" under an adjacent symbol and activate one of the more remote symbols rather than the nearest one.

This process could be controlled by presence or absence of a neurotransmitter. Favorable conditions for such a process could also be created by the "constitutional" characteristics of the cognitive system, e.g., relatively weak connections between the attribute and symbolic levels (attribute-symbol), or, on the contrary, by the relatively strong connections at the attribute level (attribute-attribute).

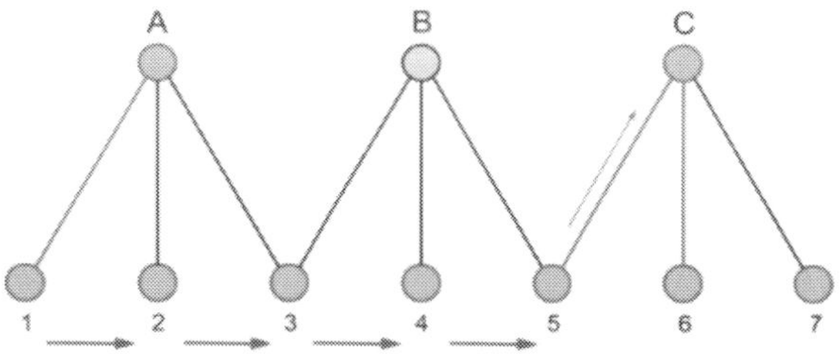

Figure 4. Flow within the cognitive system.

We would like to emphasize that Hebb's rule [10] describes the strengthening of connections between closely spaced (directly contacting) neurons. In contrast, the tunnel transition corresponds to the formation of connections between non-neighboring neurons that are not directly connected.

E. *Fusibility of thinking*

Within our model, the presence of a "neurotransmitter" in a subnet containing attributes and/or the cognitive system's constitutional features make this system more "fusible", i.e., more fluid (akin to molten metal). It would be interesting to study the "coefficient of fusibility" (K_{fus}) of a cognitive system defined as the ratio of the connection strength at the attribute level to the strength of attribute-symbol connections:

$$K_{fus} = W_{atr} / W_{symb} \qquad (1)$$

Note that mental disorders can be associated with different types of associative thinking impairment. For example, the so-called acceleration of thinking (racing thoughts) is characterized by an excessive emergence of associations. As a result, thinking becomes superficial, with attention being switched too easily.

Let us examine how the character of thinking depends on K_{fus}. The creative process involves working with associations as the mechanism of new image production. We believe that the "coefficient of fusibility" may control the ease with which associations emerge in the cognitive system. At low values of K_{fus}, the "flow" (activation of connections) between images on the same attribute level and the subsequent merging of different images into new ones is hampered, and the system becomes rigid. Such a system can only work with the images (symbols together with their attributes) it already contains. The system can analyze them, i.e., it knows the properties of each symbol and can attribute it. However, such a cognitive system is virtually incapable of synthesizing new images. As K_{fus} increases, it becomes possible for new images to appear within the cognitive system. With $K_{fus} > K_{critical}$, flow across the attribute level becomes too easy, numerous associations arise, but they are not fixed in new images. This process represents a thinking disorder.

In psychology, our concept corresponds (to some extent) to Raymond Cattell's concept [11] of fluid and crystallized intelligence, where *crystallized* intelligence is the ability to operate with already acquired knowledge, skills and experience, while *fluid* intelligence (or *fluid* reasoning) corresponds to the ability to reason and solve novel problems in new ways.

III. EXAMPLE

As an example, let us consider the poem *"The Soft Moscow Rain"* by Osip Mandelstam, translated by Richard McKane [12]:

> It shares so stingily
> its sparrow cold –
> a little for us, a little for the clumps of trees,
> a little for the cherries for the hawker's stall.
> And a bubbling grows in the darkness,
> the light fussing of tea-leaves,
> as though an ant-hill in the air
> were feasting in the dark green grass;
> fresh drops stirred
> like grapes in the grass,
> as though the hot-bed of the cold
> was revealed in web-footed Moscow.

Let us consider the main symbols and their important attributes that are mentioned in this poem.

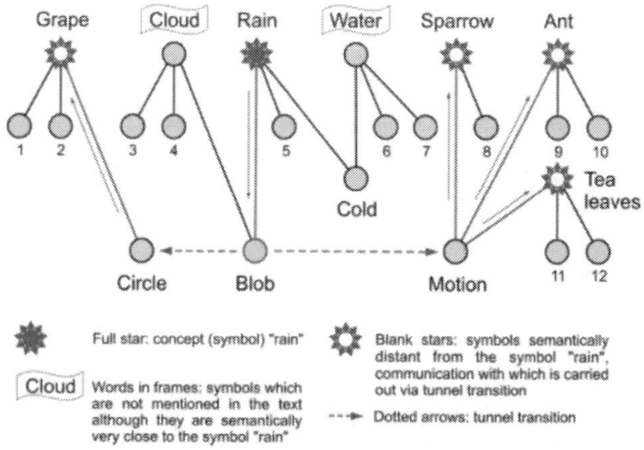

Figure 5. Semantic connections in Mandelstam's poem *The Soft Moscow rain*. "Tunnel transitions" result in unexpected combinations of symbols.

In Figure 5, we can see that symbols that are semantically close to the term "rain" (such as "cloud" and "water") do not appear in the poem. At the same time, connections are established via attribute-attribute transitions between semantically distant symbols, such as "rain", "ant-hill", "tea leaves", and "grapes". The artistic value of the poem and the fact that it is a masterpiece seems to be due to the "tunnel effect" which reveals distant connections, thus helping to communicate an impression of the rain.

IV. Conclusion

Problems associated with understanding the mechanisms of creativity and reproducing them form a barrier to creating general Artificial Intelligence (AI), which has not been overcome so far. It seems that entirely anthropomorphic AI could only be developed if artificial intelligence systems were able to think independently and perform creative tasks. To achieve this, we will have to solve the problem of generating new information in the cognitive system, which was discussed within the framework of Dynamic Theory of Information [13]. In this paper, we made an attempt to show the possible basic mechanisms of information synthesis in the cognitive system, illustrating them with some operations on graphs. The main concepts discussed in this paper are:

- formation of ensembles that combine different images;
- the "tunnel effect", i.e., the attribute-attribute transition that leads to unexpected combinations of symbols;
- the "degree of fusibility" of a cognitive system.

The formation of ensembles and the "tunnel effect" are associated with the mechanism that can transform images in the cognitive system. In the former case (the formation of ensembles), image transformation is caused by the transfer of attributes from one image to another. In the latter case (the "tunnel effect"), the attributes of semantically distant symbols are combined together. This can result not only in the enrichment of an existing image, but also in the generation of a new image (e.g., as in Mandelstam's poem, where *rain* is associated with an *ant-hill* and *grapes*). Both mechanisms are characteristic of cognitive processes, not the simple image classification provided by existing artificial neural networks. It should be emphasized that in both of the above cases, new information is generated. These mechanisms could be closely connected with the intuitive and creative thinking process.

The concept of the degree of fusibility, as well as the coefficient of fusibility introduced in this paper, when applied to an artificial cognitive system, could provide a way of controlling the rigidity of artificial cognitive systems, making them more adept at reflecting the reality or, on the contrary, more intuitive and creative.

Implementing these mechanisms could help to achieve an AI that can think creatively and has intuition. The next step would be to develop these ideas further as a mathematical model.

Acknowledgments

The author is grateful to Olga Chernavskaya, Evgeny Volovich and Artem Vorontsov for the fruitful discussions.

References

[1] What is Amazon Alexa? Available from: https://developer.amazon.com/alexa Retrieved 2018.01.09

[2] Meet your Google Assistant. Available from: https://assistant.google.com. Retrieved 2018.01.09

[3] Azuma Hikari. Official Site. Available from: http://gatebox.ai/hikari/en/ Retrieved 2018.01.09

[4] O. D. Chernavskaya, D. S. Chernavskii, V. P. Karp, A. P. Nikitin, and D. S. Shchepetov, "An architecture of thinking system within the Dynamical Theory of Information," BICA, vol. 6, pp. 147–158, 2013.

[5] O. D. Chernavskaya, D. S. Chernavskii, V. P. Karp, Ya. A. Rozhylo "An architecture of the cognitive system with account for emotional component," Biologically Inspired Cognitive Architectures, vol.12, pp. 144–154, 2015.

[6] E. D. Kazimirova, "Two-Component Scheme of Cognitive System Organization: the Hippocampus Inspired Model," The Ninth International Conference on Advanced Cognitive Technologies and Applications (COGNITIVE 2017) IARIA, Feb. 2017, pp. 21–23, ISBN: 978-1-61208-531-9

[7] E. D. Kazimirova, "Elements of the symbol-image architecture of cognition and their parallelism to certain linguistic phenomena", Neurocomputers, vol. 4, pp. 35–37, 2015. Available from: http://www.radiotec.ru/article/16364 Retrieved 2017.12.12

[8] M. Oizumi, L. Albantakis, and G. Tononi, "From the Phenomenology to the Mechanisms of Consciousness" Integrated Information Theory". Available from:

http://journals.plos.org/ploscompbiol/article?id=10.1371/journal.pcbi.1003588 Retrieved 2018.01.09.

[9] G. Lakoff and M. Johnsen, "Metaphors we live by", London: The university of Chicago Press, pp. 8–10, 2003.

Available from: http://shu.bg/tadmin/upload/storage/161.pdf Retrieved 2018.01.24

[10] D. O. Hebb. The organization of behavior: a neuro-psychological theory. New York, 2002.

[11] R. B. Cattell, "Theory of fluid and crystallized intelligence: A critical experiment", Journal of Educational Psychology, vol. 54, pp. 1–22, 1963.DOI:10.1037/h0046743

[12] Available from: http://arlindo-correia.com/200801.html Retrieved 29.01.2018

[13] D. S. Chernavsky, Synergetics and information: Dynamic Theory of Information. Moscow: URSS, 2004. (in Russian). (Sinergetica i Informaciya: Dinamicheskaya Theoriya Informacii)

On the Social Aspects of Forming the Concept of "Chef-D'oeuvre"

Olga Chernavskaya
Lebedev Physical Institute (LPI)
Moscow, Russia
E-mail: olgadmitcher@gmail.com

Yaroslav Rozhylo
BICA Labs
Kyiv, Ukraine
E-mail: yarikas@gmail.com

Abstract— **Aesthetic Emotions caused by the perception of an Artworks (music, painting, literature, architec-ture, dancing, etc.) represent the enigma, since they are quite individual and caused by (generally) no rational reasons. However, the individual concept of Chef-D'oeuvre, that is the effect of 'goose bumps', is sincere and objective since could be measured by skin sensors. In our previous works, we have proposed so-called Natural-Constructive Cognitive Architecture that is represented by the complex multilevel combination of various-type neural processors. Being based on this architecture, we have argued that the Aesthetic Emotions are connected with activation of the 'halo-neurons', those that correspond to atypical (rare) attributes of the real objects. It was shown that the personal feeling of Chef-D'oeuvre could be caused by the 'recognition paradox' effect, when the artwork seems similar to well-known patterns but is still unusual. In this paper, we consider certain social aspects of this concept's formation. It is shown that this process is also paradoxical and largely similar to the process of individual learning.**

Keywords – emotions; association; paradox; halo-neurons; core-neurons; ambiguity; expertise.

I. INTRODUCTION

Understanding and modeling emotions in artificial cognitive systems is really a challenge and attract great attention [1]—[6]. Emotions, being a more ancient way of reaction to the environment [3], than rational thinking (perhaps for this very reason) appear to be rather difficult to be conscious and formalized. This is especially so when it comes to the Aesthetic Emotions (AE), i.e., the perception of artworks and natural phenomena (fire, waterfall, etc.) [7]—[9]. In contrast to the so-called "pragmatic emotions" associated with the attainment of a specific goal, AE do not have visible rational reasons and clear criteria. Moreover, the standard division into positive and negative emotions is not applicable here, since one can only say whether they "like" or "dislike" an artwork. Thus, AE are always purely individual and sincere: strong AE are accompanied by an objective (and even measurable) effect of "goose bumps". This effect occurs when a phenomenon or an artwork is perceived as a "Chef-D'oeuvre" (ChD).

In our previous work [10], we have considered possible mechanisms and manifestations of AE in individual cognitive systems. It was shown that, in addition to the apparent influence of cultural context and public opinion, the concept of ChD is formed under the influence of

- childish vague impressions;
- personal fuzzy associations;
- the influence of cultural mini-media (family, messmates, etc.).

All these factors produce *subjective fuzzy associations*, and this is the very mechanism of artwork perception. It was shown also that, using the terminology of J. Levin ("explanatory gap between the Brain and the Mind") [11], these associations appear at the border between the Brain and the Mind.

In this paper, we consider possible mechanisms of forming the public opinion about the value of certain artwork. We employ the so-called Natural Constructive Approach to the problem of cognitive process modeling, that has been proposed and elaborated in our previous works [10][12][13]. In other words, we try to realize, how the symbol ChD could appear in the "social Mind". Thus, the paper is aimed to reveal possible "natural" mechanisms of social appreciation of a certain artwork as a ChD besides the obvious propaganda, marketing policy, etc. However, it is necessary to stress that this work is in progress yet.

The paper is organized as follows. Section II is focused on the formalization of the problem of forming the public evaluation of ChD. In Section III, a possible solution to the problem is presented. Summary and discussion of further working perspectives are presented in Section IV.

II. FORMALIZATION OF THE PROBLEM

In engaging with the problem of forming a public appraisal of a certain Artwork, we did not fully realize the whole measure of its complexity. Any Artwork, as well as the concepts of *'information'* and *'thinking'*, has both material and virtual component, and the processes of formation of their social assessment vary significantly. For example, paintings (originals) of well-known and recognized masters are valued as brands; they are so expensive because only a single copy of the work exists. Here, the laws of the market do work, which practically have no relation to the artistic content of the picture. This fact explains that musical ChDs have low material price (the notes are easily reproducible), but tickets for a concert of a famous performer can reach a fairly high price, if the performer is fashionable. But what is the mechanism of the word "fashionable"? Here again, marketing policy and propaganda do work, i.e., forcible implanting into the public consciousness the idea of "greatness" of certain pattern. To the same range of problems, the political considerations could be related. So in the Soviet Union, rather weak (untalented) and deservedly forgotten now artworks, glorifying the party and the government, were highly appreciated.

The mechanism of artificial formation of public opinion is the subject of sociology research, not cognitive science. The problem that we are trying to solve is how a natural (or "sincere") feeling that some artwork is a ChD does arise not for one individual, but for a large part of society.

One important factor should be noted. In modern society (as well as in any sufficiently developed and structured one), the professional corporations (for example, the Union of Writers, the Union of artists, the Nobel Committee, the Academy of Sciences, etc.) have a great influence. These are sufficiently closed communities that are reluctant to accept both new members and new ideas. Within these communities, certain (sometimes tacit) criteria for evaluating the artworks and the notion of "right" work are accepted, but these criteria can not guarantee that this work is a ChD .

It seems that the word "right" could not be applied to an artwork, but initially the term ChD, or *masterpiece,* had the meaning of the best example of a product made by an artisan, "an approved work sample." Only after the artisan made a ChD, he could enter the *guild* (a trade and craft corporation that united masters of one or several similar professions), open his own 'shop' (*studio*) and become a master. Thus, it was the professionals who evaluated the artwork, and often the appraisal was influenced by personal interests of the corporation's members (in other words, by intrigues). This is a good example of the emergence of *conventional information*, i.e., subjective information accepted within the given society. The mechanism of formation of subjective (conventional) information was considered within the framework of the Dynamic Information Theory [14][15], where it was shown that the choice of the society (in the given context, the choice of the ChD) should not and often is not the best. It is the result of the struggle and agreement of the community's members, which could not stand the test of time and/or be not shared by the society in a broader sense (outside professional corporations). In the days of Mozart, it was Salieri who was treated as a recognized (and highly paid) master, because he wrote the "right" music, which was familiar and pleasant hearing of the nobles, while Mozart had the reputation of a bully whose music was not serious and understandable to commoners. However, nowadays it appeared that Mozart's music (we will be bold enough to say that not all, but only several outstanding patterns like, e.g., "*Lacrimosa*") is really great, i.e., causes true and sincere "goose bumps" not only among professional musicians, but also among a lot of people far from music. Speaking about ChD we mean just this effect.

Traditionally, the problem of public acceptance of ChD was considered in the humanities, within different branches. These approaches account for, first of all, the social and historical aspects of the ChD appearance. However, within the limits of different directions of art criticism, some specific characteristics of those artworks that society recognized as a ChD are analyzed. For example, in the framework of musicology, certain laws of musical harmony [9] are trying to distinguish genius creations from simply good professional work. Similarly, within the framework of literary studies and linguistics, texts are analyzed for the correlation of different grammatical constructions in recognized ChDs, and so on. However, the problem that we set for ourselves is to highlight certain regularities in the process of shaping public opinion in the "sincere" evaluation of any ChD, regardless of whether it relates to music, painting, literature, architecture, etc.

III. Possible Solution within the Natural Constructive Approach

In our work [10], the Natural-Constructive Cognitive Architecture (NCCA) has been proposed and considered. Let us recall briefly some conclusions on the individual perception of ChD obtained in the framework of this model.

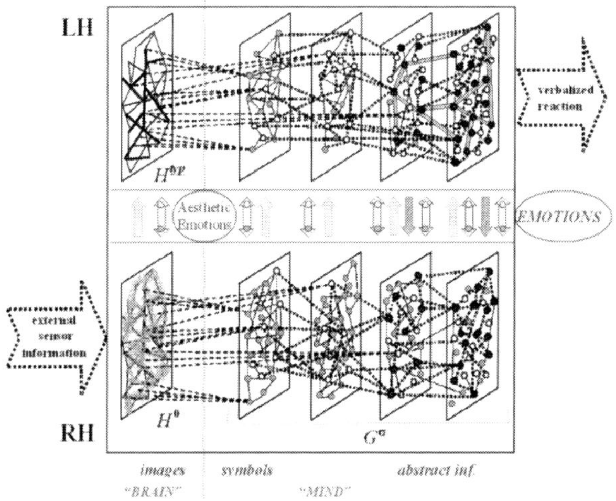

Figure 1. Schematic representation of NCCA.

One of the main principles of the Natural-Constructive Approach is that any cognitive system should be divided into two subsystems, in analogy with hemispheres of the human brain [16]. One of them, the Right Hemisphere (RH) is responsible for generating information and learning new information (it contains the necessary random factor, the "noise"), the other one, tLeft Hemisphere (LH) being responsible for processing well-known information. This specialization is ensured by the fact that the connections between the dynamic formal neurons in the RH are trained according to the Hebbian self-organization principle [17] (amplified with time), while in the LH, the strongest (black) connections are selected according to the Hopfield principle [18] "redundant cut-off".

The whole system represents a complex multi-level hierarchical structure. The main (lower) level contains imaginative information (distributed memory) ***H***, where signals from each real object activate a chain of neurons. In Levin's terminology, this level corresponds to the area of the Brain. Already at the next level, symbols [19] of typical (i.e., most clearly learned) images are formed, which themselves can form "generalized" images (chains of connected symbols). At all subsequent levels, this process is repeated, leading to the structured ensemble of neurons. We emphasize that the process of symbol's formation relates to the generation of a conventional (subjective for a given system) information. However, the chosen symbol is not necessarily (that is often impossible) *the best*, i.e., the most vivid representative of active neurons. It was obtained precisely as a result of "struggle and agreement" in the ensemble of neurons. Thus, all the symbolic information refers to the field of Mind, because it is not created objectively (in response to physiological signals), but as a result of the perception of this information in the given community of neurons.

It was noted that the scheme of NCCA in Figure 1 repeats the location of the various zones of the neocortex [13]. Emotions, as a product of the interaction between the sub-cortical structures and the neocortex, control the interaction and activation of the subsystems RH and LH. They can be indicated on the diagram only schematically, i.e., between the subsystems. In this process, the so-called pragmatic (or rational) emotions associated with the achievement of a certain (symbolic) goal, which can easily be formalized and formulated, refer to the area of Mind. In [10], we have shown that AE, which have no certain goal as well as a clear explanation, can arise on the boundary between the Brain and the Mind, i.e., when objective information obtained by the system results in generation of the subjective (conventional) information. Let us consider this process in more detail.

In the process of recording any perceived object at the lowest level of RH, there participate so-called *core*-neurons encoding typical (the most characteristic and frequently repeated attributes) of this object, and so-called *halo*-neurons corresponding to atypical (not characteristic, rare) attributes. The first are activated at any presentation of the object, and the connections between them intensify faster and become "black". After that, the image is replicated in LH, becomes a "typical image" and gets its symbol at the next hierarchy level, etc. In this process, only the core-neurons are involved in the symbol's formation, so the perception of a typical image can be formulated and verbalized, i.e., expressed by the symbol-words.

The halo-neurons are activated only at atypical (rare) representations of the object, therefore the connections between them and the core-neurons remain rather weak ("grey"). They have no connection with any symbol, so their activation leads to vague impressions that could not be formulated and expressed by words. However, the halo-neurons provide multiple associative links between images that are lost at the stage of the typical image/symbol formation. Note that the majority of halo-neurons are concentrated in the lowest level $\boldsymbol{H^0}$ in RH (that is why it was called the *"fuzzy set"*), which could be associated with human's sub-consciousness.

According to our hypothesis, it is these implicit associative connections that the Brain perceives, while the Mind do not realize, that create the "paradox of recognition" when perceiving the artworks. It is the impossibility of verbalized resolution of this paradox that leads to the effect of "goose bumps".

Let us stress that these multiple nonverbalized associations can be considered as a mechanism for the effect of "seeing the invisible, connecting the unconnectable".

How this consideration could be applied to formation of the concept of ChD in a "Social Mind"? Actually, the society represents a more primitive structure than the human's Mind, but it definitely has highly structured organization. We can suppose that the "Social Brain" can be treated as the whole (unstructured) community, the analogy to the fuzzy set $\boldsymbol{H^0}$. But what is the "Social Mind"? Paradoxically, it seems that it is presented by just the next (lowest) symbolic level, while all others correspond to the artificial "power vertical".

Of course, it is impossible to apply these arguments literally to the analysis of the process of forming the public opinion. However, certain analogies suggest themselves. Thus, professional communities can be treated as a "typical image" of the profession, and the core-neurons represent the analogy with its recognized masters. They determine the evaluation of the works in this area, i.e., just they select those works that deserve the symbol of ChD. It is conventional information of this community (corporation).

According to our hypothesis, the concept of ChD is formed as follows. First, there is a group of professionals in the art that defines the standard (pattern) of the "right" work (ChD). They play the role of core-neurons and form the *typical image* of the profession. This corporation, officially formalized (analogous to the transmission of a typical image in the LH), itself selects works that receive an assessment of ChD. At the same time, their evaluation can be influenced by corporate (however, personal) interests, so this estimate may not be related to the true value. Moreover, a really great work never corresponds to existing patterns.

We suppose that true (sincer) perception of ChD in society is provided by a group of people who have a certain and sufficient experience in this area of art and understand the subtleties and measure of paradoxicalness of ChD, which represent an analogy with the halo-neurons. Then, there is a paradoxical effect of the "unconnectable connection", i.e., personal sensation of ChD appears to be extended to all (almost) the community. However, it should be stressed that speaking about the halo-neurons we imply only those, that were involved in some (any) learning process and got certain experience (expertise) in some area of Art. Note that the process of acquiring the experience requires certain time.

An analogy to the phenomenon of "collective goose bumps" can be considered spontaneous (hysterical) popularity of certain creations (such as "Yesterday") not caused by an official propaganda. Thus, "sincere" AE and the appreciation of real ChD in the society arise in full correspondence with that in the individual cognitive system. Being provided by the excitation of halo-neurons (halo-people), this effect corresponds to the formula "to connect unconnectable".

IV. Conclusion

We have shown that, apart from obvious propaganda and marketing policy (that are not a subject of our research), there could be a "natural" mechanism of forming the public evaluation of certain artworks. It is in many respects similar to the formation of individual perception of ChD and refers to the true great artworks providing the "recognition paradox" (an object, being in many respects similar to well-known ones, still seems unusual). In the majority of cases, the impression of ChD could be expressed by the formula "to see invisible, to connect unconnectable".

According to our hypothesis, this effect is provided by forming common opinion within not the related professional communities, but in a rather large community of no professionals who nevertheless have sufficient expertise to estimate the value of ChD and the degree of its paradoxical features. This group represents an analogy to the halo-neurons in the fuzzy set $\boldsymbol{H}^0$ of individual cognitive system and could be called "the sub-consciousness of society" relating to the "Social Brain".

It is shown that ChD acceptance in the "Society Mind" requires more time, than corporative evaluation (possible, incorrect). This effect could explain certain delay in the creation and appreciation of almost all ChDs – the society should get certain expertise to value the ChD adequately.

However, there are still many open questions that do not allow us to extend the architecture of Figure 1 to human society. First of all, there is no (formal) division in a society into two subsystems, one of which generates information while the other works with well-known information. Of course, there are people more and less creative, but this does not determine the structure of society. In principle, the hierarchy of the architecture in Figure 1 recalls the hierarchical organization of power, but these problems require additional reflection and analysis.

Furthermore, the conclusions drawn should be verified by, e.g., public opinion poll in certain groups, which are not connected professionally. Thus, the work is in progress.

References

[1] A. Samsonovich, "Emotional biologically inspired cognitive architecture," BICA, vol. 6, pp. 109–125, 2013.

[2] E. Hudlyka, "Affective BICA: Challenges and open questions," BICA, vol. 7, pp. 98–125, 2014.

[3] J. Panksepp and L. Biven, The Archaeology of Mind: Neuroevolutionary Origins of Human Emotions. N.Y.: Norton, 2012.

[4] M. I. Rabinovich and M. K. Muezzinoglu, "Nonlinear dynamics of the brain: emotions and cognition," Physics-Uspehi, vol. 53, pp. 357–372, 2010.

[5] O. Larue, P. Poirier, and R. Nkambou, "The emergence of (artificial) emotions from cognitive and neurological processes," BICA, vol. 4, pp. 54–68, 2013.

[6] R. Solso, Cognitive psychology (5th ed.). Needham Heights, MA: Allyn & Bacon, 1998.

[7] J. Schmidhuber, "Simple algorithmic theory of subjective beauty, novelty, surprise, interestingness, attention, curiosity, creativity, science, music, jokes," Journal of Science, vol. 48 (1), pp. 21–32, 2009.

[8] D. Huron, Sweet Anticipation: music and physiology of expectation. MIT Press, 2006.

[9] M. Korsakova-Kreyn and W. J. Dowling, "Emotional Processing in Music: Study in Affective Responses to Tonal Modulationin Controlled Harmonic Progressions and Real Music," Psychomusicology: Music, Mind and Brain, vol. 24(1), pp. 4–20, 2014.

[10] O. D. Chernavskaya and Ya. A. Rozhylo, "On the Possibility to Interpret Aesthetic Emotions and the Concept of Chef-D'oeuvre in an Artificial Cognitive System" The Nineth Int. Conf. on Advanced Cognitive Technologies and Applications (COGNITIVE), IARIA, Feb. 19--23, pp. 24–31, 2017; Copyright (c) IARIA, 2017. ISBN: 978-1-61208-531-9 .

[11] J. Levin, "Materialism and Qualia: The Explanatory Gap," Pacific Philosophical Quarterly, vol. 64(4), pp. 354–361, 1983.

[12] O. D. Chernavskaya et al., "An architecture of the cognitive system with account for emotional component," BICA, vol.12, pp. 144–154, 2015.

[13] O. D. Chernavskaya and Ya. A. Rozhylo, "The Natural-Constructive Approach to Representation of Emotions and a Sense of Humor in an Artificial Cognitive System," IARIA Journal of Life Sciences, vol. 8(3&4), pp. 184–202, 2016.

[14] H. Haken, Information and Self-Organization: A macroscopic approach to complex systems. Springer, 2000.

[15] D. S. Chernavskii, "The origin of life and thinking from the viewpoint of modern physics", Physics-Uspekhi, vol. 43, pp. 151–176, 2000.

[16] E. Goldberg, The new executive brain. Oxford University Press, 2009.

[17] D. O. Hebb, The organization of behavior. John Wiley & Sons, 1949.

[18] J. J. Hopfield, "Neural networks and physical systems with emergent collective computational abilities," PNAS, vol. 79, pp. 2554–2558, 1982.

[19] S. Grossberg, Studies of Mind and Brain. Boston: Riedel, 1982.

A Conceptual Architecture of Cognitive Electronic Warfare System

Qinghan Xiao
Radar Electronic Warfare Section
Defence R&D Canada – Ottawa Research Centre
Ottawa, Canada
e-mail: Qinghan.Xiao@drdc-rddc.gc.ca

Abstract—**The major motivation behind research on cognitive Electronic Warfare (EW) is the requirement to defeat modern radar systems using emerging technologies, especially cognitive algorithms. Using cognition-based techniques, a radar system would be able to perceive its operational environment, fine-tune and accordingly adjust its emission parameters, such as the pulse width, pulse repetition interval, and transmitter power, to perform its assigned task optimally. It is certain that traditional EW methods, which rely on pre-programmed attack strategies, will not be able to efficiently engage with modern radar threats. Therefore, the next generation of EW systems needs to be enhanced with cognitive abilities so that they can make autonomous decisions in response to changing situations, and cope with new, unknown radar signals. In this paper, a conceptual architecture of a cognitive EW system is presented. The system consists of five major functional components, namely: environmental perception to observe the operational environment; intelligent signal analysis to assess and characterize electromagnetic spectrum signals emitted by enemy radars; a cognitive thinking module to produce close-to-optimal jamming solutions; a dynamic knowledge base that continues to grow during the operation; and a feedback loop as a facilitator of intelligence to improve the jamming performance. The system architecture and functional modules are described in detail.**

Keywords-adaprive electronic warfare; cognitive electronic warfare; machine leaning; cognitive thinking.

I. INTRODUCTION

In recent years, there are growing research interests in the development of cognitive capabilities in various electronic systems. Mitola and Maguire first introduced the concept of cognitive radio in 1999 [1]. In 2006, Haykin proposed the idea of cognitive radar, which is a dynamic system that adapts and optimizes transmitted waveforms based on the operational environment [2]. The proposed cognitive radar system is characterized by the following three key features: (1) the receiver learns, iteratively, from experience gained through interaction with the environment; (2) the transmitter adapts its illumination of the environment in an optimal manner in accordance with information about the environment passed on to it by the receiver; and (3) the feedback link coordinates and optimizes the operations of the transmitter and receiver in a synchronous manner [3]. Different from traditional radar systems, cognitive abilities could allow a radar to fine-tune and adjust its emission parameters, such as the pulse width, pulse repetition interval, power, and pulse compression technique, to perform its assigned task optimally. Therefore, to defend against cognitive radar systems, cognition is the key to the next generation Electronic Warfare (EW) system. The US Air Force Science Advisory Board carried out a study entitled, "Responding to Uncertain or Adaptive Threats in Electronic Warfare" in 2016. It pointed out that, "increasing signal density and highly variable or real-time adaptive waveforms and modalities will challenge the ability of Air Force systems to identify source and intent of signals in the Radio Frequency (RF) spectrum" [4]. Legacy EW systems that rely on databases of known threats and predefined countermeasures lack the ability to identify and respond to parameter agile radars in real time. Therefore, the front-end of EW system, Electronic Support (ES), and the back-end of the system, Electronic Attack (EA), need to be enhanced with intelligence to provide accurate situational awareness information through ES, and decide where and how to apply jamming through EA.

As shown in Figure 1, a basic cognitive EW system should include five modules: signal analysis and characterization, countermeasure preparedness and response, countermeasure effectiveness assessment, a database to hold a priori and dynamic knowledge of the operational environment and threats, and a feedback loop encompassing the environment, receiver and transmitter [5][6]. In the system, Environmental Perception focuses on sensing of the operational environment to optimize further processing procedures based on the surrounding environment. Intelligent Signal Characterization block performs pattern recognition and uses machine learning algorithms to assess and characterize electromagnetic spectrum signals emitting from enemy radars as either known or unknown threats. The objective of the Cognitive Thinking module is to synthesize close-to-optimal countermeasures subject to transceiver limitations, user-input restrictions and performance goals. The Dynamic Knowledge Base contains not only environmental, target, and other a priori information, but also information on recently learned threats. The Feedback loop plays a key role in causing the transmission parameters to be adjusted in order to improve the jamming performance in real time.

The rest of the paper is organized as follows. Section II discusses the major differences between adaptive EW and cognitive EW. Section III presents a cognitive EW system architecture, and finally, Section IV concludes the paper.

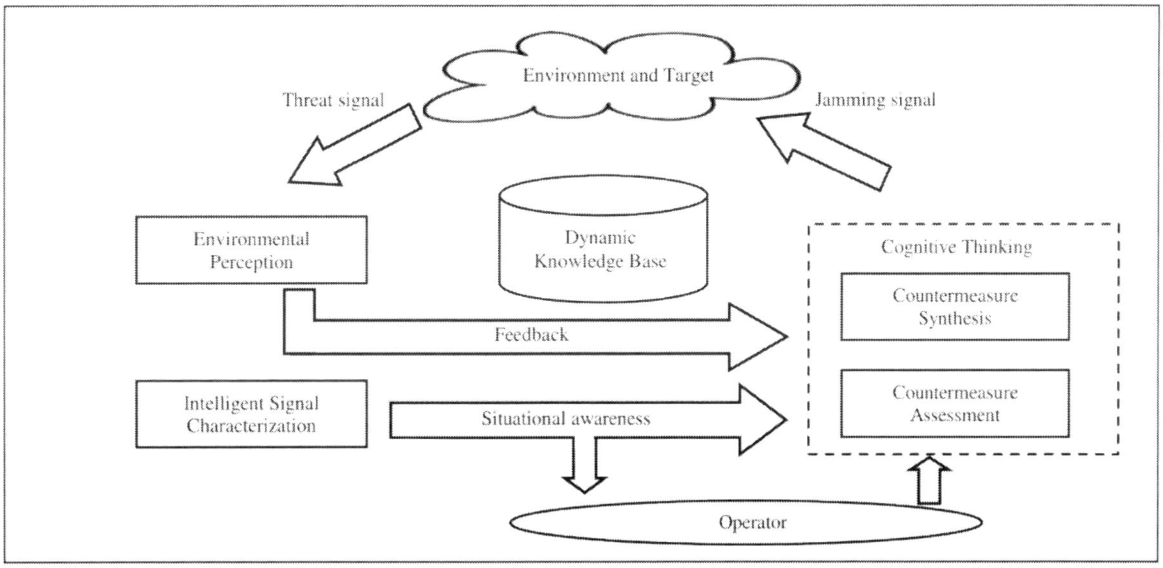

Figure 1. Basic cognitive EW system.

II. ADAPTIVE EW AND COGNITIVE EW

Over the past few years, the terms adaptive EW and cognitive EW have been used interchangeably by many people. In [7], the author raised the following questions: What is the difference between adaptive and cognitive electronic warfare? Does it even matter? This section is intended to address these questions.

A. *Adaptive EW*

The advances of digital radar technology have led to a shift in the way legacy EW is executed and raised the need for more advanced EW solutions. Adaptive EW is proposed in the literature as being capable of recognizing a change in the operating environment, and then selecting from a series of predetermined EA actions that have been deemed to be optimized in an off-line environment [7][8]. For example, when the receiver detects a target radar changing its transmit frequency, the EW system adapts the transmitter to the corresponding frequency band. The main properties are summarized as follows:

- Adaptive EW is reactive;
- ES identification relies on a pre-programmed library;
- EA responses are pre-programmed solutions; and
- The system operates with a feedback mechanism between transmitter and receiver, which is independent of the environment.

B. *Cognitive EW*

The concept of cognitive EW is based on a perception-learning-action framework, which is one step beyond that of adaptive EW (Figure 2). Not only would a cognitive EW system adapt based on what it observes, but also it should use machine learning and pattern recognition algorithms to mimic human mental processes of perception, memory, judgment, and reasoning. Cognitive EW needs to be a dynamic closed-loop feedback system that would enable an intelligent response to defeat threat radars.

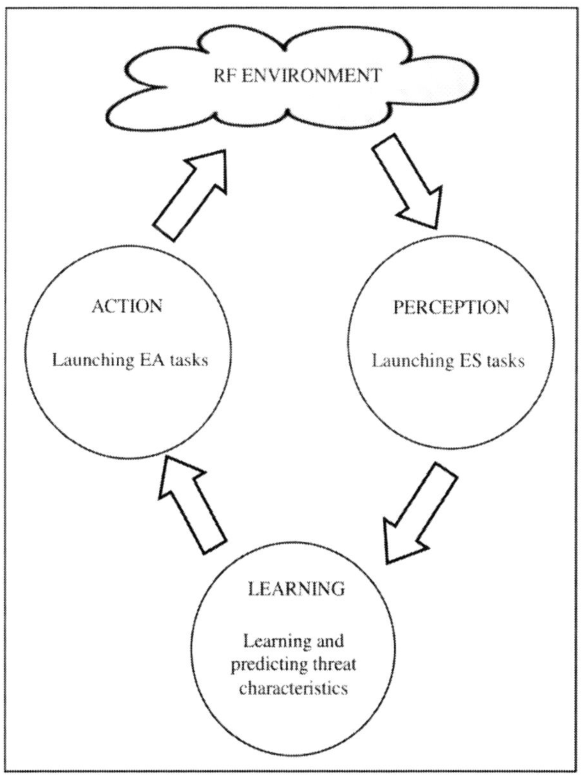

Figure 2. Perception-learning-action loop.

Artificial Intelligence (AI) and machine learning could make it possible for a cognitive EW system to exploit unknown radar waveforms that the system has never seen before. A feedback mechanism could possibly coordinate the operations of the transmitter and receiver to achieve optimal jamming performance. The following are the key features of cognitive EW with which cognitive EW needs to be proactive, i.e., it would:

- Adaptive EW is reactive;
- ES identification relies on a pre-programmed library;
- Attempt to learn the target's dynamic states and account for time-varying environmental conditions;
- Operate as a dynamic closed-loop feedback system encompassing the transmitter, environment and receiver; and
- Produce effective countermeasures against a threat radar even for a new or unknown threat.

C. *Major Differences*

As discussed in the previous sections, there are several fundamental differences between cognitive EW and adaptive EW. Mark Pomerleau stated in his article [7], "differentiating between different levels of adaptability and true cognitive EW is important", although a few experts viewed it differently [8]. An adaptive EW system adapts and responds to a threat in a pre-programmed manner, either based on rules or pre-processed knowledge obtained off-line. A cognitive EW system would overcome the limitations of the rule-based or knowledge-based adaptive EW system through machine learning to make the system better aware of the environment in which it is being used, and then characterize the threat and determine appropriate countermeasures. Let us conclude this section with three remarks:

- A cognitive EW system should continuously learn about the environment through experience gained from its interactions with the environment, and should continuously update itself with relevant information.
- The transmitter could deploy jamming signals in an intelligent manner which would:
  - take into account factors such as threat function, the relative positions and motions of targets, and construct optimal countermeasures techniques;
  - assess countermeasure effectiveness; and
  - adjust the countermeasure appropriately in order to maintain optimal effectiveness.
- The whole EW system would constitute a closed-loop dynamic system, which should encompass the transmitter, environmental, receiver, and feedback channel.

III. SYSTEM ARCHITECTURE

Based on above analysis, a conceptual architecture of a cognitive EW system is developed. Figure 3 shows a functional block diagram of the proposed system. The following important aspects distinguish a cognitive EW system from a legacy EW system.

A. *Closed-Loop*

A legacy EW system has an open-loop structure that does not assess the jamming effectiveness in real-time. A cognitive EW system needs to be a closed-loop system that performs environmental analysis, signal characterization, countermeasure synthesis, and countermeasure effectiveness assessment in real-time. It would continually adjust its jamming strategy based on feedback concerning threat behavior.

B. *Completely Automated*

In order to devise countermeasures in real-time, a cognitive EW system needs to continuously learn about the dynamically changing environment, automatically generate an optimized jamming technique and evaluate its effectiveness. Therefore, it is necessary to perform autonomous decision-making in real time.

C. *Machine Learning*

In contrast to static and adaptive EW systems that rely on pre-programmed threat libraries, a cognitive EW system needs to be able to analyze signals that have not previously been encountered, devise effective countermeasures, assess their effectiveness, and predict future threat emissions, all in real time. Therefore, machine learning is a basic ingredient of a cognitive EW system with which to learn and predict threat characteristics, and to automatically generate effective countermeasures by reasoning about past experiences.

D. *Fuzzy Reasoning*

Fuzzy Logic is an AI technique that can handle ill-defined, imprecise systems, and therefore enables a system using imprecise concepts and dependencies to reason about target systems [9]. Due to dynamic changes in the electromagnetic spectrum environment, fuzzy reasoning is a good tool to address uncertainty and deal with unexpected inputs by modeling human behavior to provide approximate reasoning when precise information is not available.

IV. CASE STUDIES

In order to gain a better understanding of the differences between cognitive EW and adaptive EW, two case studies are described and discussed in this section. The first one is about dealing with a previously unknown radar signal. As mentioned above, an adaptive EW system relies on libraries of known emitter (radar, communications, electro-optical, etc.) waveforms to identify the threat and determine the appropriate countermeasures response. To detect, deceive, and defeat enemy radar threats using new waveforms and unknown techniques, the adaptive solution involves collecting evidence and analyzing it in a laboratory for countermeasure development. There are two challenges: (1) it may take months to develop and deploy new profiles and countermeasures; and (2) when the received signal is slightly out of tolerance compared to what was recorded in

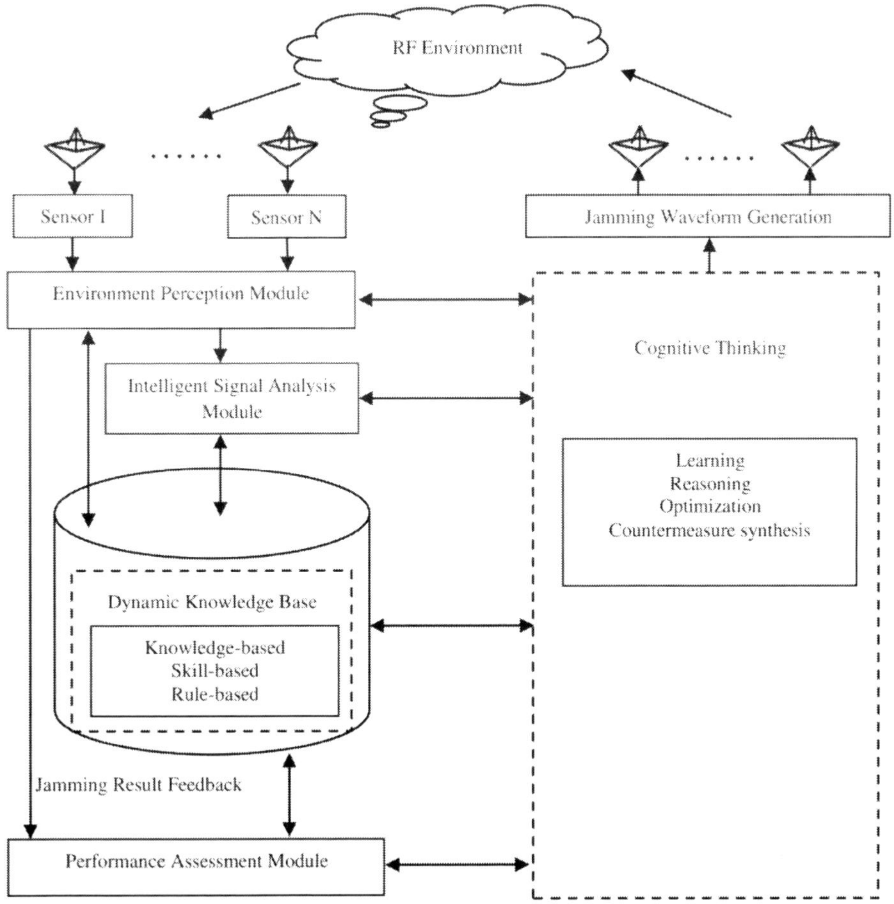

Figure 3. Functional block diagram of a cognitive EW system.

the library, the threat emitter cannot be identified and defeated. On the contrary, a cognitive EW system would use AI and machine learning to detect, characterize, and counter both known and unknown threat transmissions in real time. It would start by analyzing the electromagnetic spectrum environment. If changes are detected, then it is reasonable to conclude that new or unknown radar emitters are present. The environmental change would then be extracted for spectrum analysis. Machine learning algorithms would be used to characterize and predict the threat's properties and capabilities. The second example concerns the appropriate countermeasures response. As mentioned above, an adaptive EW system is only reactive' to the received data stream, which relies on a pre-programmed library to provide a specific, pre-determined countermeasure. With a dynamic knowledge base, a cognitive EW system would generate a dynamic action library consisting of several countermeasures options, and perform perception-learning-action feedback cycles to determine the optimal one.

V. CONCLUSIONS AND FUTURE WORKS

With the evolution of radar systems from fixed analogue systems to programmable digital variants, it is possible to endow radars with the ability to produce an almost infinite variety of signals. These developments have made legacy EW systems less and less effective against modern radar systems, especially those that are highly adaptive or cognitive [10]. The introduction of cognition into engineering systems is therefore key to the development of next generation EW systems. In this paper, a conceptual architecture of a cognitive EW system is presented, based on a perception-learning-action framework. Its major components include: an environmental perception module, an intelligent signal analysis module, a cognitive thinking module, a dynamic knowledge base, and a performance feedback module. The important aspects that distinguish a cognitive EW system from a legacy EW system are discussed in detail. This is the first step in the development of novel cognitive EW techniques. Further research will address the following issues: (1) development of analytic abilities to perceive the surrounding environment; (2)

application of machine learning techniques to characterize previously unknown radar signals; and (3) implementation of fuzzy logic techniques to deal with environmental uncertainty.

REFERENCES

[1] J. Mitola III and G. Q. Maguire, Jr., "Cognitive radio: Making software radios more personal," IEEE Personal Commun., vol. 6, no. 4, pp. 13–18, August 1999.

[2] S. Haykin, "Cognitive radar: A way of the future," IEEE Signal Processing Magazine, vol. 23, no. 1, pp. 30-40, Jauary 2006.

[3] S. Haykin, "Cognition is the key to the next generation of radar systems," Proc. of the 13th IEEE Digital Signal Processing Workshop and 5th IEEE Signal Processing Education Workshop (DSP/SPE '09), January 2009, pp. 463–467.

[4] USAF Scientific Advisory Board. *Responding to Uncertain or Adaptive Threats in Electronic Warfare*. [Online]. Available from: http://www.scientificadvisoryboard.af.mil/About-Us/Fact-Sheets/Display/Article/878167/fy16-study-tors/, (Access date: 13 September 2017).

[5] S. Cole, "Cognitive electronic warfare: Countering threats posed by adaptive radars," Military Embedded Systems, pp. 16-19, January/February 2017.

[6] B. H. Kirk, R. M. Narayanan, A. F. Martone, and K. D. Sherbondy, "Waveform design for cognitive radar: Target detection in heavy clutter," Proc. of SPIE Radar Sensor Technology XX, vol. 9829, 13 pages, 30 June 2016.

[7] M. Pomerleau, "What is the difference between adaptive and cognitive electronic warfare?" C4ISRNET. [Online]. http://www.c4isrnet.com/c2-comms/2016/12/16/what-is-the-difference-between-adaptive-and-cognitive-electronic-warfare/, (Access date: 14 September 2017).

[8] J. Knowles, "Regaining the advantage – Cognitive electronic warfare," The Journal of Electronic Defense, vol. 39, no. 12, pp. 56-62, December 2016.

[9] S. Lee-Urban, et al. "CORA: A flexible hybrid approach to building cognitive systems," Proc. of the Third Annual Conference on Advances in Cognitive Systems, Poster Collection, 2015, pp. 1-16.

[10] M. Arik and O. B. Akan, "Enabling cognition on electronic countermeasure systems against next-generation radars," Proc. IEEE Military Communications Conference 2015 (MILCOM 2015), October 2015, pp. 1103-1108.

Implementing Systemic Thinking for Automatic Schema Matching: An Agent-Based Modeling Approach

Hicham Assoudi, Hakim Lounis

Département d'Informatique
Université du Québec à Montréal
Succursale Centre-ville, H3C 3P8, Montréal, Canada
Email: assoudi.hicham@courrier.uqam.ca lounis.hakim@uqam.ca

Abstract— **Several approaches are proposed to deal with the problem of the Automatic Schema Matching (ASM). The challenges and difficulties caused by the complexity and uncertainty characterizing both the process and the outcome of Schema Matching motivated us to investigate how bio-inspired emerging paradigm can help with understanding, managing, and ultimately overcoming those challenges. In this paper, we explain how we approached Automatic Schema Matching as a systemic and Complex Adaptive System (CAS) and how we modeled it using the approach of Agent-Based Modeling and Simulation (ABMS). This effort gives birth to a tool (prototype) for schema matching called Reflex-SMAS. A set of experiments demonstrates the viability of our approach on two main aspects: (i) effectiveness (increasing the quality of the found matchings) and (ii) efficiency (reducing the effort required for this efficiency). Our approach represents a significant paradigm-shift, in the field of Automatic Schema Matching.**

Keywords- Schema Matching; Systemic Approach; Complex Adaptive Systems; Agent-Based Modelling and Simulation.

I. INTRODUCTION

Schema Matching is an important task for many applications, such as data integration, data warehousing and e-commerce. Schema matching process aims at finding a pairing of elements (or groups of elements) from the source schema and elements of the target schema such that pairs are likely to be semantically related [2] [3].

Schema matching existing approaches rely largely on human interactions, either for the matching results validation, during the post-matching phase, or for the matching process optimization, during the pre-matching phase. Although this human involvement in the automatic matching process could be considered as acceptable in a lot of matching scenarios, nevertheless it should be kept to a minimum, or even avoided, when dealing with high dynamic environments (i.e., semantic Web, Web services composition, agents communication, etc.) [1]. Thus, the existing approaches are not suited for all the matching contexts due to their intrinsic limitations. We can summarize those limitations as follows:

- Lack of autonomy to the extent that the user involvement is still needed for the results validation and analysis, but also for matching process configuration and optimization (tuning) to improve the matching result quality and then reduce uncertainty.
- Lack of adaptation in sense that the optimization task of the matching tool must be repeated and adapted manually, for every new matching scenario.

We were motivated to investigate other prospects not yet applied on Schema Matching. We try to answer the following general question: "How can we, with the help of a generic approach, better manage complexity and uncertainty inherent to the automatic matching process in general, and in the context of dynamic environments (minimal involvement of the human expert)?"

More specifically, we asked the following questions:

(i) How can we model the complexity of the matching process to help reduce uncertainty?

(ii) How can we provide the matching process of autonomy and adaptation properties with the aim to make the matching process able to adapt to each matching scenario (self-optimize)?

(iii) What would be the theoretical orientation that may be adequate to respond to the above questions?

In our work, we have investigated the use of the theory of CAS emanating from systemic thinking, to seek, far from the beaten path, innovative responses to the challenges faced by classical approaches for automatic schema matching, (e.g., complexity, uncertainty). The central idea of our work is to consider the process of matching as a CAS and to model it using the approach of ABMS. The aim being the exploitation of the intrinsic properties of the agent-based models, such as emergence, stochasticity, and self-organization, to help provide answers to better manage complexity and uncertainty of Schema Matching.

Thus, we propose a conceptual model for a multi-agent simulation for schema matching called Schema Matching as Multi-Agents Simulation (SMAS). The implementation of this conceptual model has given birth to a prototype for schema matching (Reflex-SMAS).

Our prototype Reflex-SMAS was submitted to a set of experiments, to demonstrate the viability of our approach with respect to two main aspects: (i) effectiveness (increasing the quality of the found matchings), and (ii) efficiency (reducing the effort required for this efficiency). The results came to demonstrate the viability of our approach, both in terms of effectiveness or that of efficiency.

The empirical evaluation results, as we are going to show in Section IV of this paper, were very satisfactory for both effectiveness (correct matching results found) and efficiency (no optimization needed to get good result from our tool).

The current paper is organized as follows: Section 2 discusses schema matching through a state of the art that identifies the important factors affecting the schema matching process. Section 3 presents the chosen paradigm to address the problem. Section 4 shows the results obtained by our approach, and how we can compare them to those obtained in other works. Finally, the last section concludes and summarizes this work.

II. CURRENT APPROACHES OF SCHEMA MATCHING

Many algorithms and approaches were proposed to deal with the problem of schema matching and mapping [1] [4]–[15]. Although the existing schema matching tools comprise a significant step towards fulfilling the vision of automated schema matching, it has become obvious that the user must accept a degree of imperfection in this process. A prime reason for this is the enormous ambiguity and heterogeneity of schema element names (descriptions). Thus, it could be unrealistic to expect a matching process to identify the correct matchings for any possible element in a schema [16] [17].

A comprehensive literature review, of the existing matching tools and approaches, allowed us to identify the most important factors affecting, in our opinion, the schema matching process. Moreover, some causal relationships, between those different factors, participating to the schema matching difficulties and challenges, were identified. As shown in Figure 1, the factors influencing the Schema Matching are:

- Heterogeneity: in general, the task of matching involves semantics (understanding the context) to have complete certainty about the quality of the result. The main challenge in all cases of automatic matching is to decide the right match. This is a very difficult task mainly because of the heterogeneity of the data.
- Uncertainty: the cause for this uncertainty lies mainly in the ambiguity and heterogeneity, both syntactic, and semantic, which often characterize the Schema Elements to match.
- Optimization: the uncertainty about the matching results implies the optimization of the process to improve the matching quality, and the testing of different combinations (e.g., different Similarity Measures, Aggregate Functions, and Matching Selection Strategies). Each step of the matching process involves choosing between multiple strategies, which leads to a combinatorial explosion (complexity).
- Complexity: the matching process optimization generates complexity because of the search space (combinatorial explosion). In addition, changing matching scenarios exacerbates this complexity to the extent that the result of the optimization often becomes obsolete with changing scenarios.

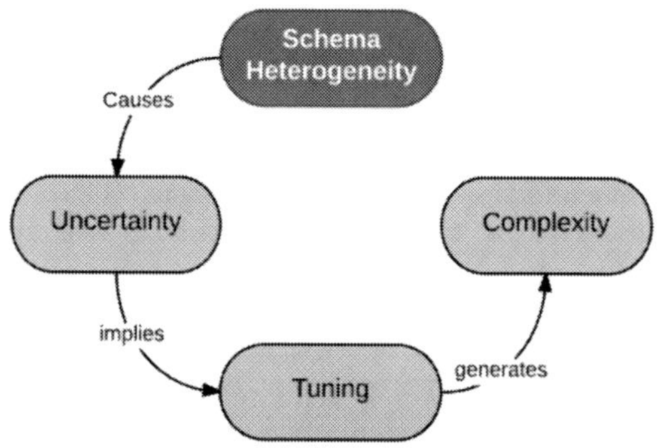

Figure 1. Schema Matching impacting factors causality diagram

One of the commonalities between all existing approaches is the thinking behind these approaches, namely reductionism (as opposed to holism). The reductionist thinking is a very common and efficient thinking approach. It is at the basis of the almost totality of previous schema matching approaches, and then, on their characteristics that are, in our view, the root causes preventing the automatic matching schemes to cope fully with the challenges and difficulties.

Reductionism, as opposed to systemic (holism), is a philosophical concept that refers both to the way of thinking solutions as well as to their modeling methodology. Reductionism advocates reducing system complexity or phenomenon to their basic elements which would then be easier to understand and study [18]. This reductionist approach, despite its high efficacy in several areas, shows, however, its limits within certain contexts. In fact, for explaining certain phenomena or solving certain problems, the approach consisting of reducing or abstracting the reality to a linearization of simple relationships of causes and effects between a complex system underlying fundamental components, appears as a highly limiting and simplifying approach.

With regard to schema matching, it seems clear, as Figure 2 illustrates it, that all current approaches follow the reductionist thinking. They abstract the matching process to a linear function with a set of inputs and outputs. This function is decomposed into a series of modules, each of which is responsible for the running of a stage of the process (e.g., selection and matching execution).

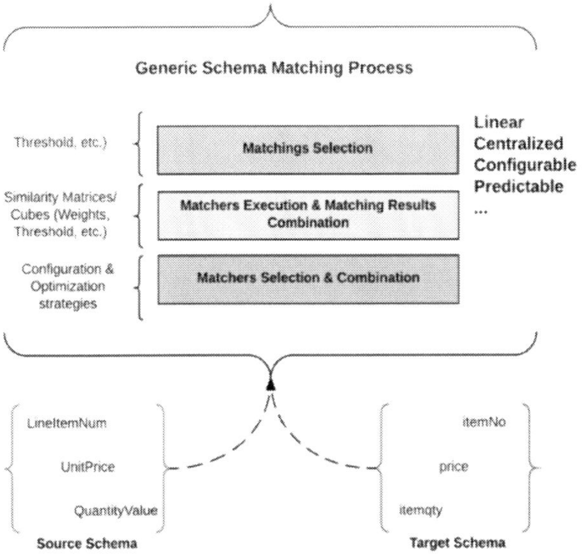

Figure 2. Generic Schema Matching process (linear process with an analytical-based resolution)

Some fundamental and intrinsic characteristics, common to all current Schema Matching systems, may partially explain their inability to overcome the limitation of the complexity and other challenges, such as uncertainty. Those characteristics are declined as following: these systems are (i) complicated and not complex, (ii) linear (analytical, deterministic and predictable) and not non-linear, (iii) centralized rather than decentralized (parallelism and emerging solutions), (iv) and finally, configurable and not adaptable (self-configuration, self-optimization).

The need to explore new approaches to make systemic and holistic responses to the problems of matching leads us to raise the question: how can we have a matching solution that could give us high-quality matching results, for different matching scenarios and this with a minimal optimization effort from the end-user?

Our premise is that a good part of the answer may come from the theory of CAS where modeling the complexity of adaptation and evolution of the systems is at the heart of this theory. Having a schema matching approach that can face and overcome the challenges facing the existing schema matching tools requires, in our view, a paradigm shift, placing the notions of adaptation, evolution, and self-organization at its center. We strongly believe that the theory of CAS, which is exploited to explain some biological, social, and economic phenomena, can be the basis of a programming paradigm for ASM tools.

III. SCHEMA MATCHING AS A SYSTEMIC APPROACH

As part of our research we investigated the use of the theory of CAS (systemic thinking), to try to find an innovative response to challenges (i.e. complexity, uncertainty) that the conventional approaches for schema matching are still facing.

We think that the CAS could bring us the adaptation capability to the realm of schema matching tools (self-configuration and self-optimization), which should relieve the user from the complexity and effort resulting from configuring and optimizing the automatic schema matching systems.

Our conceptual model for schema matching, based on the theory of complexity, sees the schema matching process as a complex adaptive system.

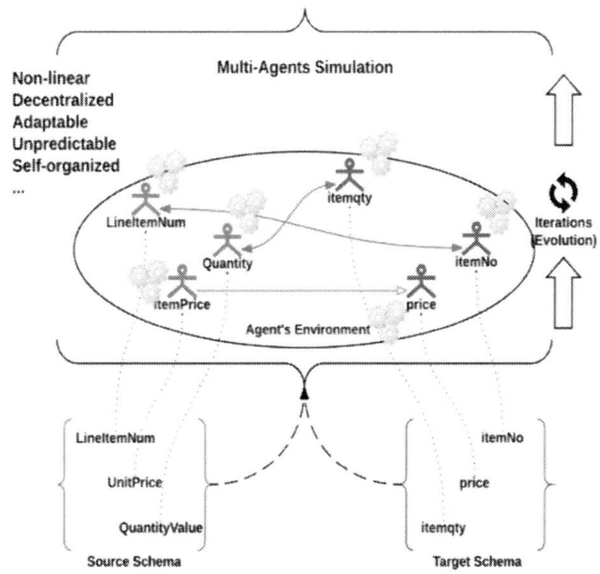

Figure 3. Schema Matching as Multi-Agents Simulation (non-linear process with emergence-based resolution)

As illustrated in Figure 3, in this model, each schema element of the schemas to match (source or target schema) is modeled as an autonomous agent, belonging to a population (source or target schema population). Each agent behaviors and interaction, at the micro level, with the other agents in the opposite population and with its environment, brings out at the macro level, a self-organized system that represents the global solution to matching problem (i.e., relationships between schemas elements). In other words, the resolution of the matching problem goes through individual effort deployed by each agent, locally, throughout the simulation to find the best match in the opposite population.

We think that many intrinsic properties of our model, derived from the ABMS modeling approach, can contribute efficiently to the increase of the matching quality and thus the decrease of the matching uncertainty. These properties are:

- Emergence: the emergence of the macro solution (schema matching) comes from local behaviors, rules and interactions between agents (micro solutions).
- Self-organization: the cooperation of source and target schema elements (represented as agents) helps to reach a consensus about their best matching.
- Stochasticity (randomness): the randomness within the model, gives the ability to perform statistical analysis on the outcome of multiple simulations (meta-simulation) for the same matching scenario.

Briefly, our idea is to model the Schema Matching process as interactions, within a self-organized environment, between agents called "Schema Attribute Agent". In the rest of the paper, we are going to refer to the "Schema Element Agent" simply as agent. Each schema element is modeled as an agent belonging to one of two populations: source or target schema group. Furthermore, the schema matching process is modeled as the interaction between the two populations of agents.

In our model, the internal architecture of the agents is Rule-based (reflexive agent). The agents have as a main goal to find the best matching agent within the other group of agents. The foundation of the rules governing the agent's behaviors is stochasticity (randomness). In fact, a certain degree of randomness is present in each step executed by each agent during the simulation.

The main random elements influencing the simulation are as follows:

- Similarity Calculation based on similarity measures selected randomly from a similarity measures list.
- Similarity Scores aggregation based on aggregation functions selected randomly from an aggregation function list (MAX, AVERAGE, WEIGHTED).
- Similarity score validation based on generated random threshold value (within interval)

As opposed to deterministic solutions for schema matching (all the existing matching solutions), the nondeterministic and stochastic nature of our agent-based simulation increase the confidence in the quality of the matching results. Even though the agent's behaviors are based on randomness (e.g., during the similarity calculation), our model can often produce the right matchings at the end of each simulation run.

Figure 4 illustrates the internal states of each agent. It allows representing the transitions between the internal states, during the perception-decision-action cycle of the agent. In the context of our operational model, the agent during the perception phase, perceives its environment by interrogating it, by performing similarity calculations (which can be considered as an act of recognition) or by capturing certain events. The result of this phase will be a set of percepts, allowing the agent to identify the agents of the other group, available for matching. The capture of events, coming from the environment, is another action of perception: for instance, the event that is triggered when the agent is chosen by another one as a matching candidate. During the decision phase, the agent from the results of the perception phase, reasons, deliberates and decides on the action to be selected. The decisions, involving the choice of actions, are the following: (i) the decision concerning the convergence of similarities and the selection of a candidate matching, (ii) the decision concerning the reset of the beliefs concerning the candidate matching, and (iii) the decision on consensual matching. During the action phase, the agent executes the actions selected during the previous phase. The current iteration of the simulation ends with this phase.

The behavior of the agent is driven by the goal of finding a consensual match. The consensus-selection approach is a naive approach, consisting of waiting for a consensus that must coincide for both agents (which may imply a longer duration for the simulation).

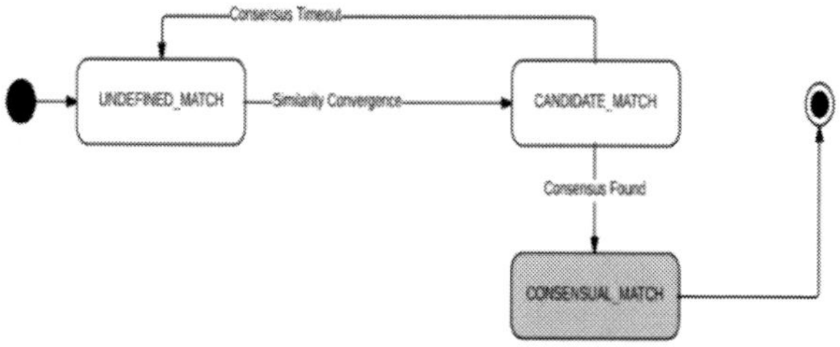

Figure 4. Agent's internal states

The main key-features of our conceptual model are summarized as follow:

- Stochastic Linguistic Matching: similarity calculation based on similarity measures selected randomly from a similarity measures list. Similarity Scores aggregation based on aggregation functions selected randomly from an aggregation function list (MAX, AVERAGE, WEIGHTED). Similarity score validation based on generated random threshold value (within interval).
- Consensual Matching Selection: to form a valid pairing/correspondence, the two agents (form opposite

populations: source and target schemas) should refer to each other as candidate match (in the same time).

- Meta-Simulations and Statistical Analysis: performing statistical analysis on multiple simulation runs data is a good way to improve the confidence in the matching result obtained from our model.

We believe that the conceptualization and the modeling of schema matching as multi-agent simulation will allow the design of a system exhibiting suitable characteristics:

(i) An easy to understand system, composed of simple reflexive "agents" interacting according to simple rules.

(ii) An effective and efficient system, autonomously changing over time, adapting, and self-organizing. A system allowing the emergence of a solution for any given matching scenario.

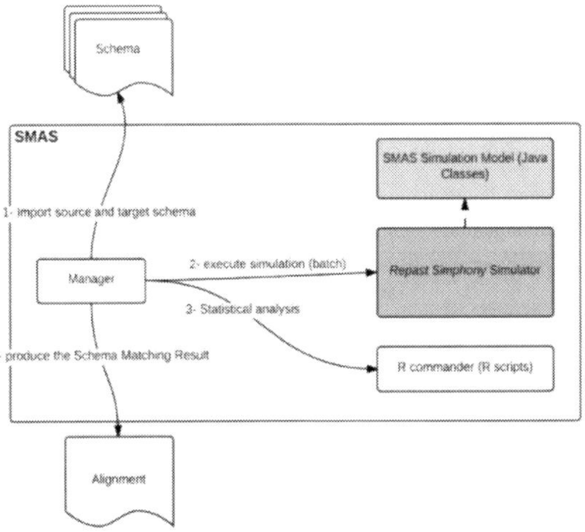

Figure 5. High-level Architecture for Reflex-SMAS

As depicted in Figure 5, our Reflex-SMAS prototype core was implemented in Java using the open source ABMS framework Repast Simphony (2.1) [19], and the open source framework for Text Similarity DKPro Similarity (2.1.0) [20]. The open source R language (R 3.1.0) [21] was used for statistical data analysis.

In the next section, we are going to describe the empirical evaluation of the prototype Reflex-SMAS.

IV. EMPIRICAL EVALUATION

The validation of agent-based simulation models is a topic that is becoming increasingly important in the literature on the field of ABMS. Three types of validation could be identified [22]: (i) Empirical Validation, (ii) Predictive Validation, and (iii) Structural Validation.

As we will see in detail, the empirical validation is the type of validation that we have adopted for the evaluation of our Agent-based Simulation Model for Schema Matching (i.e. prototype Reflex-SMAS).

First, we will start with the description of the methodology used as our validation approach, and then we continue by providing a summarized view of our validation results.

A. *Evaluation Objectives and Strategy*

We are seeking, through this empirical evaluation, to validate the following aspects of our prototype Reflex-SMAS:

- That our solution is, indeed, an effective and efficient automatic schema matching system, capable of autonomously changing behaviors and evolving over time, to adapt, and to self-organize and thus make the solution for any matching scenario to emerge.
- That our solution is easy to understand, and therefore, could display a high degree of maintainability (e.g., adding new matchers).

The proof strategy consists on conducting experiments and then collecting and analyzing data from these experiments. Thus, the validation approach that we have adopted is considered as a hybrid validation approach combining two validation approaches coming from two different fields, namely Schema Matching and ABMS. On one hand, from the field of Schema Matching, we are leveraging a popular evaluation method consisting of the comparison of results with those expected by the user [23]. On the other hand, from the field of ABMS, we are using the Empirical Validation [22] which is mainly based on the comparison among the results obtained from the model and what we can observe in the real system.

Thus, the strategy adopted for the validation of our prototype (implementing our multi-agent simulation model for schema matching) consists of:

- Defining different synthetic matching scenarios (three matching scenarios namely "Person", "Order" and "Travel") with different sizes and different level of lexical heterogeneity, so we can evaluate the prototype matching performance in different situations (adaptation).
- Conducting experiments, compiling results and evaluating the matching performance by comparing, for those three matching scenarios, the matching results (matchings) obtained from our prototype Reflex-SMAS with the results expected by the user.

In the first matching scenario "Person", we need to match two schemas with small size (i.e., six elements) showing a medium lexical heterogeneity level. The second matching scenario "Order" is composed of schemas with medium size with a high lexical heterogeneity level. The schemas in the last matching scenario "Travel" have a relatively big size with a low lexical heterogeneity level.

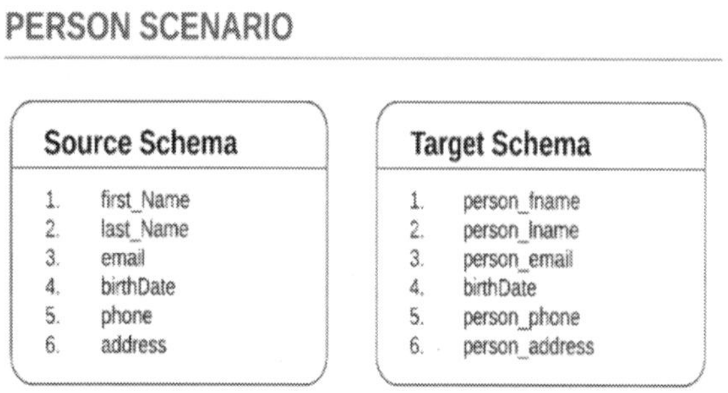

Figure 6. Matching Scenario "Person"

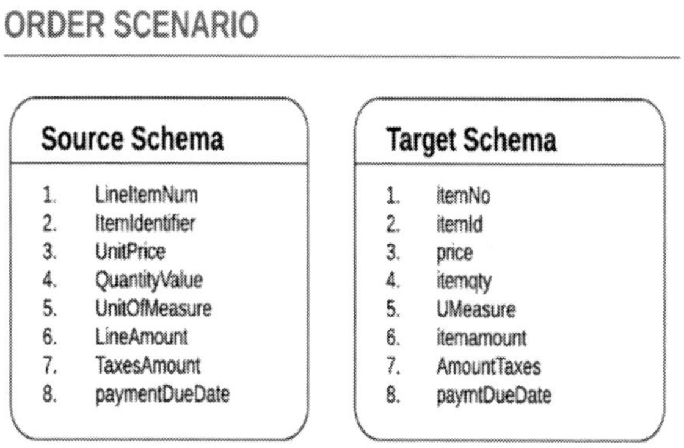

Figure 7. Matching Scenario "Order"

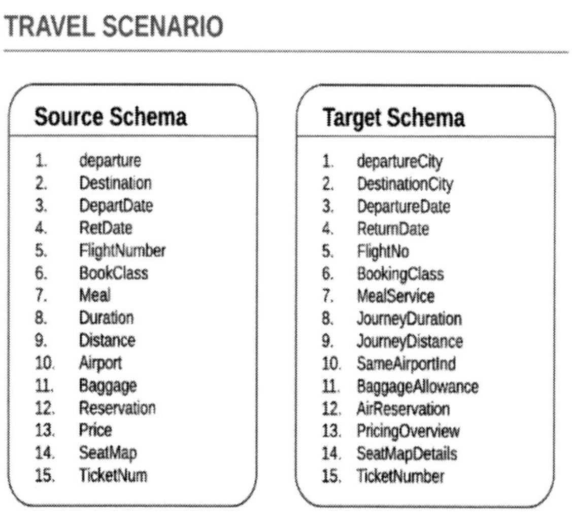

Figure 8. Matching Scenario "Travel"

In order to assess the relevance and level of difficulty that can represent those synthetic matching scenarios (i.e., "Person", "Order" and "Travel"), we decided to evaluate them, first, using the well-known matching tool COMA [24]–[26]. Since, the COMA tool was not able to resolve all the all expected matches for those scenarios, we can say that the proposed synthetic matching scenarios, should be enough challenging scenarios for our validation (from their level of heterogeneity perspective).

Regarding the experiments execution and results compilation, we have decided to run series of three meta-simulations for each scenario (each meta-simulation includes 10 simulations).

The final matching result is based on a statistical analysis of each meta-simulation outcome. In other word, the matching result relies on the calculation of the frequency of occurrence of a found match on the ten simulations composing the meta-simulation. Furthermore, executing for each scenario the meta-simulations three times is a choice that we made to help with the assessment of the experiment repeatability.

B. Experiment Results

This section summarizes the results obtained because of experiments conducted to evaluate the tool Reflex-SMAS. After executing the set of three meta-simulations for each matching scenario, we have compiled the results for the performance for each meta-simulation for all scenarios. As indicated in Table I, our tool was able to correctly find all the expected correspondence by the user (a 100% success rate) after each meta-simulation, and for each scenario.

TABLE I. REFLEX-SMAS EXPERIMENT COMBINED RESULTS

Scenario	M.S.	M. to F.	C.M.F.	% C.M.F.
Person	1	6	6	100%
Person	2	6	6	100%
Person	3	6	6	100%
Order	1	8	8	100%
Order	2	8	8	100%
Order	3	8	8	100%
Travel	1	15	15	100%
Travel	2	15	15	100%
Travel	3	15	15	100%

M.S: Meta Simulation
M. to F: Matchings to Find
C.M.F: Correct Matchings Found
% C.M.F: % Correct Matchings Found

Now, if we compare the results of our Reflex-SMAS prototype with COMA tool results, we can clearly notice that our tool outperformed the COMA tool in all the syntactic matching scenarios. Table II shows the compared result for Reflex-SMAS vs. COMA.

TABLE II. REFLEX-SMAS VS. COMA EXPERIMENT COMBINED RESULTS

		Reflex-SMAS		*COMA*	
Scenario	**M. to F.**	**C.M.F.**	**% C.M. F.**	**C.M.F.**	**% C.M.F.**
Person	6	6	100%	5	83%
Order	8	8	100%	6	75%
Travel	15	15	100%	13	87%

Figure 9 shows a comparison of the performance obtained for scenarios "Person", "Order" and "Travel" with our prototype compared to those obtained with the COMA tool.

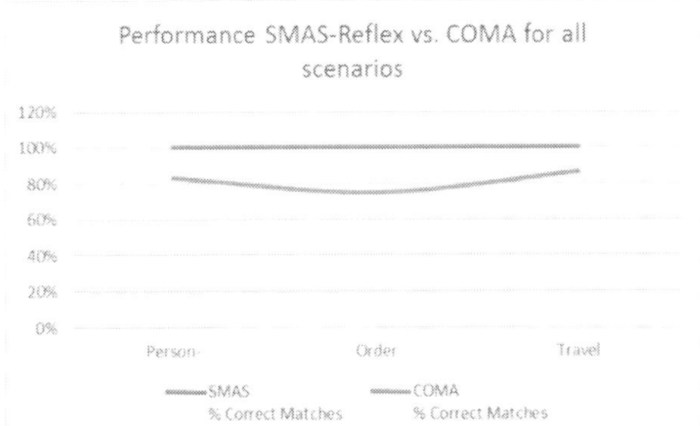

Figure 9. Comparative result between Reflex-SMAS and COMA

To challenge the "perfect" results obtained with our tool Reflex-SMAS for the synthetic matching scenarios, we were curious to know to what extent the performance obtained at the meta-simulations, may be impacted by a reduction in the number of individual simulations composing a meta-simulation. Therefore, we decided to conduct further experimentation, reducing, this time, the number of individual simulations of a meta-simulation from ten simulations to only three simulations.

As we can notice in Figure 10, the performance obtained in the experiment with the meta-simulations composed of three individual simulations instead of ten, has dropped for the scenarios "Order" and "Travel". It means that our matching tool Reflex-SMAS was not able to find all the expected matchings during some of the meta-simulations for those two scenarios (due to the high level of heterogeneity of the scenario "Order" and the big size of the scenario "Travel"). Unquestionably, we can conclude that the number of individual simulations, composing the meta-simulation is an important factor to ensure good matching performance (better quantification of the uncertainty regarding the outcome of the matching process) especially when it comes to scenarios involving large schemas and/or having a high level of heterogeneity.

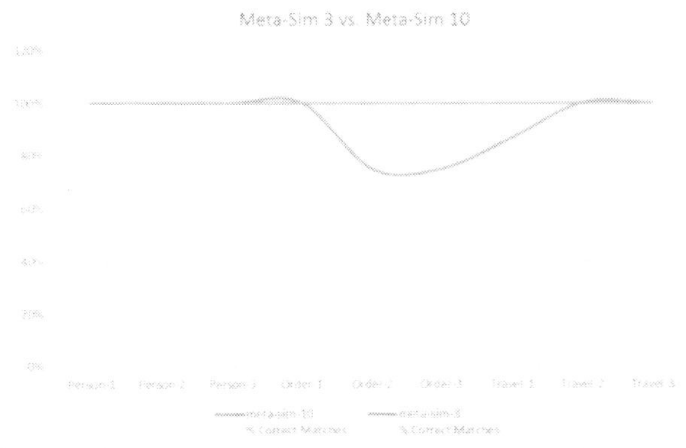

Figure 10. Meta-simulation with 3 vs. 10 individual simulations

V. CONCLUSION AND FUTURE WORKS

Our prototype (Reflex-SMAS) empirical evaluation showed us clearly its capability of providing a high-quality result for different schema matching scenarios without any optimization or tuning from the end-user. The experiments results are very satisfactory. Thus, we can conclude that approaching the schema matching as a CAS and modeling it as ABMS is a viable and very promising approach that could greatly help to overcome the problems of uncertainty and complexity in the field of schema matching.

Our approach represents a significant paradigm-shift, in the field of ASM. In fact, to the best of our knowledge, never the ASM problem has been addressed by adopting systemic thinking (holistic approach) or has been considered as a CAS and modeled using ABMS modeling approach.

As future work, we are planning to enhance the conceptual model of our prototype to tackle challenges, such as complex schema (*n:m* cardinalities) by exploiting other Similarity Measures, such as Structural Similarities (schemas structures). On the other hand, in order to open up new perspectives and to overcome the limits of purely reactive behavior, we are thinking on a "conceptual" evolution of the internal architecture of our agent, evolving it from a reactive agent to an agent of rational type. This evolution consists in the implementation of a decision-making model under uncertainty, at the level of the decision-making phase of the agent, giving it the ability to reason and to choose between conflicting actions. The rational agent we are aiming for, should have a memory, a partial representation of its environment and other agents (its perception), and a capacity for reasoning, allowing it to make a rational choice (to choose the action with the greatest utility) that can guarantee it to maximize its satisfaction (measure of performance). The result of this conceptual evolution could give rise to a new version of our prototype.

REFERENCES

[1] E. Rahm and P. A. Bernstein, "A survey of approaches to automatic schema matching", in the International Journal of Very Large Data Bases, vol. 10, no. 4, pp. 334–350, 2001.

[2] P. Bohannon, E. Elnahrawy, W. Fan, and M. Flaster, "Putting context into schema matching", in proceedings of the 32nd International Conference on Very Large Data Bases, pp. 307–318, 2006.

[3] V. Cross, "Uncertainty in the automation of ontology matching," in proceedings of the 4th International Symposium on Uncertainty Modeling and Analysis, pp. 135–140, 2003.

[4] J. Madhavan, P. A. Bernstein, and E. Rahm, "Generic schema matching with cupid", in proceedings of the 27th Conference on Very Large Data Bases, pp. 49–58, 2001.

[5] B. Villanyi, P. Martinek, and A. Szamos, "Voting based fuzzy linguistic matching", in proceedings of the 15th IEEE International Symposium on Computational Intelligence and Informatics (CINTI), pp. 27–32, 2014.

[6] F. Duchateau and Z. Bellahsene, "Designing a benchmark for the assessment of schema matching tools", in the Open Journal Databases OJDB, vol. 1, no. 1, pp. 3–25, 2014.

[7] C. J. Zhang, L. Chen, H. V. Jagadish, and C. C. Cao, "Reducing uncertainty of schema matching via crowdsourcing", in proceedings of the VLDB Endowment, vol. 6, no. 9, pp. 757–768, 2013.

[8] H. N. Q. Viet, H. X. Luong, Z. Miklos, K. Aberer, and T. T. Quan, "A MAS Negotiation Support Tool for Schema Matching", in the 12th International Conference on Autonomous Agents and Multiagent Systems, pp. 1391-1392, 2013.

[9] P. Shvaiko and J. Euzenat, "Ontology matching: state of the art and future challenges", in the IEEE Transactions on Knowledge and Data Engineering, vol. 25, no. 1, pp. 158–176, 2013.

[10] E. Peukert, "Process-based Schema Matching: From Manual Design to Adaptive Process Construction", Thesis Dissertation, University of Leipzig, 2013.

[11] E. Peukert, J. Eberius, and E. Rahm, "A self-configuring schema matching system", in proceedings of the 28th IEEE International Conference on Data Engineering (ICDE), pp. 306–317, 2012.

[12] W. Nian-Feng and D. Xing-Chun, "Uncertain Schema Matching Based on Interval Fuzzy Similarities", in the International Journal of Advanced Computer Technology, vol. 4, no. 1, pp. 163-171, 2012.

[13] D. Ngo and Z. Bellahsene, "YAM++: a multi-strategy-based approach for ontology matching task", in proceedings of the 18th Conference on Knowledge Engineering and Knowledge Management, Springer, pp. 421–425, 2012.

[14] J. Gong, R. Cheng, and D. W. Cheung, "Efficient management of uncertainty in XML schema matching", in the International Journal of Very Large Data Bases, vol. 21, no. 3, pp. 385–409, 2012.

[15] A. D. Sarma, X. L. Dong, and A. Y. Halevy, "Uncertainty in data integration and dataspace support platforms", in Schema Matching and Mapping. Data-Centric Systems and Applications. Springer, pp. 75–108, 2011.

[16] A. Gal, "Managing uncertainty in schema matching with top-k schema mappings", in Journal on Data Semantics VI, Lecture Notes in Computer Science, vol. 4090. Springer, pp. 90–114, 2006.

[17] A. Gal, "Uncertain schema matching", in Synthesis Lectures on Data Management, vol. 3, no. 1, pp. 1–97, 2011.

[18] R. Fortin, "Comprendre la complexité: introduction à La Méthode d'Edgar Morin", Presses Université Laval, 2005.

[19] M. J. North, E. Tatara, N. T. Collier, and J. Ozik, "Visual agent-based model development with repast simphony", in proceedings of the Agent Conference: Complex Interaction and Social Emergence, pp. 173-192, 2007.

[20] D. Bär, T. Zesch, and I. Gurevych, "DKPro Similarity: An Open Source Framework for Text Similarity", in proceedings of the 51st Annual Meeting of the Association for Computational Linguistics: System Demonstrations, pp. 121–126, 2013.

[21] R. C. Team, "R: A language and environment for statistical computing. R Foundation for Statistical Computing, Vienna, Austria", Open Access Available at: http://www.R-project.org/, 2014.

[22] M. Remondino and G. Correndo, "Mabs validation through repeated execution and data mining analysis", in the International Journal of Simulation, vol. 7, no. 6, pp. 10-21, 2006.

[23] Z. Bellahsene, A. Bonifati, F. Duchateau, and Y. Velegrakis, "On evaluating schema matching and mapping", in Schema matching and mapping, Springer, pp. 253–291, 2011.

[24] H.-H. Do and E. Rahm, "COMA: a system for flexible combination of schema matching approaches", in proceedings of the 28th international conference on Very Large Data Bases, pp. 610–621, 2002.

[25] D. Aumueller, H.H. Do, S. Massmann, and E. Rahm, "Schema and ontology matching with COMA++", in proceedings of the ACM SIGMOD International Conference on Management of Data, pp. 906–908, 2005.

[26] S. Massmann, S. Raunich, D. Aumüller, P. Arnold, and E. Rahm, "Evolution of the COMA match system", in proceedings of the 6th International Conference on Ontology Matching, Volume 814, pp. 49-60, 2011.

Subjective Evaluation on Three Types of Cognitive Load and its Learning Effects

Kazuhisa Miwa
Graduate School of Information Science
Nagoya University
Nagoya, Japan 464-8601
e-mail: miwa@is.nagoya-ua.jp

Hitoshi Terai
Faculty of Human-oriented Science
Kindai University
Iizuka, Japan 820-8555
e-mail: terai@fuk.kindai.ac.jp

Kazuaki Kojima
Learning Technology Lab.
Teikyo University
Utsunomiya, Japan 320-8551
e-mail: kojima@lt-lab.teikyo-u.ac.jp

***Abstract*—Cognitive Load Theory (CLT) distinguishes between three types of cognitive loads: intrinsic, extraneous, and germane. The present study primarily seeks to examine whether participants evaluate cognitive loads correctly when the extraneous and intrinsic cognitive loads are experimentally manipulated. The results showed that the participants evaluated the intrinsic and extraneous cognitive loads correctly, and also evaluated the germane load based on the manipulation of the extraneous load. The study also seeks to identify the type of cognitive load that contributes to learning effects; the results indicate that greater germane and lesser extraneous loads contribute to learning effects. However, the learning effects were not noticeable when far transfer problems were used.**

Keywords* - *Cognitive Loads; Intrinsic; Extraneous; Germane

I. INTRODUCTION

Cognitive Load Theory (CLT) plays a central role in the process of designing learning environments [1][2]. The theory distinguishes between three types of cognitive loads: intrinsic, extraneous, and germane. Previous studies about CLT have focused on the distinction between intrinsic and extraneous loads [1]. Intrinsic load is the basic cognitive load required to perform a particular task. Conversely, extraneous load is the cognitive load that is unrelated to, and hence wasted in, primary cognitive activities. Therefore, extraneous load may have a negative impact on learning activities. In the mid-1990s, it was found that positive cognitive load increases learning effects. Some studies reported significant learning gains upon the imposition of a large cognitive load on participants assigned to the experimental group [2][3], and this type of cognitive load came to be known as the germane load, which is used for learning [4][5].

Several methods have been proposed for the measurement of the three cognitive loads [6]-[11]. A representative method entails the evaluation of the response time for a secondary task—a longer response time indicates the emergence of high cognitive load in the performance of a primary task. Alternatively, it is also common to use a questionnaire to elicit the participants' subjective evaluation; the questionnaire typically consists of question items related to one of the three types of cognitive loads. However, the reliability of the subjective evaluation method has been called into question as results of multiple evaluations using questionnaires have been inconsistent. Moreover, some studies also imply that it is difficult for naive participants to evaluate each of the three types of cognitive loads individually.

The present study primarily seeks to examine whether participants evaluate cognitive loads correctly when the extraneous and intrinsic cognitive loads are experimentally manipulated. Based on the results of this examination, the relations between extraneous, intrinsic, and germane cognitive loads in the context of subjective estimation are also investigated.

The study also seeks to identify the type of cognitive load that contributes to learning effects. The learning effects are measured based on the increase in the post-test scores, as compared to the pre-test scores. The present study also evaluates the relations between learning gains and the subjective evaluation scores of each of the three cognitive loads measured using a questionnaire developed by the authors.

We explain an experimental design in Section 2, report the experimental results in Section 3, and summarize our conclusions in Section 4.

II. EXPERIMENT

In this section, we will explain the summary of our experiment.

A. Task

The task used in this study involved an 8-by-8, computer-based Reversi game, for which a Reversi-based learning environment was developed by the authors [12][13]. Figure 1 represents the overall configuration of the experimental system. Participants played 8-by-8 Reversi games on a computer against a computerized opponent (i.e., opponent agent) in the experimental environment. Participants were assisted by a partner, also computerized (i.e., partner agent), to selecting winning moves. The opponent agent and the partner agent were both controlled by Edax, a Reversi engine, which suggested the best moves by assessing future states of the game. The partner agent typically recommends candidate moves among valid squares before the participant makes a move.

B. Procedure

In order to determine the baseline for the measurement of learning gains, the participants were involved in a pre-test, which consisted of 12 problems. Following this, the participants took part in the learning (training) phase, which involved

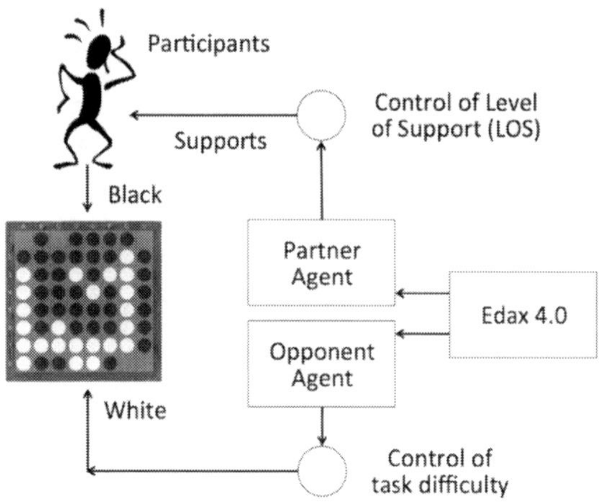

Figure 1. Overall Configuration of the Reversi-based learning environment

16 games. This phase was set up such that the participants had access only to games that were already in progress; as a result, nearly half of the discs were already placed on the board. The learning phase consisted of four blocks, and the participants were required to play four games in each block. A set of winning strategies is proposed; and the training for each block enabled the participants to learn one of the strategies. The discs were arranged in an identical manner for the first three games in each block, whereas the arrangement was altered for the fourth (final) game. The participants were then required to work with the questionnaire designed to evaluate cognitive loads; they were also required to take part in the post-test, which consisted of the same 12 problems as the pre-test.

C. Questionnaire for cognitive load evaluation

We developed a new questionnaire for cognitive load evaluation by drawing from the questionnaires used in previous studies. The questionnaire used in the present study consists of the following ten items (E, I, and G indicate items related to extraneous, intrinsic, and germane loads respectively). The following examples were translated from Japanese version of the questionnaire that was actually used in the experiment.

- It is difficult to search for possible moves. (I)
- It is difficult to search for the best move. (I)
- It is difficult to look ahead. (I)
- It is difficult to understand the arrangements of the discs on the board. (E)
- The representation of the arrangement of discs is inadequate for learning. (E)
- Great effort is required to perform a task given the inadequate representation. (E)
- I try to find heuristics for winning. (G)
- I try to understand the other party's intention. (G)
- I make great effort to find heuristics for wining. (G)
- I concentrate on my performance in the game. (G)

D. Manipulated factors

The following two factors were applied for manipulation: (i) the disc representation factor and (ii) the hint information factor. The first factor was expected to manipulate the extraneous load, whereas the second factor was expected to manipulate the intrinsic load.

1) Disc representation factor: Figure 2 presents a sample disc arrangement typical of the Black and White and the L and rL (reversal L) conditions.

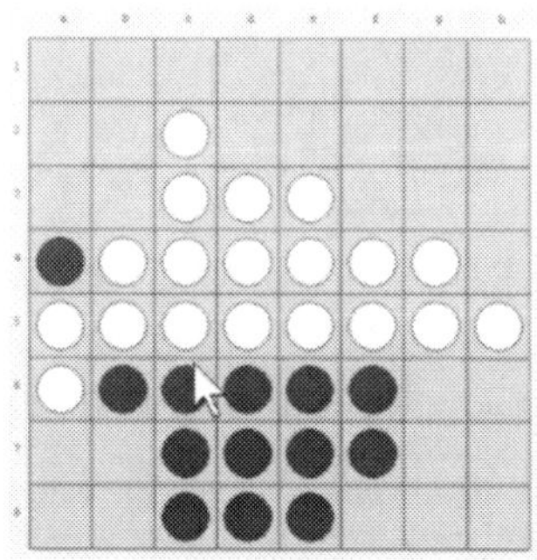

(a) Black and White condition

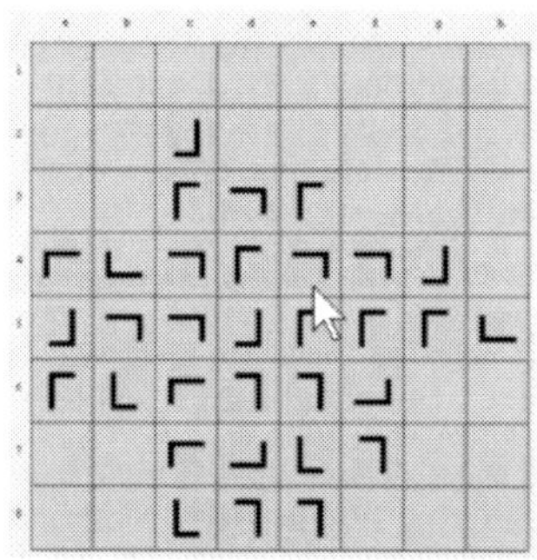

(b) L and reversal L condition

Figure 2. A screenshot of the game board in the Black and White and L and rL (reversal L) conditions

When the Black and White condition was considered, the Black and White discs were used in the arrangement, whereas when the L and rL condition was considered, the Ls or rotated Ls (black discs) and the mirror reversal Ls or rotated reversal Ls (white discs) were used in the arrangement. In order to perceive the status of the disc arrangement and decide the best move in the L and rL condition, participants had to imagine the rotation of the L or reversal L images during each trial, thus causing a significant extraneous load. As a result, the L and rL condition increased the extraneous load more than the Black and White condition.

2) Hint information factor: For each trial of the game, the main task was to choose the best winning move. In order to do so, the participants had to understand the status of the disc arrangement, search the problem space, and estimate the best move, thus increasing intrinsic load. The computerized partner agent suggested the best moves to the participants in the hint presentation condition (see Figure 3), whereas under the no hint condition, no such information was presented. This suggests that the intrinsic load of the participants was lower in the hint presentation condition than in the no hint condition.

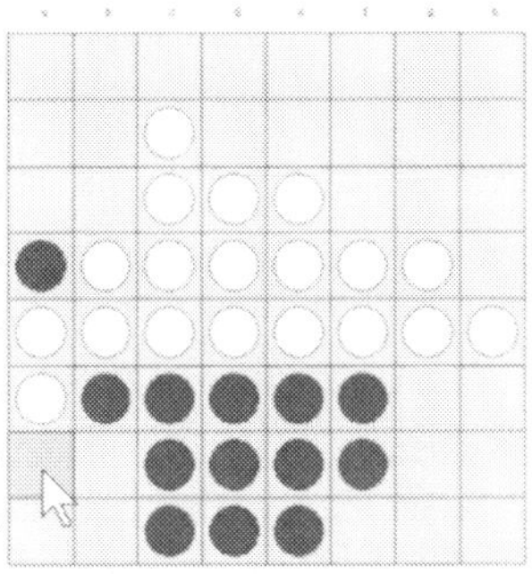

Figure 3. A screenshot of the game board when hint information is presented

E. *Learning gains*

Pre and post-tests were conducted to evaluate the learning gains, and each test consisted of the same 12 problems. In each problem, the participants were presented with a disc arrangement, after which they were required to determine the best possible move. The 12 problems were grouped into the following three categories, each of which in turn consisted of four problems:

1) Identical problems: This disc arrangements presented here were identical to those used in the training phase.

2) Near transfer problems: For this category, the disc arrangements used for the learning phase were modified. More specifically, they were rotated 90, 180, or 270 degrees from their original position or mirror-reversed from the rotated arrangements.

3) Far transfer problems: New disc arrangements were presented for this category. The participants were able to determine the best possible move based on the strategies they were trained in during the learning phase.

As the number of problems in each category was four, the full score was also determined to be four. In the present study, the difference between the pre-test and post-test scores, more particularly, the increase in the post-test scores, were used as learning gains.

F. *Participants*

81 undergraduates from Nagoya University participated in this study. Although all the participants had played Reversi prior to their involvement in the study, they were not experts. The participants were divided into three groups: 21 participants were assigned to the no hint and Black and White condition; 19 were assigned to the hint presentation and Black and White condition; 20 were assigned to the no hint and L and rL condition, and 21 participants were assigned to the hint presentation and L and rL condition.

III. RESULTS

First, we examined whether participants evaluate cognitive loads correctly when the extraneous and intrinsic cognitive loads are manipulated. Figure 4 presents the results of the questionnaire used to measure each type of cognitive load.

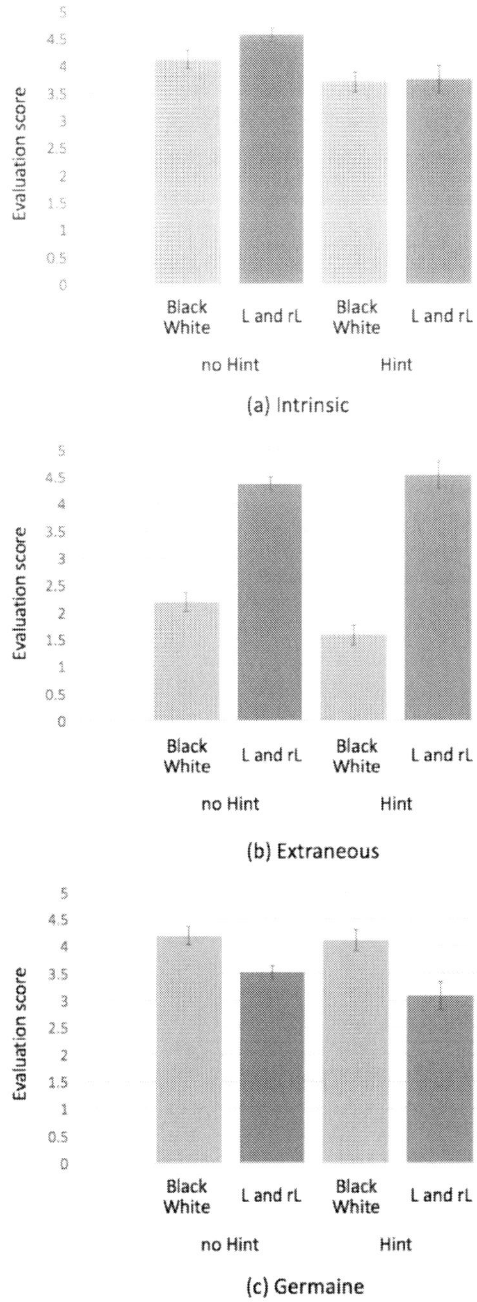

Figure 4. Results of participants' subjective evaluation for the three cognitive loads

In the intrinsic load, a two (hint information: Hint and No hint) × two (disc representation: Black/white and L/rL) ANOVA revealed a significant main effect of the hint information factor ($F(1, 77) = 9.59, p < 0.01$), but neither the main effect of the disc representation factor nor the interaction of the two factors reached a significant level ($F(1, 77) = 1.58$, n.s.; $F(1, 77) = 1.07$, n.s.).

In the extraneous load, the same ANOVA revealed a great

TABLE I. CORRELATION OF THE EVALUATION SCORE OF EACH COGNITIVE LOAD AND THE DIFFERENCE BETWEEN THE PRE-TEST AND POST-TEST SCORES

Problem type	Intrinsic	Extraneous	Germane
Identical	n.s.	r=-0.385, $p < 0.01$	r=0.279, $p < 0.05$
Near transfer	n.s.	r=-0.294, $p < 0.01$	n.s.
Far transfer	n.s.	n.s.	n.s.

significant main effect of the disc representation factor ($F(1, 77) = 520.43$, $p < 0.01$) but the main effect of the hint information factor did not reach a significant level ($F(1, 77) = 3.79$, n.s.). The interaction of the two factors, however, was found to be significant ($F(1, 77) = 12.13$, $p < 0.01$).

In the germane load, the same ANOVA revealed a significant main effect of the disc representation factor ($F(1, 77) = 35.13$, $p < 0.01$), but neither the main effect of the hint information factor nor the interaction of the two factors reached a significant level ($F(1, 77) = 3.21$, n.s.; $F(1, 77) = 1.43$, n.s.).

Second, we sought to identify the type of cognitive load that contributes to learning effects. We analyzed the relations between the evaluation score of each cognitive load in the questionnaire and the increase in the post-test scores as compared to the pre-test scores. Table 1 presents the results of this analysis. We found a positive correlation between germane load and learning gains, but only in the identical problems that were tested. Negative correlations were found between extraneous load and learning gains in the identical and near transfer problems. However, the relations were not noticeable when the far transfer problems were tested.

IV. CONCLUSION

Our first research question involved examining whether participants evaluate cognitive loads correctly when the extraneous and intrinsic cognitive loads are experimentally manipulated. The results indicate that they accurately and consistently evaluated extraneous and intrinsic loads with the experimental manipulation. In the current study, the germane load was estimated based not on intrinsic load manipulation, but on extraneous load manipulation.

The second research question pertained to identifying the type of cognitive load that contributes to learning effects. The results showed that greater germane load contributed to learning effects when identical problems were used in the test phase. This effect, however, was not noticeable when transfer problems were used.

It takes a lot of training and time to acquire skills and expertise to play the games [14]. For the purposes of this experiment, only 16 games were used for training. It is possible that this limitation did not cause learning effects in the transfer problems.

Interestingly, the results also clearly showed that less extraneous load contributed to learning, whereas greater intrinsic load did not. This would depend on the much greater extraneous load caused by the L and rL disc representation. The results highlight the harmful effect of extraneous load on learning activities, which is consistent with the findings of previous studies [2][8][15][16].

The functions of intrinsic load in learning processes still remain unclear; we have, therefore, identified the investigation of its functions as a key objective of our future studies.

REFERENCES

[1] J. Sweller, "Cognitvei load during problem solving: Effects on learning," Cognitive Science, vol. 12, no. 2, 1988, pp. 257–285.

[2] J. Sweller, J. J. Van Merrienboer, and F. G. Paas, "Cognitive architecture and instructional design," Educational psychology review, vol. 10, no. 3, 1998, pp. 251–296.

[3] F. G. Paas and J. J. Van Merrienboer, "Variability of worked examples and transfer of geometrical problem-solving skills: A cognitive-load approach," Journal of Educational Psychology, vol. 86, no. 1, 1994, pp. 122–133.

[4] F. Paas and T. van Gog, "Optimising worked example instruction: Different ways to increase germane cognitive load," Learning and Instruction, vol. 16, no. 2, 2006, pp. 87 – 91.

[5] P. Ayres and T. van Gog, "State of the art research into cognitive load theory," Computers in Human Behavior, vol. 25, 2009, pp. 253–257.

[6] P. Ayres, "Using subjective measures to detect variations of intrinsic cognitive load within problems," Learning and instruction, vol. 16, no. 5, 2006, pp. 389–400.

[7] K. E. DeLeeuw and R. E. Mayer, "A comparison of three measures of cognitive load: Evidence for separable measures of intrinsic, extraneous, and germane load," Journal of educational psychology, vol. 100, no. 1, 2008, pp. 223–234.

[8] G. Cierniak, K. Scheiter, and P. Gerjets, "Explaining the split-attention effect: Is the reduction of extraneous cognitive load accompanied by an increase in germane cognitive load?" Computers in Human Behavior, vol. 25, no. 2, 2009, pp. 315–324.

[9] T. H. S. Eysink, T. de Jong, K. Berthold, B. Kolloffel, M. Opfermann, and P. Wouters, "Learner performance in multimedia learning arrangements: An analysis across instructional approaches," American Educational Research Journal, vol. 46, no. 4, 2009, pp. 1107–1149.

[10] E. Galy, M. Cariou, and C. Mélan, "What is the relationship between mental workload factors and cognitive load types?" International Journal of Psychophysiology, vol. 83, no. 3, 2012, pp. 269–275.

[11] J. Leppink, F. Paas, T. van Gog, C. P. van der Vleuten, and J. J. van Merrinboer, "Effects of pairs of problems and examples on task performance and different types of cognitive load," Learning and Instruction, vol. 30, 2014, pp. 32 – 42.

[12] K. Miwa, K. Kojima, and H. Terai, "An experimental investigation on learning activities inhibition hypothesis in cognitive disuse atrophy," in Proceedings of the Seventh International Conference on Advanced Cognitive Technologies and Applications (Cognitive 2015), 2015, pp. 66–71.

[13] ——, "Measuring cognitive loads based on the mental chronometry paradigm," in Proceedings of the Eighth International Conference on Advanced Cognitive Technologies and Applications (Cognitive 2016), 2016, pp. 38–41.

[14] K. A. Ericsson, The road to excellence: The acquisition of expert performance in the arts and sciences, sports, and games. Psychology Press, 2014.

[15] R. E. Mayer and R. Moreno, "A split-attention effect in multimedia learning: Evidence for dual processing systems in working memory," Journal of Educational Psychology, vol. 90, no. 2, 1998, pp. 312–320.

[16] ——, "Nine ways to reduce cognitive load in multimedia learning," Educational Psychologist, vol. 38, no. 1, 2003, pp. 43–52.

EEG based Valence Recognition using Convolutional Kernel on Time-Frequency axis

Jun-Su Kang and Minho Lee
School of Electronics Engineering, Kyungpook National University
Taegu, South Korea
E-mails: {wkjuns, mholee}@gmail.com

Abstract—**In this study, we present an emotion recognition model, namely valence recognition, based on convolutional kernel on time-frequency axis. Our proposed model uses convolutional kernel on Time-Frequency axis for Convolutional Neural Network (CNN). In order to compare our results with previous ones, we use the DEAP dataset that represents the benchmark for emotion classification research. The preliminary results show that the proposed model has a potential for positive and negative emotion recognition when compared to conventional studies.**

Keywords-EEG; valence recognition; convolutional neural network; long-short term memory; spectrogram.

I. INTRODUCTION

Emotion is one of the most central and pervasive aspects of human experience. Normal people 'feel' and 'express' a wide range of emotions. While emotions deepen and enrich human experience, they also have profound affected on other cognitive functions such as decision-making, reasoning, language comprehension, etc.[1] It has been argued that cognition and emotion are complimentary to each other and one cannot be properly understood or modeled without understanding the other. Especially, at a time when technology is moving towards advanced intelligent systems and smarter robots, this fundamental aspect of human nature cannot be overlooked. Therefore, to develop 'human like intelligence' and/or for a 'qualitative human-machine interaction', it is important that machines also be trained to understand, if not feel, human emotions.

Human emotion is elicited by external stimuli such as image, sound, smell, texture, etc.[2] For understanding the human emotion, we need to catch the internal and external cues from human. For the external cues, there are facial expression, gesture, voice. For the internal cues, we can record the brain or bio signals by attaching sensors to the brain or body. Each modality has its own strength and weakness as shown in Table 1.

TABLE 1. PROS AND CONS FOR RECOGNIZING HUMAN EMOTION

Modality	Pros	Cons
Facial expression	Easy to use	Easy to deceive
Gesture	Easy to use	Easy to deceive
Speech/voice signal	Easy to use	Easy to deceive
Bio-signal	Hard to deceive	Hard to get good signal
Brain signal	Hard to deceive	Hard to get good signal

Among several modalities, we choose electroencephalography (EEG) signals to recognize human valence emotion as 2 classes (positive and negative). EEG signal is a measurement of the brain's electrical activity and provides good temporal resolution. Many prior studies show that EEG power and power asymmetry are related to the emotional valence[3]. The EEG signal with high alpha activity is shown to be an indication of low brain activity, whilst gamma band EEG is connected to high cognitive processes [4]. In this study, we use gamma band power spectrogram as the input of our proposed network. Because, the results of gamma band from the prior studies were better than the results of other frequency bands [5-7]. The rest of the paper is organized as follows: in the next section, the related works are presented. In the section 3, we explain our proposed method for preprocessing and model design. In section 4, the results of the experiment is given. In the last section, we conclude our results and present our future plans.

II. RELATED WORKS

There are many works in the field of emotion recognition. Many studies have tried to extract important emotional features from raw EEG data in the time and frequency domain. Table 2 shows the used feature set of the prior studies.

TABLE 2. FEATURES OF THE PRIOR STUDIES

Prior study	Features	Performance (%)
[8]	440 features (power spectral density(PSD), time domain feature), window size: 50[s], 10[s]	Valence: 78.75
[9]	425 features (PSD, time domain feature), window size: 60[s]	Valence: 76.02
	425 features, window size: 6[s]	Valence: 80.09
[10]	PSD	Valence: 57.60

For time domain features, entropy, kurtosis and zero crossing rate were well used to recognize human emotion. As for frequency domain features, power spectral density (PSD), power subtraction between left and right hemisphere were well used. Feature-based analysis makes it easy to interpret/understand the phenomenon, however, it takes a lot of effort to calculate all those features. Furthermore, the calculation method is very complex. In this study, we only use the spectrogram (gamma band) as the input data.

III. METHOD

We propose an emotion recognition model based on CNN, which attempts to determine the negative and positive emotional state from EEG signals.

A. *Dataset description*

We used the DEAP dataset, which represents the benchmark for emotion classification research. The data were taken from [10] and included responses of 32 participants (seventeen males, fifteen females). Their mean age was 27.197 years (SD = 4.446) and each subject watched 40 music videos of 60 seconds each with the goal of inducing positive/negative valence emotion. After watching the movie, the subjects were asked to rate the video on a continuous scale ranging from 1 to 9. If the response score of a subject is over 5, we consider it as positive status, otherwise, it's considered negative.

B. *Preprocessing of EEG data*

We downloaded the preprocessing EEG dataset from [10], but there still are noises such as eye movement. Because of that, we considered Independent Component Analysis (ICA) as a noise removing algorithm [11]. After removing the major noise components with ICA, Short-Time Fourier Transform (STFT) is applied to obtain the spectrogram. The STFT uses a 3 [sec] window to divide the time series data. After dividing the time series data, 1 [sec] window is applied to get the spectrogram from each 3 [sec] windows with overlap ratio of 87.5%.

C. *Model design*

In order to understand the human emotion from the spectrogram data, convolution kernels on time-frequency axis are used in the CNN structure. In the CNN structure, there are two sub-CNN networks (CNN with convolutional kernel on time axis and CNN with convolutional kernel on frequency axis). Both CNN networks have 6 convolutional layers with 4 drop connections from the 2nd to the 6th layer for increasing the generalization performance [12]. After the 6th convolutional layer, the feature moves to a fully connected layer. The fully connected layer consisted of 3 layers and the output of the 2nd fully connected layer (time/frequency network) is concatenated into one vector. This concatenated feature is moved to the softmax function. Figure 1 shows the part of the proposed CNN structure.

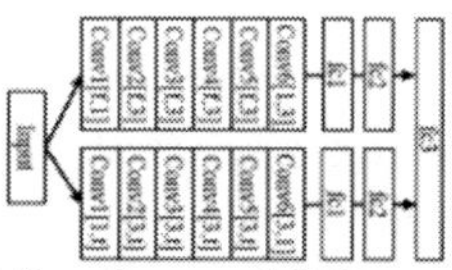

Figure 1. Part of proposed CNN structure

IV. RESULTS

When testing the proposed model, we preliminary test to the 9 subjects among 32 subjects. To increase the regularization performance, l2 regularization is used with weight decay factor of 1e-2, and dropout ratio of 50%. Learning rate is used with 6e-6. For reducing the data bias, 5-fold cross validation is applied (train: data of 32 movies, test: data of 8 movies, 1 fold: data of 8 movies). Figure 2 shows the 9 subject-wise average train and test performance for 5-fold cross validation. The proposed model shows 71.367%(±5.469%) average test accuracy for the 32 subjects.

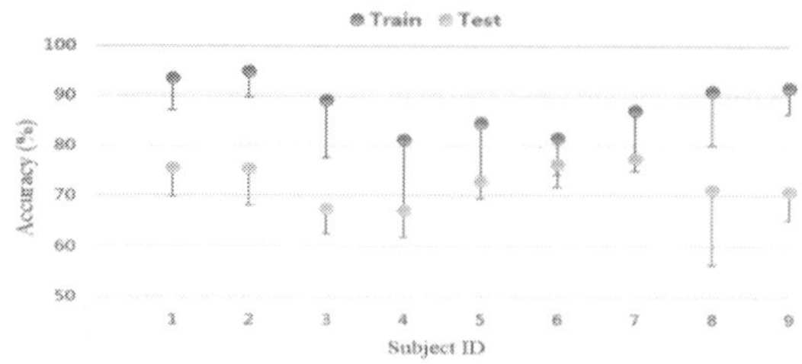

Figure 2. 9 Subject-wise train and test performance (dot means the average accuracy and vertical bar means the standard deviation)

V. CONCLUSION

The characteristics of EEG signal is needed to understand both the time-domain pattern and frequency-domain pattern. Because of that, we design the time-frequency axis convolution kernels for understanding the EEG spectrogram. For future work, the data for other subjects should be considered and also an expansion emotion's dimensions.

ACKNOWLEDGMENT

This work was supported by the National Research Foundation of Korea (NRF) grant funded by the Korea government (MSIP) (No. NRF-2016R1A2A2A05921679).

REFERENCES

[1] L. Pessoa, The cognitive-emotional brain: From interactions to integration: MIT press, 2013..

[2] H. Leventhal, "A perceptual-motor theory of emotion," Advances in experimental social psychology, vol. 17, pp. 117-182, 1984.

[3] Q. Zhang, S. Jeong, and M. Lee, "Autonomous emotion development using incremental modified adaptive neuro-fuzzy inference system", Neurocomputing, vol. 86, pp. 33-44, 2012.

[4] M. Li and B.-L. Lu, "Emotion classification based on gamma-band EEG," in Engineering in Medicine and Biology Society, 2009. EMBC 2009. Annual International Conference of the IEEE, 2009, pp. 1223-1226.

[5] N. Jatupaiboon, S. Pan-ngum, and P. Israsena, "Emotion classification using minimal EEG channels and frequency bands", in Proceedings of the 10th international joint conference on computer science and software engineering (JCSSE), 2013, pp. 21-24.

[6] W.-L. Zheng, J.-Y. Zhu, Y. Peng, and B.-L. Lu, "EEG-based emotion classification using deep belief networks", in Proceeding of IEEE international conference on Multimedia and Expo (ICME), 2014, pp. 1-6.

[7] R.-N. Duan, J.-Y. Zhu, and B.-L. Lu, "Differential entropy feature for EEG-based emotion classification", in Proceeding of 6th international IEEE/EMBS conference on Neural Engineering (NER), 2013, pp. 81-84.

[8] Z. Yin, Y. Wang, L. Liu, W. Zhang, and J. Zhang, "Cross-subject EEG feature selection for emotion recognition using transfer recursive feature elimination," Frontiers in neurorobotics, vol. 11, pp. 1-16, 2017.

[9] Z. Yin, M. Zhao, Y. Wang, J. Yang, and J. Zhang, "Recognition of emotions using multimodal physiological signals and an ensemble deep learning model," Computer Methods and Programs in Biomedicine, vol. 140, pp. 93-110, 2017.

[10] S. Koelstra, et al., "Deap: A database for emotion analysis; using physiological signals," IEEE Transactions on Affective Computing, vol. 3, pp. 18-31, 2012.

[11] M. Chaumon, D. V. Bishop, and N. A. Busch, "A practical guide to the selection of independent components of the electroencephalogram for artifact correction," Journal of neuroscience methods, vol. 250, pp. 47-63, 2015.

[12] L. Wan, M. Zeiler, S. Zhang, Y. L. Cun, and R. Fergus, "Regularization of neural networks using dropconnect," in Proceedings of the 30th international conference on machine learning (ICML-13), 2013, pp. 1058-1066.

A Model of Free Will for Artificial Entities

Eric Sanchis
University of Toulouse Capitole
Toulouse, France
e-mail: eric.sanchis@iut-rodez.fr

Abstract—**The impression of free will is the feeling according to which our choices are neither imposed from our inside nor from outside. It is the sense we are the ultimate cause of our acts. In direct opposition with the universal determinism, the existence of free will continues to be discussed. In this paper, free will is linked to a decisional mechanism: an agent is provided with free will if having performed a predictable choice C, it can immediately perform another choice C' in a random way. The intangible "feeling" of free will is replaced by a decision-making process including a predictable decision-making process immediately followed by an unpredictable decisional one.**

Keywords-free will; artificial entities; three-step decisionnal process; synthetic property.

I. INTRODUCTION

Concepts produced by the human mind to characterize its own functioning, such as the properties of *intelligence*, *autonomy* or *free will* have a particularly important influence in our comprehension of the world. For this reason, they are continuously being revisited by philosophy, psychology, neurosciences, cognitive sciences but also computer sciences. In this latter area, it is undoubtedly the property of *intelligence* which has been the most studied in Artificial Intelligence, particularly in its most classical branch. Other properties, such as *autonomy* are studied in other fields of computer sciences (*Software Agent*, *Multi-Agent Systems* or *Robotics*), each one with their own issues.

More complex, *free will* is the property according to which the human being would be the first source of his choices. No internal or external force would impose him a choice rather than another. In other words, only the individual would be at the origin of his acts. After the first characterizations of this property, a question immediately emerged: does *free will* exist? This question has fuelled the philosophical debate for several centuries with no satisfactory solution found [1]. Many philosophers, such as Spinoza or Nietzsche, refuted its existence. Others, such as Sartre, did not feel that way. Others still have or have had a mitigated opinion. Studies of *free will* carried out by neuroscientists since the end of the last century, such as those achieved by B. Libet [2], although informative on certain points, did not give a definitive answer either.

Contrary to *intelligence* or *autonomy*, *free will* has received little attention in the computer science domain. A. Krausová and H. Hazan [3] examined the relevance to study *free will* within the *General Artificial Intelligence* field and answered by the affirmative. J. McCarthy [4] and R. Manzotti [5] tackled the *free will* problem within the classical Artificial Intelligence framework, the first via a logical formalization of the property reduced to a rational choice, the second by proposing a model sketch.

The model of *free will* which is proposed in this paper results from previous work related to the *autonomy* of software agents [6]. That is not completely surprising because these two properties have common characteristics, such as the plurality of possibilities and freedom of choice. *Free will* is considered as a decision-making process structured in three stages, where an agent makes a first choice that is immediately called into question by making a second choice randomly selected.

The paper is structured as follows. First, various aspects of *free will* are sketched, related to its nature and problems involved in the implementation of this property inside an artificial entity. The second section introduces a class of models called *Two-Stage Models of Free Will*. These models include the creation of the possible choices and the selection of the final choice. Sections 3 and 4 present the decision-making process at the heart of the *Three-Stage Model of Free Will*. In conclusion, entities being able to be provided with *free will* and the needed conditions are identified.

II. THE FREE WILL PROBE

Free will is a complex property which creates several questions. The first one is the following: how to characterize the property of free will in a precise way? In fact, there is no single definition! Indeed, depending on the language, certain formulations of the property name will privilege the aspect of choice (in French, *libre arbitre*), others the aspect of will (in English, *free will*). It would rather be a perception, a sense that our choices belong to us, that they are not imposed to us neither from the outside, nor by an interior force which we would not control. It is the feeling that we are the main cause of our acts. Free will is mentally defined by physical, emotional and intellectual sensations that a person feels, giving birth to a specific global "feeling". In the case of free will, this "sense" is expressed in terms of freedom, will and choice, a concise formulation of which could be: my will is free to choose.

The second question is: why *free will* is so important? It is possible to identify at least two main reasons:

- *Free will* is considered as a specific property to humankind. As our knowledge progresses on the animal societies, other properties we believed to be specific to human beings appear to be in fact … much less specific! Let us mention for example the capacity to use a complex language, to have empathy, to use a technical knowledge in tools construction.

- *Free will* constitutes a social pillar. Because we are provided with *free will* we are *morally responsible* for our acts and *criminally liable* before society. Moreover, various studies showed that people had a more social behaviour when they believed in the existence of *free will* [7]. Denying the existence of *free will* is undermining one of the human society bases.

The third question is certainly the most important: does *free will* actually exist? Serious arguments denying its existence were put forward by philosophers and scientists. The threat mainly comes from the *universal determinism* posed as the world's general functioning principle. This is why the contents of this principle must be examined before any study of the property of *free will*.

A. *Determinism and free will*

The concept of *determinism* is closely associated with the *principle of causality* (there cannot be an effect without a cause). *Determinism* is a *janusian* concept, i.e., a concept which has two faces like the Roman god Janus. Indeed, two kinds of determinisms can be distinguished: *concrete determinisms* and *speculative determinisms*.

Concrete determinisms are determinisms whose existence could be proven in the form of a natural law (e.g., the law of gravitation) or explicitly built (e.g., a computer program).

Speculative determinisms are not supported by any proof of their existence. Only a body of facts and evidence suggest that they can exist. Examples of *speculative determinisms* are *social determinisms* and the most representative of them: the *universal determinism*.

The *universal determinism* is the principle according to which the succession of each event in the universe results from the *principle of causality*, the *past* and *natural laws*. According to the *universal determinism*, all is predetermined. That means that each event in the universe is given before it occurs. Thus, the existence of *free will* would be an illusion produced by our ignorance of the *past* and *natural laws*. On the other hand, the *universal determinism* is a fertile methodological framework because it is an essential engine of the scientific investigation.

As part of the *universal determinism*, it is important to distinguish the occurrence of an event from its predictability. Although an event is predetermined, its predictability may not be effective as it appears in chaotic systems. This absence of predictability is often justified as being due to a lack of information. This lack of information is also used to deny the existence of *indeterminism* or to interpret *chance*. As a result, a system can be *deterministic and predictable*, *deterministic and not predictable* or *not deterministic* (thus not predictable) if the *universal determinism* is refuted.

In short, the *universal determinism* (metaphysical principle) induces a methodology (scientific approach), which demonstrates the existence of *concrete determinisms* (natural laws). But it is also a fossilizing metaphysical principle, which denies that our experience as a person is the first source of our choices.

As neither the existence of the *universal determinism* nor the existence of *free will* can be demonstrated, philosophers have summarized the relationship between these two concepts with two points of view:

- *Incompatibilism*: the existence of a deterministic universe is in complete contradiction with the existence of *free will*. Between the two, it is necessary to choose.
- *Compatibilism*: there is no total opposition between a deterministic universe and *free will*. In particular, it is possible to freely act in a deterministic world.

B. *The notion of cause*

Using the *law of causality*, *determinism* invokes the concept of *cause*. But is this notion actually easy to handle?

The concept of cause

- returns to the past, most of the time unknowable: when we have a thought *T* or we have carried out an action *A*, we cannot specify in an irrefutable manner what all their causes were.
- is a multilevel concept: it applies at the same time at the social, psychological, biological and physical levels. We generally do not know how these various causal levels overlap.
- is protean: in each context where it appears, it presents itself in a different form.
- leads to a regression ad infinitum: the event *E* is the result of cause *C*, which is the result of cause *CC*, etc.

Like *determinism*, the notion of *cause* also presents two faces:

- it can be an enlightening explanation of a precise experiment. For example, when I drop a stone it falls (effect) because the stone is subject to the gravitation law (cause).
- it can be unknowable due to an unknown past and composite contents.

It results that in many cases, the general concept of cause brings more problems than solutions.

In conclusion, the model suggested to interpret and implement the property of *free will* within an artificial entity will replace the problematic concept of *cause* by the concrete concepts of *inputs* and *influences* while the couple *determinism/indeterminism* will be replaced by the concepts of *predictability/unpredictability*.

III. THE TWO-STAGE MODELS OF FREE WILL

The characterization of *free will* in the form of a process including two stages [8] is assigned to the American philosopher and psychologist W. James.

In this model of *free will*, a process is sequentially executed in two steps:

- At the first step, a certain number of possibilities are generated (some of them can be randomly created). Several futures are then possible: it is the *freedom* aspect of the agent which is expressed.
- in the second stage, one of these possibilities is chosen, choice in which the chance does not intervene any more : it is the *will* part of the agent (Figure 1).

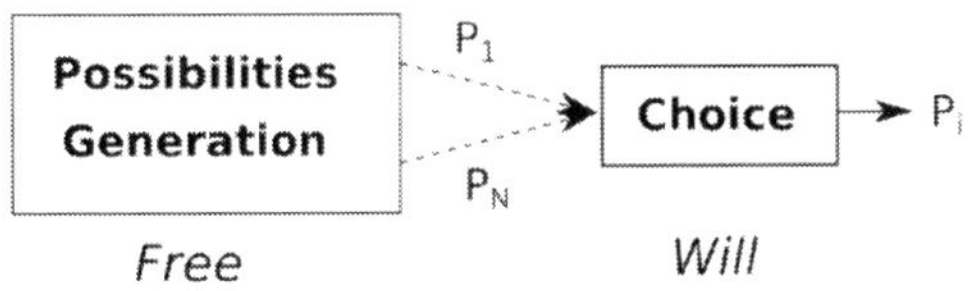

Figure 1. Two-Stage Model of Free Will

Since then, this model has been taken up directly or indirectly by several philosophers and scientists. B. Doyle listed a large number of these interpretations of *free will* that he classified under the generic expression *Two-Stage Models of Free Will* [9].

In Computer Science, J. McCarthy proposed a formalization of the concept which can also be considered as a *Two-Stage Model of Free Will*:

"*We present a theory of simple deterministic free will (SDFW) in a deterministic world. The theory splits the mechanism that determines action into two parts. The first part computes possible actions and their consequences. Then the second part decides which action is most preferable and does it*" [4].

The important common points to the different *Two-Stage Models of Free Will* are the following:

- The generation of the future possible choices and the creation of the selection function are parts of the *free will* process.
- There is only one phase of choice that ends the process associated with *free will*.
- In addition to the concept of *will*, these models use in the first stage properties difficult to characterize with precision, such as *intelligence* or *creativity*.

IV. FROM THE "FEELING" OF FREE WILL TO THE "MECHANISM" OF FREE WILL

Free will is a complex property, i.e., it is difficult even impossible to have a thorough knowledge of it. It is a property with vague and elastic contours, with their contents changing according to the point of view that one can have. It authorizes different interpretations (ex: various *Two-stage Models of the Free Will*), when these interpretations are not contradictory. Lastly, for some *free will* exists, for others it does not exist.

Tackling *free will* by considering only the "feeling" associated to it or the "impression" it causes poses problems because it requires to use concepts which raise the same type of problems of definition and scope (ex: *conscience*, *will*, *freedom*, *first cause* of an act).

In order to solve these various problems, the model of *free will* described in the next section is based on the following points:

- *Conscience* and *free will* are decoupled. That means the implementation of *free will* in an entity does not require that this entity is provided with a brain or an advanced mental system.
- The *choice* aspect of *free will* is privileged over the *will* aspect. Indeed, the concept of *choice* can be defined with more precision than the concept of *will*.
- The *origin* and the *nature* of the causes related to a choice are ignored. The concept of *cause* is replaced by the concepts of *inputs* and *influences*.
- *Free will* is considered as a precise *decision-making process*. *Free will* is interpreted as the possibility to question a first choice by combining in the same decision-making process a *predictable choice* and a *random choice*.

V. A THREE-STAGE MODEL OF FREE WILL

The suggested characterization of *free will* is the following: **an agent is provided with *free will* if, after having made a predictable choice *C*, it can immediately make another choice C' in a random way**. In other words, the impalpable "feeling" of *free will* is replaced by a *two-component decision-making process* including a *predictable decision-making process* immediately followed by a *unpredictable decision-making* one.

A. *Model*

The *Three-Stage Model of free will* implements two modules sequentially executed, a *predictable module* and a *unpredictable module*, driven by *causes* modelled in the form of *inputs* and *influences*.

1) Inputs and influences

We will say that a component (or module) has a *predictable behaviour* if the same *entries* applied to it always generate the same *outputs*.

The term of *input* must be understood in its most general signification (internal or external conditions, stimuli, states, etc). It was chosen for simplicity reasons: the concept of *input* has the advantage of making the nature of the *causes* it summarizes transparent.

A module has an *unpredictable behaviour* if the same *inputs* applied to it at two different moments can produce different *outputs*.

When an *input* must be represented but with no or little information about it the term of *influence* will be used. An *influence* materializes the complex aspect of a property by circumscribing its complexity in precise points of the model.

In the *Three-Stage Model of Free Will*, *influences* are only present in the *unpredictable component* (Figure 2).

Hereafter, the concept of *entry* will be only used to represent well-identified information having an effect on a choice module. Otherwise, the term *influence* will be chosen.

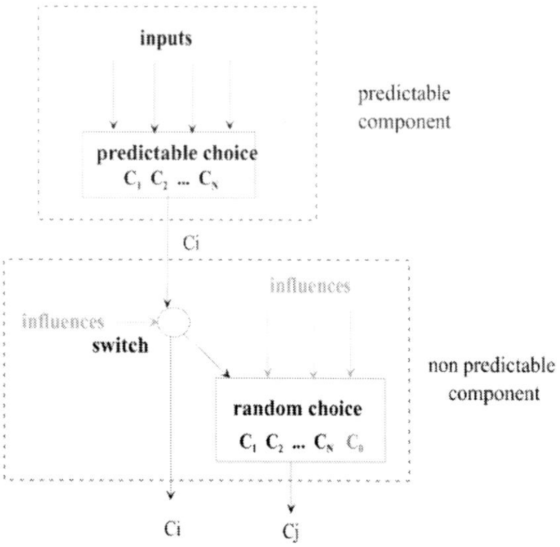

Figure 2. Three-Stage Model of Free Will

2) The predictable component

The *predictable component* provides an artificial entity with a *regular behaviour*: this module can implement a *rational choice* (e.g., in situation *A*, my interest is to make choice *C*) or an *automatic behaviour* (ex: each time I am in such a situation, I make this choice). In the first case, it is a thoughtful behaviour: the situation will be evaluated and the selected choice will be determined by taking into account various parameters, such as preferences, probabilities of occurrences of events, evaluation of consequences. In the last case, it is a constrained behaviour.

The presence of the *predictable module* also materializes the coherent behaviour of the agent: some sense pre-exists to the selected choice.

From a formal point of view, the *predictable module* is characterized by a *set of choices* C_p $(1 \leq p \leq N, N>1)$, a *selection function* and a *set of inputs*. From the *N* possible *choices*, the *selection function* and the *inputs*, the *predictable module* selects a choice C_i.

Contrary to the various *Two-Stage Models of Free Will*, processes involved in the development of these *N* choices, the selection function and its inputs are considered being external to the property of *free will*. This means that it is necessary to have at one's disposal a set of choices, an associated selection function and the values of inputs before *free will* can appear.

The *predictable decision-making process* begins with the execution of the selection function. It is the first stage of the general process related to *free will*.

To illustrate the key elements of a *predictable module* we will use the following example. Let us suppose that one task of an agent *A* is to go to a point *P* no more than ten kilometres.

A *regular* behaviour of *A* could be: if it rains agent *A* uses its car, if it does not rain and the sky is grey, *A* uses its bicycle. If the weather is nice, *A* reaches point *P* on foot.

The choice function of the agent is controlled by a unique input: the weather state. The three possible choices are: to go by car, to use its bicycle, to walk.

3) The unpredictable component

This module includes two elements:

- A *switch*, which, either does not interfere on choice *Ci* resulting from the *predictable component*, or activates an *unpredictable choice function*. In the first case, *Ci* is the final choice. In the latter case, the final choice could be different.
- An *unpredictable choice function*, which carries out a random choice on the *N* choices available during the execution of the *predictable component* plus an *additional choice* noted C_0 called *empty choice*. This choice means that no choice is performed by the agent. It illustrates the situation where there is an inhibition of the choice resulting from the *predictable component*. Consequently, after the activation of the *unpredictable component*, the final choice *Cj* $(0 \leq j \leq N)$ may differ from choice *Ci* selected by the *predictable component*. In particular, if $j=0$ there is inhibition of the choice resulting from the *predictable module*.

The following points must also be noted:

- There is no creation or development of new choices by the *unpredictable component*.
- Without context it is difficult to associate a precise meaning to the *empty choice* C_0. According to the situations, it can be interpreted in various manners like "*no choice must be made*" or "*it is a veto*".
- The activation details of the *switch* and *random choice function* can be partially or completely unknown to the agent. This is why their conditions of activation are represented in the form of *influences*.

Let us assume that in the previous example, the sun is shining. The *predictable component* invites agent *A* to reach point *P* on foot. But *A* can decide for reasons (*influences)* which are partly or completely unknown to it to call this choice into question: the *switch* is triggered. Then, *A* decides to select by random a choice among four: the three previous choices and the choice to remain where it is (C_0 choice). This *unpredictable choice* can be accomplished for example by using an appropriate computer program. It should be noted that the quality of the random choice function has a secondary importance in the global decision-making process.

In this precise example, the concept of *influence* makes it possible to represent an intuition as well as a change of mood of *A* having caused the switch triggering.

4) A Three-Stage decision-making process

To sum up, the decision-making process associated to *free will* is structured by three moments (Figure 3):

- The moment t_D when the execution of the *predictable choice function* begins. The *first stage* ends with the selection of a choice C_i.
- The moment t_S when the entity decides to put into question the choice C_i. It is the *second step* of the decisional process.
- The moment t_U when the execution of the *unpredictable choice function* begins, leading to the final choice C.

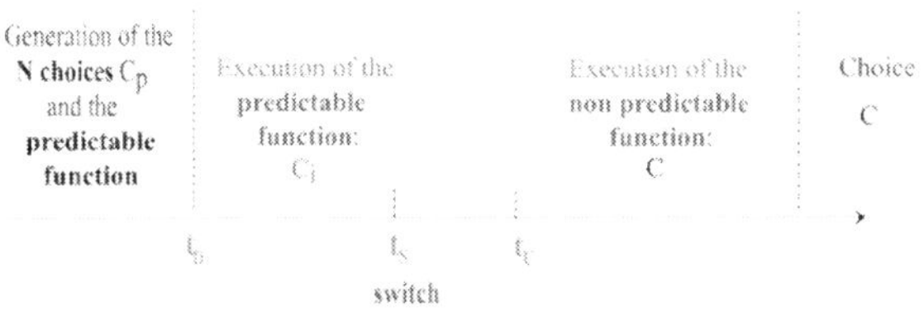

Figure 3. Temporal pattern of the decision-making process associated to free will

The agent has expressed its *free will* when the three moments t_D, t_S and t_U took place. This process will be qualitatively different according to the nature of the agent. If the agent is an individual, these three moments will be lived more or less consciously. For an artificial agent, the decision-making process associated to *free will* is simply executed.

B. Discussion

1) Model justification

a) Components articulation

Let us justify the role of the model elements and their articulation.

If the decision-making process associated to *free will* implemented only the *predictable choice module*, the agent executing this decision-making process would be comparable to a classical program like an accounting programme or a flight tickets booking program.

If the *unpredictable component* were the only one there, the agent would be stripped of rationality and condemned to an erratic functioning.

Let us suppose that the two modules of choice are reversed. Firstly, subjected to *influences*, the agent performs an *unpredictable choice*. In a second step, according to *influences*, the *switch* can give access to the *predictable choice module*, which according to the *inputs*, will select the rational choice. That means that the trigger of a coherent behaviour of the agent is controlled by *influences*, which is a very unsatisfactory functioning.

If there were no *switch*, the two modules would be sequentially executed. In this case, only the result of the last executed choice module would be considered. In one case, it boils down to always having a rational behaviour, in the other case to systematically exhibiting a random behaviour.

Lastly, the delicate concept of *ultimate cause* is replaced by the concrete notions of *input* and *influence*. Their values characterise the *current state* of the agent. The double advantage of the *current state* notion is that it avoids any reference to the origin of an event while synthesizing the agent's history.

b) The feeling of free will

The choice to favour the *decision-making* aspect of *free will* rather than the *will* aspect makes it possible to design a model of this complex property. Conversely, the following question is worth asking: is this model compatible with the concept of *free will*? Formulated in another manner, the question becomes: does the proposed mechanism make it possible to recompose, at least partially, the feeling of *free will*?

From a human point of view, it is undeniable that this *three-stage decision-making process* can give an individual the feeling that he is provided with *free will* since he has the impression of being the source triggering the *unpredictable component*. However, that does not mean that it is the unique situation where an individual can have the feeling to be provided with *free will*.

2) Comparison between Two-Stage and Three-stage Models

Several aspects deeply differentiate *Two-Stage* and *Three-Stage Models* (Figure 4).

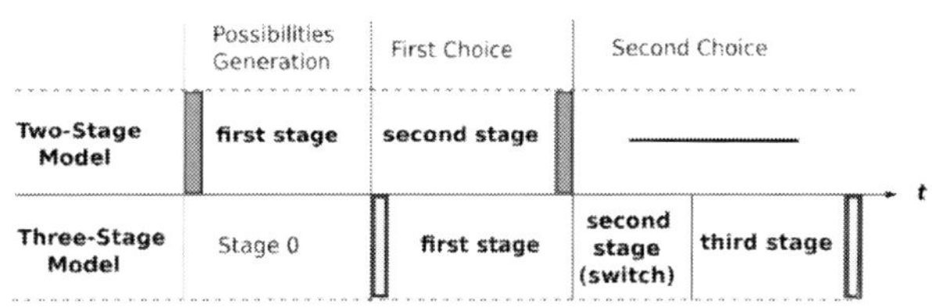

Figure 4. Two-Stage Model vs. Three-Stage Model

In the *Two-Stage Model*, the properties of *intelligence* and *creativity* intervene in the first phase of the model because the creation of the possible choices is part of the process related to *free will*. *Free will* can thus be seen as a composition of heterogeneous properties which are complex to represent. In the *Three-Stage Model*, choices creation is not part of the *free will* process. This possibilities generation step (*Stage 0*) takes place before the expression *of free will*. The result is a much finer granularity of the *Three-Stage Model* than that of the *Two-Stage Model*.

The *Two-Stage Model* only contains one phase of choice. This choice can be rational or not. It expresses the *will* aspect of the entity. The *Three-Stage Model* utilizes two consecutive choices, a predictable choice followed by a random choice. However, the concept of *choice* is much simpler to implement than the concept of *will*.

Lastly, the main weakness of the *Two-Stage Model* is not discriminating enough. Let us take as example a chess program. First, it will analyse the chess position, will generate the different possibilities and will choose the best move. The program functioning corresponds perfectly to the *Two-Stage Model of Free Will*. It is then legitimate to conclude that a chess program is provided with *Free Will*. According to the *Three-Stage Model*, a chess program is not provided with *Free Will*.

3) Model utilization

a) A critical analysis of a philosophical concept from a computational point of view

The human cognitive system produces complex *mental concepts*, such as the concepts of *conscience*, *will*, *autonomy* and *free will*, partly characterized by other *mental concepts* with vague contents.

The computational approach of a concept, such as *free will* imposes a clarification of the essential components of the property to obtain an operational model of this concept. This clarification concerns at the same time the choice of the selected elements, their contents and their relationship.

Although this method leads to a simplified representation of the concept, it has the advantage of distinguishing with precision what was kept and what was left out of the property. When new knowledge is available or when the importance given to some features of the concept is changed, it will still be possible to update the model.

Conversely, reasoning about the model makes it possible on the one hand to identify, reduce and isolate the fuzzy areas of the property, and on the other hand to address its paradoxical aspects.

The result is a bidirectional questioning leading to a reciprocal enrichment between concept and model.

b) Design of a synthetic property

The pursued approach is similar to that of synthetic biology: developing a *synthetic property* starting from data related to a precise philosophical concept. It is an engineering approach, which consists in improving the understanding of a property by disassembling and rebuilding it in a computational form after identifying its essential aspects.

It will be possible to put together this *synthetic property* with other *synthetic properties* in order to create *artificial characters*.

c) Creation of artificial characters

The architecture of the *unpredictable component* provides a great flexibility to the creator of *synthetic characters*. Indeed, the concepts of *influence*, *switch* and *unpredictable choice* can be interpreted in various ways. This interpretative wealth allows the implementation of a broad spectrum of software agents.

For example, the agent's *unpredictable component* could be influenced by an *emotional module*. According to the composition of this module and its interconnection with the *unpredictable component*, various levels of steerability of the agent could be simulated. In this context, a second aspect, which could also be studied, is the degree of coupling between *emotions* and *free will*.

VI. CONCLUSION

How to answer the question "Does *free will* exist?" It depends on the selected meaning of this property.

According to the meaning presented in this paper, *free will* exists because it is associated with a precise decision-making process. But as *free will* is a complex property with contradictory interpretations, it is not possible to give an absolute answer.

The *Three-Stage Model of Free Will* is a decision-making process relying on a mechanism that is possible to implement in an artificial entity: this model presupposes neither the existence of a brain nor a spirit. Consequently, a natural or artificial entity that is able to exhibit this decision-making process structured by these three moments will be considered as being provided with *free will*. According to this model, *free will* is a *global property* of the agent: either the agent possesses this property or it does not have it.

To the best of the author's knowledge, among the living beings, only humans are able to trigger this structured decision-making process and consequently are provided with *free will*.

REFERENCES

[1] R. Kane (ed.), The Oxford Handbook of Free Will, 2nd Ed. Oxford University Press, Oxford, 2011.

[2] B. Libet, C.A. Gleason, E.W. Wright, and D.K. Pearl, "Time of conscious intention to act in relation to onset of cerebral activity (readiness-potential). The unconscious initiation of a freely voluntary act", *Brain* (1983) 106: pp. 623- 642.

[3] A. Krausová and H. Hazan, "Creating Free Will in Artificial Intelligence". In Beyond AI: Artificial Golem Intelligence, pp 96-109, 2013.

[4] J. McCarthy, "Simple Deterministic Free Will", 2005. [Online] [retrieved: 12, 2017]. Available from:
http://www-formal.stanford.edu/jmc/freewill2/freewill2.html
http://informationphilosopher.com/solutions/scientists/mccarthy/SDFW.pdf

[5] R. Manzotti, "Machine free will: is free will a necessary ingredient of machine consciousness?". In: Hernández C. et al. (eds) From Brains to Systems. Advances in Experimental Medicine and Biology, vol 718 (2011), pp. 181-191. Springer, New York, NY. doi: 10.1007/978-1-4614-0164-3_15.

[6] E. Sanchis, "Autonomy with Regard to an Attribute", IEEE/WIC/ACM International Conference on Intelligent Agent Technology 2007 (IAT 2007), Silicon Valley, California (USA), pp. 39-42, 2007, doi:10.1109/IAT.2007.110.

[7] K. D. Vohs and J. W. Schooler, "The value of believing in free will: encouraging a belief in determinism increases cheating", Psychol Sci. 2008 Jan;19(1): pp. 49-54. doi: 10.1111/j.1467-9280.2008.02045.x.

[8] W. James, "The Dilemma of Determinism". In The Will to Believe and Other Essays in Popular Philosophy. Longmans Green and Co, New York, 1897.

[9] B. Doyle, Free Will: The Scandal in Philosophy. Information Philosopher, 2011. [Online] [retrieved: 12, 2017]. Available from:
http://www.informationphilosopher.com/books/scandal/

A Multilayer Architecture for Cognitive Systems

Supporting well-defined processes that are partially executed manually in technical work places

Veronika Thurner
Munich University of Applied Sciences
Department of Computer Science and Mathematics
Munich, Germany
Email: veronika.thurner@hm.edu

Thorsten Gressling
ARS Computer und Consulting GmbH
Munich, Germany
Email: thorsten.gressling@ars.de

***Abstract*—Many technical work places, such as laboratories or test beds, are the setting for well-defined processes requiring both high precision and extensive documentation, to ensure accuracy and support accountability that often is required by law, science, or both. In this type of scenario, it is desirable to delegate certain routine tasks, such as documentation or preparatory next steps, to some sort of automated assistant, in order to increase precision and reduce the required amount of manual labor in one fell swoop. At the same time, this automated assistant should be able to interact adequately with the human worker, to ensure that the human worker receives exactly the kind of support that is required in a certain context. To achieve this, we introduce a multilayer architecture for cognitive systems that structures the system's computation and reasoning across well-defined levels of abstraction, from mass signal processing up to organization-wide, intention-driven reasoning. By partitioning the architecture into well-defined, distinct layers, we reduce complexity and thus facilitate both the implementation and the training of the cognitive system. On this basis, we outline the functional modules of a cognitive system supporting the execution of partially manual processes in technical work places.**

***Index Terms*—Cognitive system; Multilayer architecture; Technical work place; Machine learning; Context sensitive; Neural network.**

I. Motivation

Many technical work places, such as laboratories or test beds, are the setting for series of well-defined, repetitive actions requiring high precision in their execution, as well as extensive documentation of every process step. Both are necessary to ensure accuracy on the one hand, and on the other hand to support accountability that often is required by law, science, or both. Typical examples are laboratories for micro-biological analysis or chemical experiments, premises of optometrists or hearing aid acousticians, or test beds for the quality inspection of produced goods, such as measuring vehicle exhaust fumes or assessing nutritional values of food.

All these settings share a number of commonalities. For one thing, within each of these working settings a human being interacts extensively with technical devices, such as measuring instruments or sensors. For another thing, processing follows a well-defined routine, or even precisely specified interaction protocols. Finally, to ensure that results are reproducible, the different steps and achieved results usually have to be documented extensively and in a precise way.

Especially in scenarios that execute a well-defined series of actions, it is desirable to delegate certain routine tasks, such as documentation or preparatory next steps, to some sort of automated assistant, in order to increase precision and reduce the required amount of manual labor in one fell swoop. At the same time, this automated assistant should be able to interact adequately with the human worker, to ensure that the human worker receives exactly the kind of support that is required in a certain context. To achieve this, the assistant needs to be context aware, i.e., equipped with cognitive input channels. As well, the assistant is expected to learn new behavioral patterns from previous experience.

Traditional software systems for process control or workflow management are well able to support a set of well-defined processes that has been explicitly specified in advance. However, in situations that were not foreseen initially, or that were not explicitly specified because they were deemed to be highly unlikely to happen, these systems quickly meet their limits, requiring human take-over and problem solving abilities in expert mode.

The increasing capabilities of cognitive systems imply the potential for a new generation of systems that offer context sensitive reasoning on a scale hitherto unknown in machines and software systems. We exploit these possibilities by devising a cognitive hardware-software-system for supporting the execution of hybrid (i.e., partly manual and partly automated) processes in technical environments, in a manner that combines the respective strengths of human-expert-like cognition and reasoning with machine-like processing power, to improve performance, efficiency, accuracy and security issues.

By *cognitive system*, we denote a system that is capable of sensory perception and of expressing itself via technical devices, analogously to corresponding abilities found in biological organisms. Furthermore, it comprises an internal representation that is comparable to emotions. However, as system boundaries and internal states of an artificial intelligence differ greatly from those of humans beings and animals, its underlying system of values and beliefs in general differs from that of biological organisms.

After this initial motivation, we review related literature and briefly sketch the goals of our research in section 2. In section 3, we introduce the physical architecture of our cognitive system, followed by a logical architecture in section 4. The core element of the logical architeture are building blocks, whose structure is presented in section 5. To illustrate the processing of our cognitive system and the interaction of the building blocks on the different layers, we present an example execution in section 6. Section 7 sketches the prototypical implementation that we realized as a proof of concept. Finally, we critically discuss our work in section 8, before summarizing it in section 9.

II. State of the Art and Goals

Research has already elicited several aspects that are relevant in this context. An overview of existing approaches to computation and information architecture is provided by [1], distinguishing among others the different types of information that are processed, from subsymbolic computation focusing on data and signal processing to symbolic computation that processes data structures, thus reflecting different levels of abstraction. In [2], patterns for cognitive systems are investigated into, focusing on systems that process textual information, yet indicating that other kind of information, such as cognitively interpreted sensory data, will be addressed by cognitive systems in the near future, thus entering into new dimensions of machine cognition.

Approaches for systematic process support through Context Aware Assistive Systems (CAAS) are discusses in [3], [4] and [5], in the context of manufacturing on the shop floor and human interaction with the production line. Identifying human actions observed via cameras and relating them to the manufacturing process are a crucial issue in these Context Aware Assistive Systems.

The research from [6], [7] and [8] focusses on the usage of augmented reality in intelligent assistant systems, discussing among others digital projections into the current working situation, to guide the human workers through their share of the working process.

Anderson et al. [9] introduce the cognitive architecture ACT-R, which implements artificial intelligence in a symbolic way. In contrast to this, in our approach we combine symbolic and connectionistic aspects.

So far, existing supportive systems for processes that are partially executed manually in technical work places are realized mainly in a rule oriented way and implemented by algorithms. As a consequence, they cover only those situations, states and actions that have been anticipated in advance. However, they only have limited ability to learn from experience.

Recently, research on context awareness significantly progressed towards identifying a specific situation from a predefined set of possibilities in a given context and well-defined surroundings, incorporating cognition and artificial reasoning on a single level of abstraction. This single level of abstraction is then realized as a monolithic block of neural networks. However, this monolithic block needs to deal with the entire complexity by itself, which would require an extreme amount of training that exceeds what can be handled even by modern hardware.

Therefore, as a next step, we introduce an architecture for cognitive systems that expands cognition and reasoning across several levels of abstraction, to support a wide range of assistant services ranging from small actions to strategic processes. By partitioning the systems's cognition and reasoning into separate levels of abstraction (rather than implementing them as a single monolithic block), we reduce both implementation complexity and training effort. Thus, it is possible to tackle even very complex problems, which would exceed the capacity of a monolithic approach.

We discuss the applicability of our approach in the context of a cognitive system that supports hybrid processes involving manual tasks within technical surroundings.

III. Physical Architecture

Physically, a technical work place comprises a variety of technical devices, as a relevant tool set to execute, or support the execution of, actions involved in the processes at the work place. Typical examples for, e.g., a chemical laboratory are electronic high precision scales, a centrifuge, a power supply or a fume hood. Some of these devices are connected to computational hardware (e.g., a remote server), either directly or via a data network. In contrast to this, other devices such as a traditional heater, operate in an isolated way, without any direct data exchange with the computational hardware. Furthermore, the work place comprises a variety of tools and devices for manual tasks, such as pipettes or glassware, as well as other materials, e.g., chemical or biological substances to be processed or analyzed.

In addition, to evolve from a technology interspersed work place towards an intelligent assistant, the work place must be equipped with devices that enable the system's cognition, as well as its interaction with the human user that executes the manual process steps. Traditionally, cognitively exploitable input devices are, for example, a microphone (with subsequent speech analysis) or a camera (with subsequent image processing). In addition to this traditional notion of audio-visual cognition, sensors and other technical measuring devices provide additional cognitive channels that supply the system with information on the current situation at the work place.

Communication from the system towards the human user is realized, e.g., via a monitor, a loudspeaker or a projector that focusses its beam of light on the tool to be used next, or that displays instructions on the process step that should be executed next. Other, more sophisticated devices arise continuously, such as mixed reality smart glasses for displaying instructions directly into the field of vision, activity tracking bracelets that combine skin and body sensors with functionality for alerting its wearer, or even EEGs for integrating information on the human user's brain activity into the system's data pool.

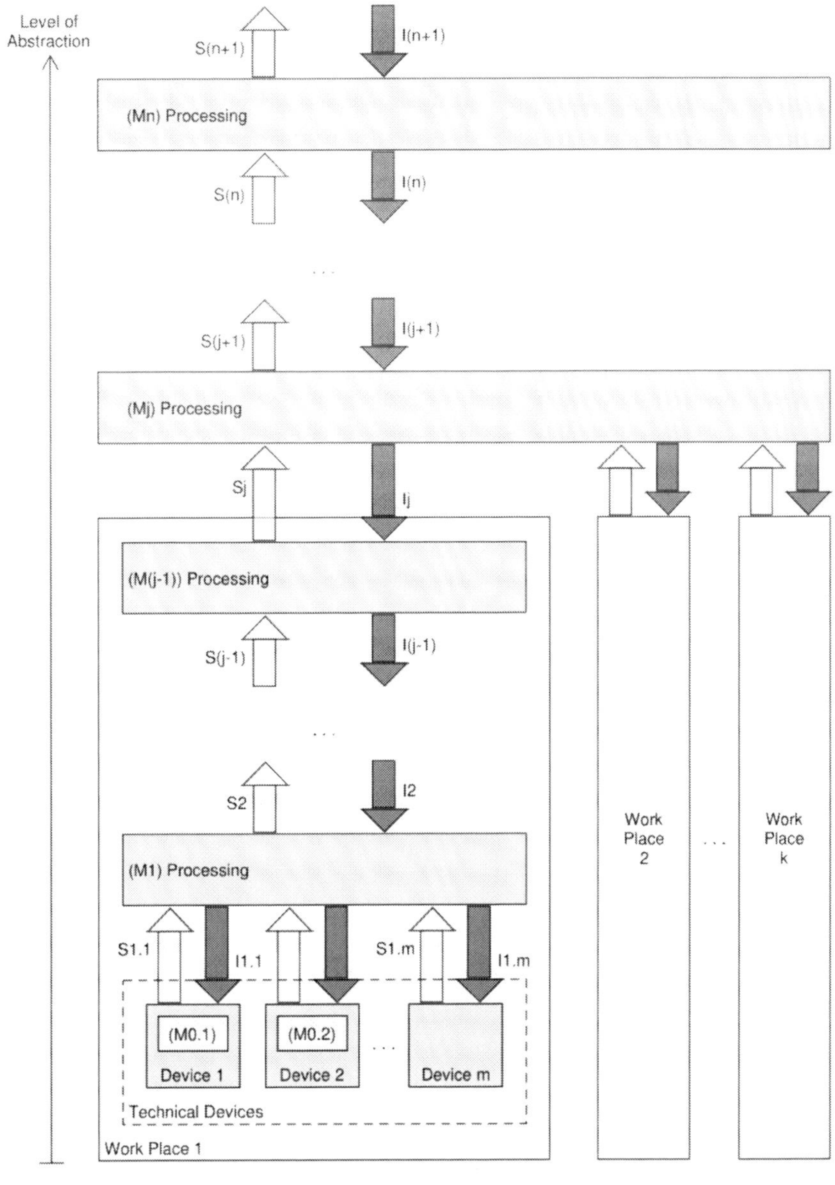

Fig. 1. Multilayer architecture of cognitive systems for supporting hybrid processes in technical work places.

Note that some of these technical devices may include their own data storage, as well as computational hardware, thus being able to directly aggregate and process the data they collected, before passing it on to more sophisticated computational hardware for integration with the data from other devices and subsequent further processing.

IV. Logical Architecture

The cognitive system that we devise to support process execution is embedded into this technical work place.

Logically, we design a multilayer architecture that structures the cognitive system into different levels of abstraction (see Figure 1), rising from concrete at the bottom towards more and more abstract as we move upwards on the processing level stack. Thus, each layer Mj encapsulates processing on a specific level of abstraction, and focuses on different tasks. By structuring the overall system into logical processing layers, it is possible to train each layer individually for its respective tasks. Furthermore, modularizing the overall system improves performance by reducing processing time, as the different layers can be run in parallel.

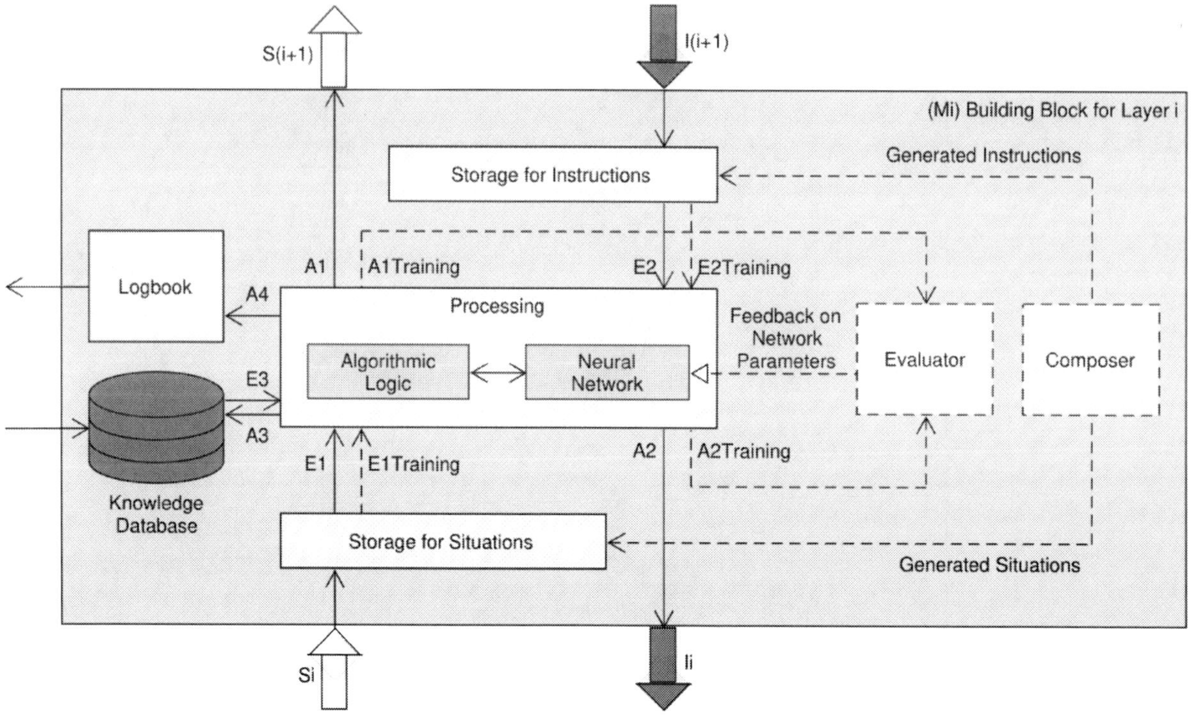

Fig. 2. Pattern of building block that implements each layer.

Processing involves the analysis of incoming data, which is synthesized and analyzed to identify the situation that the work place is in, corresponding to an overall system state in the context of the executed processes. From the identified situation, processing derives which actions should be taken as next steps, and passes these on as instructions to other layers, systems, technical devices or – via output devices – to the human user. Thus, the cognitive system is able to effectively support the human user in a context sensitive way. Note that these suggested actions are determined by aggregated conclusions that the system draws from its analysis.

Layers are interconnected by communication channels. Note that the information on situations flows upwards in the processing layer stack via channels S (white block arrows in Figure 1), whereas instructions are passed down from layer to layer via channels I (black block arrows).

The processing layer stack is based on a layer of technical devices $D1, \ldots, Dm$ as described above. These devices collect data on the work place and enter these into the cognitive system as situation information via channels $S1.i$, with $1 <= i <= m$. Some of these devices (such as Dm in Figure 1) merely collect data, e.g., by simple measuring, and pass them straight on to the first processing layer $M1$. Other devices (such as $D1$ and $D2$ in Figure 1) comprise an independent processing component ($M0.1$ or $M0.2$, respectively), which preprocesses the data before entering it into the first processing layer.

Moving upwards on the processing layer stack, situation information is aggregated from separate small snippets of measured data into larger contexts, such as actions, sequences of actions or even entire processes. Analogously, abstract instructions that are passed from top to bottom are made more and more specific from layer to layer, down to signals that operate a specific technical device in the bottom layer.

On each layer, processing takes into account the situation information that is entered into the layer from below, as well as the instruction information that is passed to the layer from above. Thus, situations are interpreted in the light of instructions that reflect the larger context of the overall system, as identified on the higher levels of abstraction.

As depicted for layer Mj in Figure 1, a processing layer can merge several process layer stacks, each representing a different work place. Thus, their information flows are integrated and consolidated, allowing for integrated information processing on a cross-organizational level of abstraction.

V. Building Blocks

Each layer in Figure 1 is implemented by a building block that follows the architectural pattern depicted in Figure 2 for a building block i, with $0 <= i <= n$, in a cognitive system that comprises $n >= 1$ processing layers stacked on top of one layer of technical devices.

Building block i is linked with the building blocks of its surrounding processing levels $i-1$ and $i+1$ via communication channels, depicted as block arrows in Figure 2. Thus, the situation information perceived by building block $i-1$ is passed on via channel Si to building block i, which stores the information in its storage for situations. Analogously, instructions issued by building block $i+1$ are passed on via channel $I(i+1)$ to building block i, which stores the information in its storage for instructions.

The central part of each building block is its processing unit, which comprises both aspects of algorithmic logic and of artificial intelligence (implemented via one or more neural networks), in varying proportions (see Figure 3). On the lower levels of abstraction, the major part of processing is accomplished by algorithmic logic, whereas on the higher levels of abstraction, aspects of artificial intelligence dominate the processing.

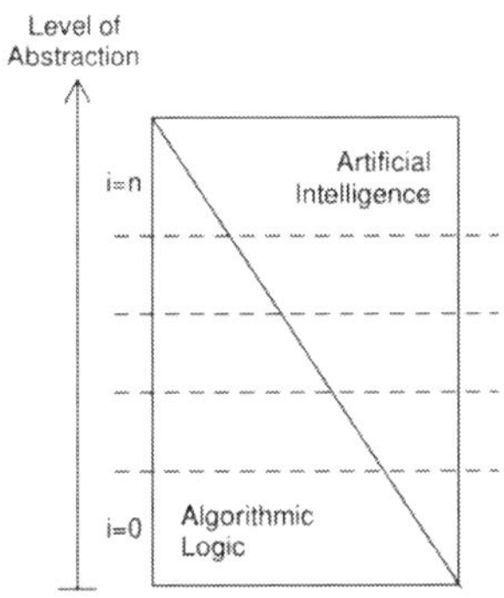

Fig. 3. Varying proportions of algorithmic logic and artificial intelligence.

The processing unit works on three different kinds of input:

- $E1$: Information on situations
- $E2$: Information on instructions
- $E3$: Relevant general factual knowledge, stored as rules in the knowledge database

Based on these inputs, the processing unit analyses the incoming information, interprets it and synthesizes it into its interpretation of the situation, thus lifting the previous information on the situation onto a higher level of abstraction. For example, on layer $M1$, short snippets of data that were measured by the technical devices (e.g., an electronic scale and a heater) in the underlying physical layer are gathered, consolidated and then passed on to layer $M2$. On layer $M2$, this consolidated data is then merged and interpreted to build a larger semantic context, e.g., a certain step in a chemical experiment where a certain amount of substance must be added to an existing mixture, and then heated to a specific temperature. In order to properly identify the semantic context correctly, the processing unit in layer $M2$ incorporates known "recipes" of chemical experiments that are stored within the knowledge database of layer $M2$.

Thus, the processing unit generates four different kinds of output:

- $A1$: Information on the synthesized, interpreted situation, passed on as input to the next higher layer ($i+1$), if present
- $A2$: Set of instructions that is passed down to the next lower layer ($i-1$), if present, or that is addressed directly to the technical devices, if $i=0$
- $A3$: Newly gathered knowledge rules for the knowledge database
- $A4$: Information on all inputs, processing steps and generated outputs, as well as on all modifications that were induced in the parameters of the neural network, to be documented in the logbook

Within the processing unit, algorithmic logic and neural networks can be combined in many different topologies to build the processing unit. In particular, they can be connected in series or in parallel, or in a combination of both, involving one or more instances of both algorithmic logic and neural network.

For example, a modern thermometer which includes both a temperature sensor and some form of algorithmic logic could monitor whether the current temperature exceeds a previously defined threshold. If the threshold value is exceeded, the algorithmic logic passes the history of measured values on to the neural network, which synthesizes and analyses this data in order to identify the current situation.

Another example for a neural network connected in-series to a subsequent algorithmic logic (i.e., the other way round from the above example), would be to enter a variety of measured data from different devices into the neural network, which derives from this data the overall situation of the work place. After the neural network classified and identified the situation, this information on the situation is passed on to an algorithmic logic that executes the predefined process that deals with this type of situation.

An example for running algorithmic logic and neural network in parallel, followed by a second algorithmic logic that is connected in series, would be some sort of security mechanism, where both algorithmic logic and neural network process the same input data individually and independently of each other. After both components reached their classification result, a subsequent algorithmic logic compares the individual results and decides on further processing steps.

For training purposes, the building block provides another two components: a composer and an evaluator, depicted in Figure 2 by dashed lines. The composer generates instructions and situations and inserts them into the respective storages as training data. To achieve this, the composer can either generate this new data from scratch, or cut and paste snippets of "real" data from the storages into new sequences.

During training mode, the processing unit works on this training data $E1Training$ and $E2Training$ and processes it into the resulting answers $A1Training$ and $A2Training$, which are then passed on to the evaluator. The evaluator's resulting verdict is re-entered into the neural network, to adapt the parameters within the neural network, as necessary. The criteria that form the basis for the evaluator's assessment are specified by a set of rules, reflecting goals and basic values. For example, they can postulate the maximization of security, or the minimization of costs.

Note that composer and evaluator are active only during training of the neural network, but not during operations.

VI. Example Execution

To illustrate which kinds of tasks are dealt with on the different layers and what kind of information is processed, Figure 4 visualizes the information flow over time for an example system and a specific exemplary situation.

The physical layer of our example work place contains seven devices, six of which are directly connected to the cognitive system: a thermometer $D1$, three cameras $D2$, $D3$ and $D4$, a loudspeaker $D5$ and an e-mail system $D6$. In addition, the work place comprises a traditional heater $D7$, which is not data connected to the cognitive system, but observed by thermometer $D1$ and the three cameras.

Adhering to the generalized architecture in Figure 1, our exemplary cognitive system is structured into four processing layers: $M1$ for signal processing close to the technical devices, $M2$ for reactions which combines short signal snippets into larger situation contexts, $M3$ for drawing conclusions and $M4$ for overall organization. Note that layer $M4$ merges several work places ($WP2$ and $WP3$), in addition to the work place in focus.

In the diagram, time is discretized into time steps, progressing from top to bottom for reasons of readability. (As a consequence, processing layers are arranged vertically, with abstraction increasing from left to right.) Within each time step, all processing actions are executed in parallel. Note that the diagram in Figure 4 abstracts from the processing time that is required in each processing layer. Consider processing to take place at the transition from each time step to its successor, in parallel for each processing layer.

In time step 1, the technical devices pass the data they observed on to layer $M1$ for signal processing, as situation information. More precisely, thermometer $D1$ communicates a series of measured temperature values, each labeled with a time stamp. All three cameras continuously gather images from their respective sections of the work place. Each camera contains basic image processing facilities, which allow for identification of previously registered work place personnel. Thus, cameras $D2$ and $D3$ communicate that they identified person "Klaus" at a certain position in the work place. In contrast to this, camera $D4$ did not identify any persons in the section of the work place that it observes.

Layer $M1$ receives this situation information from the technical devices and stores it in its storage for situations. On this basis, it aggregates the gathered information and synthesizes it into a more complex understanding and larger context of a situation, thus increasing the level of abstraction. Here, layer $M1$ realizes that both cameras $D2$ and $D3$ identified the same person, Klaus, and calculates the position of Klaus in the work place. Furthermore, layer $M1$ analyzes the sequence of temperature information measured by the thermometer. Here, layer $M1$ realizes that the temperature rises really quickly. This aggregated information is then passed on to layer $M2$ for reactions in time step 2. Information is organized according to the syntactic pattern of type of device, time stamp and two more items of structured information, whose syntax and semantics are relative to the type of the device.

The knowledge database of layer $M2$ contains information on the experiments that are carried out within the work place, referenced as DoE (i.e., design of experiments) in Figure 4. From previous context information, layer $M2$ is aware that DoE 89 is currently processed. $M2$ realizes that the measured temperature rises both faster and higher than specified in the "recipe" that is defined in DoE 89, and that the thermometer T is correlated with the heater $D7$. As well, $M2$ identifies that the thermometer T is merely a sensor and thus cannot be regulated, whereas the heater $D7$ can be regulated. Furthermore, $M2$ identifies that person Klaus is located close to the heater $D7$. All this synthesized situation information is passed on to layer $M3$ for conclusions in time step 3, and stored there in $M3$'s storage for situations. In addition, the technical devices keep sending situation information towards level $M1$ continuously. In Figure 4, this information flow is indicated as well for time step 3.

As a next step, layer $M3$ deduces from the situation information that device $D7$ is about to overheat and that Klaus is still present and able to act. Furthermore, experience gathered from previous situations indicates that in experiments that are executed according to DoE 89, temperature problems arise rather frequently, independently of the current human operator. In addition, $M3$ realizes that heater and thermometer work fine in other experiments, and thus seem to be in order technically. As a result, in time step 4 layer $M3$ communicates as instructions to level $M2$ that the heater $D7$ must be regulated, and that Klaus should act to regulate the heater. In addition, $M3$ communicates to level $M4$ for organization that temperature problems occur frequently when executing DoE 89. In addition, during time step 4 layer $M1$ passes on its newly aggregated situation information on to level $M2$, indicating that the temperature is still rising and that Klaus has moved towards the heater. As layer $M4$ for organization joins the information of several work places, additional information arrives as input from other work places during time step 4.

Based on all this situation information, layer $M4$ for organization deduces that there might exist a systematic problem in the documentation of DoE 89, such as wrong instructions. As well, $M4$ identifies that the situation in work place 1 is highly critical. Therefore, $M4$ specifies suitable instructions and passes them down to level $M3$ during time step 5. In parallel, layer $M2$ processes the newly arrived situation

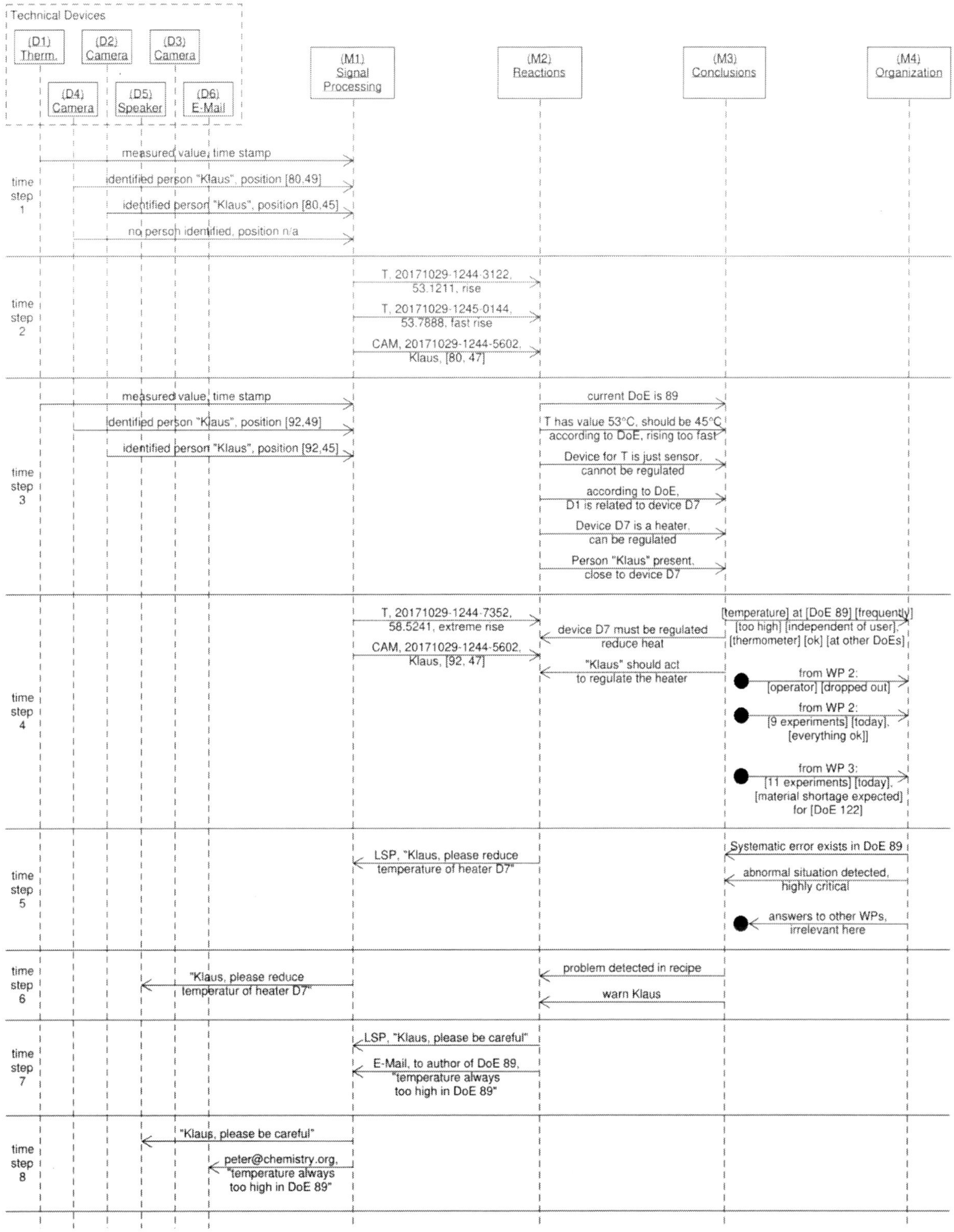

Fig. 4. Information flows between processing layers, for an exemplary execution of the system.

information in the light of the instructions that were handed down towards layer $M2$ during time step 4. As the temperature is still rising rapidly, $M2$ passes down to layer $M1$ the instruction that the loud speaker $D5$ should instruct Klaus to reduce the temperature of heater $D7$.

This instruction is translated by layer $M1$ into appropriate signals for the loud speaker $D5$, which are transferred to $D5$ during time step 6. In addition, layer $M3$ for conclusions derives from the instructions received from $M4$, in combination with the information on the ongoing situation, that a problem was detected in the recipe of DoE 89 and that Klaus has to be warned about the critical situation. Corresponding instructions are passed from $M3$ to $M2$ during time step 6.

$M2$ translates these abstract instructions into device specific instructions and passes them down to signal processing $M1$ during time step 7.

Finally, $M1$ generates the appropriate, device specific signals for the loud speaker $D5$ and for the e-mail system $D6$, respectively, and passes them down to their respective recipients, which execute them appropriately.

VII. Prototypical Proof of Concept

A prototypical proof of concept addressing the lower layers of the example presented here was realized as a show case, using IBM Watson as well as Tensorflow for the neural network processing.

In this prototypical realization, the layer $M0$ comprises a variety of cognitive channels implemented via IoT hardware: three cameras, one projector, one microfone, speakers addressed via five Raspberry PI (based on Python), one ph-Meter, one scale, and temperature sensors addressed via three ESP8266 (based on Lua). A selection of IBM Watson services is used to realize cognitive abilities on this layer (STT speech to text, TTS text to speech, and visual recognition via REST).

Both layers $M1$ and $M2$ are realized in the cloud. Processing is based on IBM Bluemix Services that are implemented in TypeScript. In addition, more complex cognitive abilities from the IBM Watson portolio are included on layer $M2$, e.g., NLC natural language classifier, which is addressed via REST as well. Furthermore, the storage for situations on layer $M2$ is realized via a NoSQL Couch database.

Layer $M3$ runs on local hardware. Processing logic is implemented in Python. Situation information is retrieved from $M2$ by download. Within the prototype, test cases were classified by hand and are processed by a convolutional neural network (based on MNIST implementation) in Tensorflow, using two convolutional / pooling layers and the dense layer with ten cases. Classification results are uploaded manually to layer $M2$.

In spite of the rather small numer of test cases, the system achieves good classification results. Note that for layer $M3$ to deliver more comprehensive classification results, a much larger amount of data would have to be collected on level $M2$, comprising at least 1000 laboratory days. Nonetheless, by this prototypical realization and the test cases under consideration, it was possible to validate the feasibility of our architecture.

VIII. Critical Discussion

In principle, it would be possible to implement a cognitive assistant system with matching abilities as a monolithic block of neural networks, rather than using our multilayer architecture. However, this monolithic block would have to handle the entire complexity by itself, thus requiring an extreme amount of training that greatly exceeds what can be handled even by modern hardware. This complexity can be handled only by partitioning the system into smaller parts that are implemented and trained separately.

All in all, the structure of the building blocks ensures that the system corresponds to a sequence of symbolic components (for persistently storing information on situations and instructions) and subsymbolic, algorithmic components that process this information. Thus, the overall processing is clearly structured into distinct layers, which facilitates the implementation of processing units and allows for their individual training, as well as for the analysis of the resulting information.

Note that the layering we suggest does *not* replicate the layers of the human brain. Rather, it creates levels of abstraction that are tailored to meet the specific requirements of the technical system. As a consequence, the system's cognition and thus its awareness will differ from that of a human being.

As any artificial intelligence, the system has an error margin that depends, e.g., on the noisy environment, changing illumination, the possible novelty of input sequences, as well as on the imperfection of the decision system itself. Thus, it is possible that the system misinterprets a situation.

If, for example, the system's task is to identify a person "Klaus" based on data gathered by cameras and microphones, it can indeed happen that Klaus is not recognized, or that a wrong person is recognized as "Klaus" (although it is, in fact, "Peter"). In the first case, the system is aware that something did not work properly; in the second case, it is not.

Strategies for dealing with the first error case range from *retry* (i.e., issuing instructions to present oneself to the camera again) to *comment*, thus informing the user as comprehensively as necessary that something unexpected has happened. The second case, where the system is unaware of its error, is more severe. Although it cannot be entirely avoided, its possibility can be significantly reduced by sufficient training.

IX. Conclusions and Future Work

We introduced a multilayer architecture for cognitive systems that support the operation of technical work places, in which hybrid processes (partially executed manually, and partially using technical devices) are executed. To ensure efficiency and adaptability, we structured this architecture into separate layers on different levels of abstraction. Each layer deals with specific kinds of tasks and processes the corresponding kind of information, which again is organized into different levels of abstraction.

Each layer of the conceptual architecture is realized by a building block, which incorporates aspects of both algorithmic logic and artificial intelligence. We provided a template defining the glass box view of these building blocks. Based on this template and the conceptual architecture, it is possible to develop cognitive systems that scale appropriately, to meet the demands of the application context under consideration.

As a next step, we demonstrated the interaction and cooperation of the different layers for a concrete example, specified from the context of a chemical laboratory. Furthermore, we sketched a prototypical proof of concept that addresses the lower layers of the presented example. This prototype was run on a small number of test cases, to validate the feasibility of our architecture.

For extending the prototypical system towards a more comprehensive classification of situations and recommendations of instructions, extensive laboratory data will have to be collected, as a basis for properly training the cognitive system.

Parts of this work are closely related to an innovation that is covered by the German patent application 10 2017 126 457.4.

REFERENCES

[1] M. Burgin and G. Dodig-Crnkovic, "A Taxonomy of Computation and Information Architecture," in *ECSAW, Dubrovnik, Croatia*. ACM, 2015, pp. 7:1–7:8, DOI: 10.1145/2797433.2797440.

[2] C. Leibold and M. Spies, "Towards a Pattern Language for Cognitive Systems Integration," in *EuroPLoP, Irsee, Germany*. ACM, 2014, pp. 17:1–17:9, DOI: 10.1145/2721956.2721968.

[3] M. Aehnelt and B. Urban, "The knowledge gap: Providing situation-aware information assistance on the shop floor," in *HCI, Los Angeles, USA*. Springer, 2015, pp. 232–243, DOI: 10.1007/978-3-319-20895-4_22.

[4] O. Korn, M. Funk, and A. Schmidt, *Assistive systems for the workplace*. IGI Global, 2015, pp. 121–135, DOI: 10.4018/978-1-4666-8200-9.ch097.

[5] T. Kosch, Y. Abdelrahman, M. Funk, and A. Schmidt, "One size does not fit all – Challenges of providing interactive worker assistance in industrial settings," in *UbiComp/ISWC, Maui, USA*. ACM, 2017, pp. 1006–1011, DOI: 10.1145/3123024.3124395.

[6] A. Srivastava and P. Yammiyavar, "Design of multimodal instructional tutoring agents using augmented reality and smart learning objects," in *ICMI, Tokyo, Japan*. ACM, 2016, pp. 421–422, DOI: 10.1145/2993148.2998531.

[7] M. Funk, T. Kosch, and A. Schmidt, "Interactive worker assistance: Comparing the effects of in-situ projection, head-mounted displays, tablet, and paper instructions," in *UbiComp*. ACM, 2016, pp. 934–939, DOI: 10.1145/2971648.2971706.

[8] S. Büttner, O. Sand, and C. Rocker, "Exploring design opportunities for intelligent worker assistance: a new approach using projetion-based AR and a novel hand-tracking algorithm," in *AmI, Malaga, Spain*. Springer, 2017, pp. 33–45, DOI: 10.1007/978-3-319-56997-0_3.

[9] J. Anderson, M. Matessa, and C. Lebiere, "ACT-R: A Theory of Higher Level Cognition and its Relation to Visual Attention," *Human–Computer Interaction*, 1997.

Human and Machine Capabilities for Place Recognition: a Comparison Study

Carlos A. Martínez-Miwa, Mario Castelán, L. Abril Torres-Méndez and Alejandro Maldonado-Ramírez
Robotics and Advanced Manufacturing Group
CINVESTAV Campus Saltillo
Ramos Arizpe, Coahuila, México
Email: carlosmiwa_18@hotmail.com; {abril.torres;mario.castelan}@cinvestav.mx; alejandro.maldonado.ramirez@gmail.com

Abstract—**This paper is aimed at exploring the way humans perceive previously visited places under challenging circumstances while driving a car. The term challenging refers to scenarios that do not contain specially rich visual information. We developed a series of experiments to investigate the performance of humans and computer vision algorithms, in order to recall locations in video sequences that were gathered with a camera mounted on a car. Our experiments reveal that the state of the art in machine vision fails against humans for identifying places where subtle changes occur, for instance, when illumination varies depending on the daytime. However, machines do present greater capabilities than humans when the reference image appears within a video sequence that does not exhibit spatial and daytime variations.**

Keywords—Place recognition; Human-machine capabilities; Computer Vision; Feature detection.

I. Introduction

Visual recognition of previous visited places is a fundamental part of our daily life. The study of how living beings recognize places, considering the fact that moving to one location to another is involved, has a long history in neuroscience [1][2]. Discoveries have provided a physiological grounding on the representation of spatial locations in our brain [3][4]. Our mind assembles "percepts" from memory (abstract thoughts) into internal images that are exactly experienced as images arising from the senses [5]. In other words, the mind feeds upon its own constructed images. We consider ourselves to be well adapted and skilled to navigate through even previously unvisited places if our interpretation about the environment matches a certain amount of already seen features. This might be because, we have mentally built an internal representation of what the action of navigating means in our mind, so that we associate past memories to the current navigation task by assigning the label: *"this is a new place"*. In this way, our brain could start the building of a visual representation for a new place. To this end, we may first need to select features that define such place in a unique way, though this selection may not result straightforward. We have been taught in our early years to pay conscious attention into what we were doing; when we do so, neurons cells start firing together and strong connections about recognizing a place occur. In addition, if perceptual changes in the environment exist due to conditions such as time of day, source of illumination, weather conditions, etc., the process of selecting good discriminative and invariant features that characterize that place turns complex. When we navigate a place for the first time, we seem more attentive on details that we believe will define it. We want those details to be distinctive enough so that a strong association is created. In that way, when we return to this location in the future, even when different conditions are present, the selected features that describe it can be fired up distinctively and thus achieve a precise recognition. Yet today, it is not clear how the learning process towards the detection of special features for place recognition is carried out in humans. However, by performing experiments we may be able to better understand human perceptual and cognitive abilities. Interestingly, from a psychophysics perspective there is not enough work that has addressed the problem of place recognition. An exception could be [6], where an approach to human perception-action, more appropriate for complex cognitive functions, such as object recognition and spatial cognition, has been studied through experiments in virtual envionments. The decision of using virtual reality is because of its ability to provide subjects with a level of sensory realism and dynamic sensory feedback that emulates their experiences in the real world. As far as computer algorithms are concerned, a survey has been recently published in [7], where an extense analysis about place recognition is presented. In this research work, we are interested in analyzing human performance for place recognition tasks compared to the performance of computational algorithms, which are based in combinations of detectors and descriptors. We are interested in evaluating how attention and previous knowledge is linked to perception when the goal is to recognize a place in challenging conditions. The combinations that were used in this work were chosen primarily due to their relevance in other computer vision tasks, such as appearance-based mapping [8], and their availability in the OpenCV Libraries. We have used features that are defined as real-valued vectors, such as SURF [9], SIFT [10] or KAZE [11]. SIFT and SURF have been widely used in the computer vision community as a benchmark for comparison using visual features, however KAZE has shown results that outperform both of them as shown in [11]. Other important branch of methods for extracting visual features are the ones defined in terms of binary values, which have shown a benefit, especially in terms of processing time. For example, ORB [12] and AKAZE [13] have been successfully applied to the problem of Real-time Vision-based Simultaneous Localization and Mapping (SLAM) as it is presented in [14]. BRISK [15] and ORB have also been applied to the task of efficient image retrieval [16].

Besides the above feature detectors and descriptors, we have also used algorithms that focus on detecting keypoints without describing them. For example Good Features to Track (GFTT) [17], FAST [18] and STAR [19]. As we are comparing the capabilities of computers and humans for place recognition, we have included a method (AVA) [20], which is based in the influential work of Itti *et al.* [21] about computational visual attention. These kind of algorithms emphasize the detection of image regions that are likely to draw the attention of humans. The outline of this paper is as follows: in Section II, we evaluate human perception for recognizing already seen places while driving; Section III describes computer vision algorithms performance for detecting previously visited locations; Section IV presents a comparison between results of both, humans and machines; finally, conclusions derived form these experiments and future work are presented in Section V.

II. Experiments on Human Perception

Our experiment is aimed at exploring the way humans perceive previously visited places under challenging circumstances while driving a car. The term challenging refers to scenarios that do not contain specially rich visual information, for example, streets that do not present striking landmarks such as store facades, graffiti, advertisements etc. In this sense, we chose blocks that people could identify as belonging to a generic neighborhood of the city.

Three different video sequences were recorded, each at a different time of the day (7h, 13h and 19h), from a 0.8 km route at a velocity of 30km/h. The camera used was a GoPro Hero4, which was mounted on a Chevrolet Cruze vehicle. Figure 1 shows examples of images of the same place taken at different times of the day. For evaluating purposes, each of the recorded videos was cut in five 10s fragments, and included on a game-like user interface designed on a Matlab GUI. Evaluation involved 60 participants: 30 women aged 34 ± 14 and 30 men aged 27 ± 6 (the average age of the total set of participants was of 30 ± 11). All of them were selected based on this profile: they had to be car drivers, be in a range of ages between 20 and 50 and their driver's license needed to be valid.

Each subject was given the following instructions: first, a 10s video sequence of an urban environment was displayed. Every video was loaded only once, so that each participant had to focus her attention completely on that opportunity. As soon as the reproduction was over, a random (reference) image was shown to the subject. Then, she was asked to carefully watch that image and determine whether or not it represented a scene within the video. If the answer was negative, another reference image appeared. Conversely, if the user was sure that the place in the picture corresponded to a location exhibited in the video, she would have to search, one-by-one, for the video frame that best matched the reference image. This process was held three times per video, until a total of 15 video sequences were displayed. It is to note that every subject was given three trials before the experiment started, so that she could get familiar to both, the interface and the test. The procedure is described in Figure 2.

Figure 1. Images of the same place taken at different times of the day (Group 2). The top image was recorded at 13h while the bottom image was recorded at 19h.

Aware of the existence of cognitive bias, we decided to perform our experiments in a relaxing environment - a Mexican-style coffee shop, during off-peak times. As a way of motivation, every person was told that she would get a reward at the end of the test. We did not establish a control group as such as the only variable to measure was a yes/no reply. However, we carefully supervised that subjects were not randomly selecting answers. For example, at least 10 subjects did not correctly pick the two answers of the "obvious" Group 4. For these subjects, we also noted that they were easily distracted or eager to finish the experiment. For this reason we decided not to trust those cases, keeping only the results from the other 50 cases (25 men and 25 women).

A total of 45 reference images were presented to each subject. Four main sets were used: Group 1 contained 16 reference images that were extracted from the shown video, *i.e.*, the reference image appeared exactly as one of the frames in the video; Group 2 contained 12 reference images representing places in the video recorded at a different time of the day, where spatial, environmental or lightning variations occurred (see Figure 1); Group 3 showed locations that could be found in the complete route but that were not contained in the video (see Figure 3); the 2 remaining images (Group 4), were totally random, exhibited just to relax and reduce possible tiredness of the subjects.

Quantitative results obtained by this experiment are depicted through Figure 4. The color yellow represents a *Yes* answer and the red a *No* answer. The figure is divided into the four groups described above, where Group 1 appears at the top, Group at the middle and Groups 3 and 4 at the bottom of the figure. Note how, for Groups 1 and 2, it was expected that subjects identified the reference image within the shown video, thus a 100% success decision rate would have meant a full

Algorithm 1: Game-like test

- **Input:** One video sequence
  Three reference images
- **Output:** Decision array

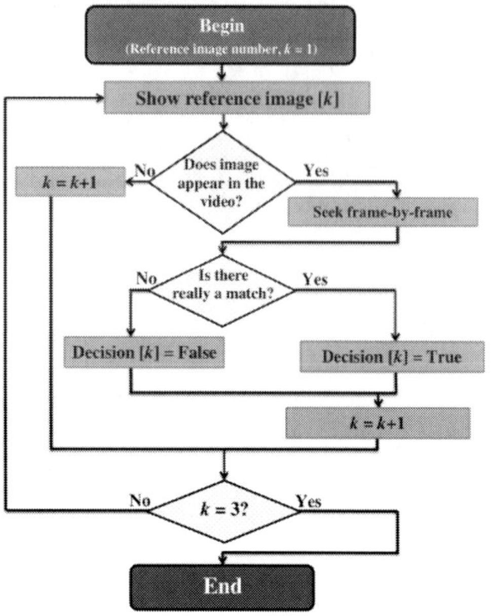

Figure 2. Flow diagram describing the steps followed by the participants. This represents one of fifteen cycles, for a total of 15 videos × 3 reference images = 45 attempts per subject. The average duration of each test was of 15 min.

(positive) yellow bar. As far as Groups 3 and 4 are concerned, the expected answers were negative, leading to a majorly red area. Percentages of success of 86 ± 7, 79 ± 11, 89 ± 6 and 99 ± 1 were achieved for Groups 1 though 4, respectively. The global mean percentage of success for the whole experiment was 86 ± 9 %.

TABLE I: FEATURES THAT, IN ACCORDANCE WITH PARTICIPANTS, HELPED THEM TO RECOGNIZE A PLACE. PV: PERCENTAGE WITH RESPECT TO THE TOTAL NUMBER OF VOTES. TS: TRAFFIC SIGNALS.

Feature	Buildings	Trees	TS	Other (20)	Color	Cars
PV(%)	25.97	22.07	16.88	16.23	15.58	3.24

As human attention is one of the main topics of our research, right after every participant completed the test, they were asked to choose from a list the features that grabbed the most of their attention. The list can be found with the results of this survey in Table I. It is important to note that the category "Other" contains all the elements that subjects expressed were helpful but were not listed in the survey. These items included benches, park games, wastelands, mountains, dumps, the driving way of the street, lampposts, etc.

III. Experiments on Machine Perception

For testing computational place recognition capabilities, the same 15 video sequences and 45 reference images as in

Figure 3. Example of an image that could be found in the complete 0.8 km route but that was not contained in the 10 s video (Group 3). The top image represents a scene in the video sequence, while the bottom one was the reference image shown to the participant.

the human perception evaluation were used. Each video was divided into 10 frames (1 frame per second), in order to follow the same way as human experiments. We tested 22 combinations of feature detectors and descriptors for a total of 9,900 comparisons. The methodology implemented, in all cases, is described as follows: first, a reference image and its 10 respective video frames were introduced as inputs to each algorithm. Then, the corresponding feature detector extracted the most relevant information from the reference image and each of the video frames. These features were explained by a descriptor, which assigned a unique feature vector for each image so that it could be identified among the rest. Next, the vector of the reference image was compared with the vector of each video frame, in order to find a best match. Once the 22 algorithms were evaluated with respect to all the 45 reference images, a threshold was applied to each detector-descriptor combination to determine wether this was a positive match or not. For threshold setting, we chose an 80% of the highest number of features found, *i.e.*, for each detector-descriptor combination there were a total of 450 evaluations. From these comparisons, we picked the image with the maximum number of correspondences as the 100% of success rate. In this way, we discarded as successful cases any images whose number of correspondences represented less than the 80% of the recorded maximum.

The above process was evaluated for each of the 22 algorithms. The efectiveness of each pair of algorithms to correctly identify wether a reference image was included in its corresponding video sequence or not is shown in Table II. From the table it is noticeable how 7 out of the 22 combinations obtained the highest success rate while the poorest performance was exhibited by other 7 combinations. It is important to mention

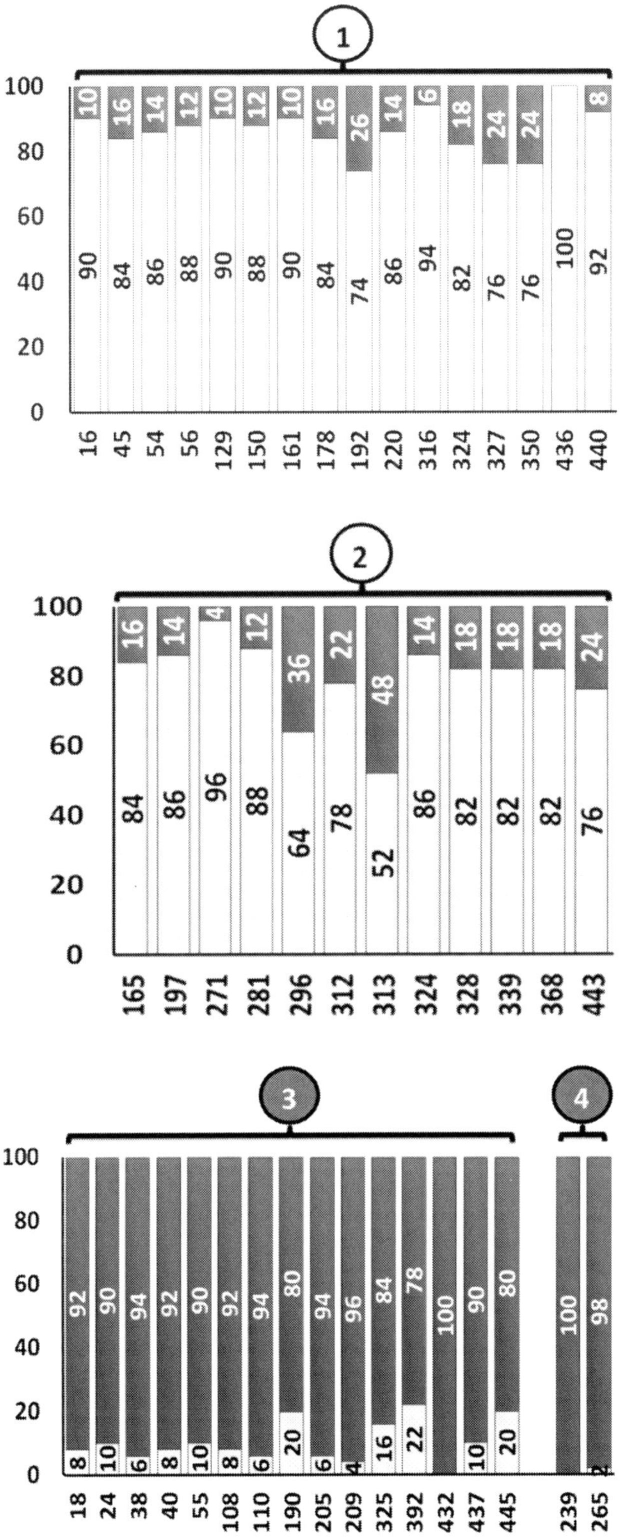

Figure 4. Human perception-Relationship between each reference image and the success rate of the experiment. For each diagram, the x-axis refers to the image number while the y-axis refers to the percentage of success rate.

TABLE II: LIST OF THE 22 DETECTOR-DESCRIPTOR COMBINATIONS USED IN OUR EXPERIMENT. THE GLOBAL PERCENTAGE OF SUCCESS WAS OF 54±41%.

Detector - Descriptor	Succes Rate (%)
AVA-ORB	73.33
AVA-SIFT	73.33
AVA-SURF	73.33
GFTT-BRISK	73.33
GFTT-ORB	73.33
GFTT-SIFT	73.33
GFTT-SURF	73.33
ORB-ORB	73.33
AVA-BRISK	51.11
STAR-BRISK	46.66
STAR-ORB	46.66
STAR-SIFT	46.66
STAR-SURF	46.66
KAZE-KAZE	44.44
AKAZE-AKAZE	42.22
BRISK-BRISK	40
FAST-BRISK	40
FAST-ORB	40
FAST-SIFT	40
FAST-SURF	40
SIFT-SIFT	40
SURF-SURF	40

that, for the 4 groups in the database none of the algorithms in the state of the art outperformed humans.

A further representation of the experiment is visually provided through Figure 5. The arrengement is similar to that of Figure 4, where results for Group 1 are shown at the top, for Group 2 at the middle, and for Groups 3 and 4 at the bottom of the figure. Here, it is to note that machines performed considerably worse than humans for Group 1, while for Group 2, where illumination changes happened, computer algorithms failed in all cases. Nonetheless, for Group 3, where humans obtained an 89% of success rate, machines achieved a complete 100%. This might suggest that the state of the art in computer vision is more effective at discriminating places that do not belong to a certain path than at recognizing previously visited places.

It is fair to comment further on the results presented in Figure 5, where machine capabilities for place recognition are depicted. For the cases of Groups 3 and 4, a 100% of correct answers for all detector-descriptor pairs was achieved; conversely, Group 2 denotes a complete fail among all of the combinations; thus, Group 1 is the only group that allows an individual evaluation of the performance for each pair. Besides, it is noticeable how the best 7 methods outperformed humans for Group 1 by achieving a 100% success rate. This means that the 7 following algorithms: AVA-ORB, AVA-SIFT, AVA-SURF, GFTT-BRISK, GFTT-ORB, GFTT-SIFT, GFTT-SURF and ORB-ORB, surpassed the capabilities of humans for Groups 1 and 3, although exhibiting a complete failure for Group 2.

IV. Discussion

From the experiments above, it is possible to discuss further on the capabilities of humans and machines for place recognition in challenging driving environments. When comparing humans and machines, it is important to focus on certain nuances. For example, in Figures 4 and 5, it is noticeable how, while humans exhibit variations in their decisions, machines show uniform results. These discrepancies could be a consequence of human visual memory. Hayhoe [22] has defined human vision "as if our conscious experience were the ultimate end-product of visual processing". However, sometimes visual perception is not sufficient, and the need of a visual memory arises, which in accordance with Palmer [23] is "the preservation of visual information after the optical source of that information is no longer available to the visual system". All things in the world are separated by time or space so, as mentioned in [24], visual memory is needed to retain information about one thing in order to relate it to another thing. In addition, as things move around, they can occlude each other, and here is where visual memory helps to overcome the temporary loss of visual information. Nonetheless, although the process of recognizing a location by remembering and identifying just specific landmarks or features could produce a sufficient accurate and robust response [25], the lack of a reference might derive on a confussion for humans.

For the case of machines, images and videos are processed at a uniform resolution, so there is no notion of saccades to shift the center of high-resolution processing. Thus, there is no need for visual memory as a buffer for integration of information over saccades [24]. The behavior computer vision methods demonstrated appears to be similar between them when the task resembles image retrieval. However, as computer vision methods mostly rely on data, when there exists subtle changes between two images, machines struggle to find correspondences, even if both images are taken from the same location.

Outstanding cases of human perception can be analyzed in Figures 6 and 7. Machine perception cases are not shown due to the uniformity of its results, *i.e.*, for each group all methods achieved either 100% accuracy or 100% failure.

The best and worst performances for human perception in Group 1 are represented by Figure 6. At the first row it can be noticed how the existence of few, but representative items in the environment, such as a white fence, a pink wall and a tree with a particular shape (which can be associated with common day things like a corn) may help humans to remember and identify previously visited places. However, the second row of the figure suggests that if there exist similar features in two different places, or too many elements within a scene, subjects are prone to get confused. For example, in this case, the presence of trees, or a similar color of fences and walls in both images, might had been the reason of failure among participants.

Similarly, Figure 7 describes the best and worst results for humans in Groups 2 and 3, respectively. The top row corresponds to the best performance. Again, it can be observed that if there exist just a few characteristic elements in a scene, it could be simpler for humans to remember and recognize such scene, even if daylight or spatial variations occur. In the

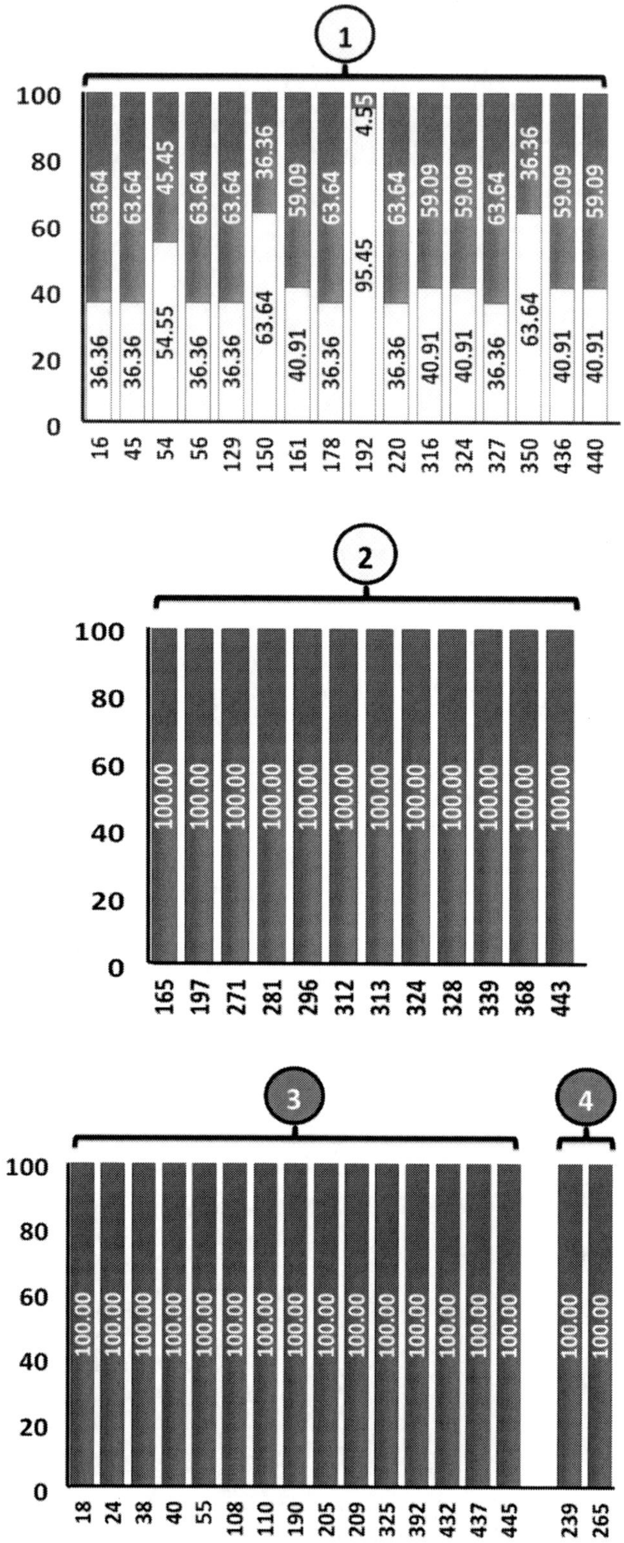

Figure 5. Machine perception-Relationship between each reference image and the success rate of the experiment. The x-axis represents the image numbers, while y-axis the percentage of success rate.

Figure 6. Best and worst cases for humans in Group 1 (top and bottom row respectively).

Figure 7. Images that represented the best performance for humans in Group 2 (top row), and the worst in Group 3 (bottom row).

figure, a single house at the left of the road, and the absence of items at the right, appeared to be enough for subjects to identify the location. Nevertheless, the bottom row shows, as it was mentioned above, that the presence of similar features can affect human perception. Here, we can see that the existence of fences that look alike could had been a cause for subjects to fail.

V. Conclusions and Future work

This paper is aimed at exploring and analyzing the way humans perceive previously visited places, while driving through urban environments under challenging conditions. An experimental setup was designed to evaluate human capabilities for place recognition. The same experiments were tested on state of the art visual place recognition algorithms. From experimental results, it can be observed that humans demonstrated a greater ability to identify scenarios with subtle changes, such as illumination or spatial variations, as opposed to machines, which did not accomplish positive results at all for these cases. However, machines outperformed humans when the problem became that of image retrieval, *i.e.*, when the reference image appeared without changes within the video.

As a future work it would be interesting to study in depth the weaknesses of computer vision algorithms so as to improve their robustness from the way humans perceive subtle changes.

References

[1] M. Riddoch and G. Humphreys, *Neuropsychology of visual perception*. Hillsdale: Lawrence Erlbaum Associates, 1989.

[2] R. G. Golledge, *Do people understand spatial concepts: The case of first-order primitives*. Berlin, Heidelberg: Springer Berlin Heidelberg, 1992, pp. 1–21.

[3] J. O'Keefe and L. Nadel, *The Hippocampus as a Cognitive Map*. Oxford: Clarendon Press, 1978. [Online]. Available: http://hdl.handle.net/10150/620894

[4] A. D. Redish and D. S. Touretzky, "Cognitive maps beyond the hippocampus," pp. 15–35, 1997.

[5] J. F. Sowa, *Conceptual Structures – Information processing in mind and machine*. Addison-Wesley Systems Programming Series Reading, 1984.

[6] H. H. Bulthoff and H. A. van Vee, "Vision and action in virtual environments: Modern psychophysics in spatial cognition research," in *Vision and Attention*. Springer, 2001, pp. 233–252.

[7] S. Lowry *et al.*, "Visual place recognition: A survey," *IEEE Transactions on Robotics*, vol. 32, no. 1, pp. 1–19, 2016.

[8] M. Cummins and P. Newman, "Fab-map: Probabilistic localization and mapping in the space of appearance," *The International Journal of Robotics Research*, vol. 27, no. 6, pp. 647–665, 2008.

[9] H. Bay, A. Ess, T. Tuytelaars, and L. Van Gool, "Speeded-up robust features (surf)," *Computer vision and image understanding*, vol. 110, no. 3, pp. 346–359, 2008.

[10] D. G. Lowe, "Distinctive image features from scale-invariant keypoints," *International journal of computer vision*, vol. 60, no. 2, pp. 91–110, 2004.

[11] P. F. Alcantarilla, A. Bartoli, and A. J. Davison, "Kaze features," in *European Conference on Computer Vision*. Springer, 2012, pp. 214–227.

[12] E. Rublee, V. Rabaud, K. Konolige, and G. Bradski, "Orb: An efficient alternative to sift or surf," in *Computer Vision (ICCV), 2011 IEEE international conference on*. IEEE, 2011, pp. 2564–2571.

[13] P. F. Alcantarilla and T. Solutions, "Fast explicit diffusion for accelerated features in nonlinear scale spaces," *IEEE Trans. Patt. Anal. Mach. Intell*, vol. 34, no. 7, pp. 1281–1298, 2011.

[14] L. Caramazana, R. Arroyo, and L. M. Bergasa, "Visual odometry correction based on loop closure detection," in *Open Conference on Future Trends in Robotics (RoboCity16)*, 2016, pp. 97–104.

[15] S. Leutenegger, M. Chli, and R. Y. Siegwart, "Brisk: Binary robust invariant scalable keypoints," in *Computer Vision (ICCV), 2011 IEEE International Conference on*. IEEE, 2011, pp. 2548–2555.

[16] Y. Uchida, S. Sakazawa, and S. Satoh, "Image retrieval with fisher vectors of binary features," *ITE Transactions on Media Technology and Applications*, vol. 4, no. 4, pp. 326–336, 2016.

[17] J. Shi *et al.*, "Good features to track," in *Computer Vision and Pattern Recognition, 1994. Proceedings CVPR'94., 1994 IEEE Computer Society Conference on*. IEEE, 1994, pp. 593–600.

[18] E. Rosten and T. Drummond, "Machine learning for high-speed corner detection," *Computer Vision–ECCV 2006*, pp. 430–443, 2006.

[19] M. Agrawal, K. Konolige, and M. R. Blas, "Censure: Center surround extremas for realtime feature detection and matching," in *European Conference on Computer Vision*. Springer, 2008, pp. 102–115.

[20] A. Maldonado-Ramírez and L. A. Torres-Méndez, "Robotic visual tracking of relevant cues in underwater environments with poor visibility conditions," *Journal of Sensors*, vol. 2016, 2016, 16 pages.

[21] L. Itti, C. Koch, and E. Niebur, "A model of saliency-based visual attention for rapid scene analysis," *IEEE Transactions on pattern analysis and machine intelligence*, vol. 20, no. 11, pp. 1254–1259, 1998.

[22] M. Hayhoe, "Visual memory in motor planning and action," in *The visual world in memory*. Psychology Press, 2017, pp. 117–139.

[23] S. Palmer, *Vision Science: Photons to Phenomenology*. MIT Press, 1999. [Online]. Available: https://books.google.com.mx/books?id=mNrxCwAAQBAJ

[24] S. Lallee, C. Tan, and B. Mandal, "Vision and memory: Looking beyond immediate visual perception," in *Computational and Cognitive Neuroscience of Vision, Cognitive Science and Technology*. Springer, 2017, pp. 195–219.

[25] C. Siagian and L. Itti, "Impact of neuroscience in robotic vision localization and navigation," in *Computational and Cognitive Neuroscience of Vision, Cognitive Science and Technology*. Springer, 2017, pp. 235–276.

NiHA: A Conscious Agent

Wajahat Mahmood Qazi
Intelligent Machines & Robotics,
Department of Computer Science,
COMSATS Institute of Information Technology,
Lahore, Pakistan
e-mail: wmqazi@ciitlahore.edu.pk

Syed Tanweer Shah Bukhari
Intelligent Machines & Robotics,
Department of Computer Science,
COMSATS Institute of Information Technology,
Lahore, Pakistan
Department of Computer Science,
University of South Asia,
Lahore, Pakistan
e-mail: stsbukhari@gmail.com

Jonathan Andrew Ware
Faculty of Computing, Engineering, and Science
University of South Wales,
Wales, United Kingdom
e-mail: andrew.ware@southwales.ac.uk

Atifa Athar
Intelligent Machines & Robotics,
Department of Computer Science,
COMSATS Institute of Information Technology,
Lahore, Pakistan
e-mail: atifaathar@ciitlahore.edu.pk

***Abstract*— This paper reports ongoing work in the development of self-aware artificial general intelligence, called Nature-inspired Humanoid Cognitive Computing Platform for Self-aware and Conscious Agent (NiHA). It is based on a quantum and bio-inspired cognitive architecture for machine consciousness and artificial intelligence. So far, a number of different cognitive features have been implemented to help facilitate the realization of NiHA. These implemented features include imaginations, dreams, personal semantics, psycho-psychological based motivations and ethics. Apart from these, some industrial applications are also underway. The review of the results obtained from these applications is encouraging and supports the potential to achieve a certain level of consciousness.**

Keywords-machine consciousness; NiHA; cognitive machines

I. Introduction

Recent years have witnessed exceptional progress in the field of Artificial General Intelligence (AGI) and Machine Consciousness (MC). Considering the current pace of technological evolution, it is envisaged by some that in the future, machines will become self-aware and even potentially become part of a man-machine society. The idea of implementing consciousness in machines is thus not new [1]-[5]. It does, however, raise several philosophical and computational issues [5]-[7]. Addressing these issues requires the unification of different knowledge domains such as physical sciences, neuroscience, psychology, and computer sciences [8]. Consequently, it has resulted in the establishment of computational theories of the mind [8]-[11], and domains which include both bio-inspired [11] and quantum-inspired methods [8][12]-[17]. Various researchers have contributed to the construction of computational equivalent of the human mind/brain [7]-[8][18]-[24]. In this regard, several projects have been initiated which include the Blue Brain Project [25]; the Human Brain Project [26]; DARPA and the Brain Initiative [27]. In addition to these projects, there have been recent corporate efforts by the likes of Google [28]-[30], Facebook [31]-[34], and IBM [35].

A roadmap for addressing the challenges of bio-inspired modeling is shown in Figure 1. One of the most challenging of these is getting humans to accept them as co-workers (socio-cognitive agents) [11][36].

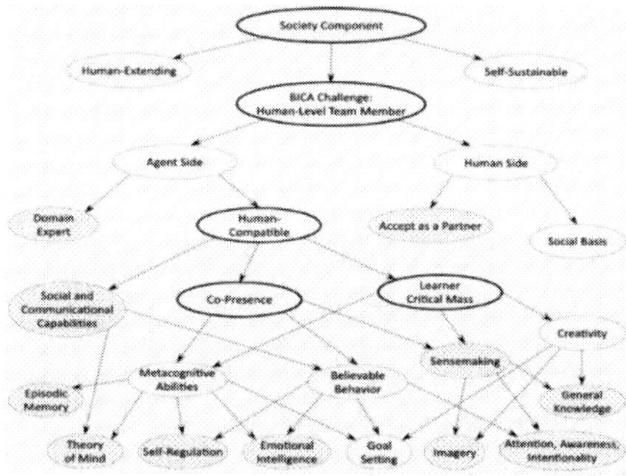

Figure 1 - Roadmap for the Bio-inspired Challenge [11]

From the roadmap, it can be seen that these socio-cognitive agents must be capable of producing believable conscious-like behavior and a sense of their presence in their human co-workers [11]. The benefit of such behavior is clear when considering socio-assistive robots, domestic robots, and personal robots. Examples of such machines acting as co-workers have long appeared in entertainment films (for example, 'Geminoid F' an actoroid, acted in the film 'Sayônara, 2015'), and more recently a robot named Sophia, was awarded citizenship by Saudi Arabia [37]. Moreover, significant work has been done in the form of cognitive computing which includes IDA [9], LIDA [38], WATSON [35], CLARION [39], SIRI [40] and CORTANA [41].

Although current progress is encouraging, there are still many issues that need to be addressed before reaching the point where it can be claimed that the presence of phenomenal consciousness [7] in machines has been achieved. Simply to achieve functional consciousness [7] the agent must demonstrate voluntary control of attention, intention, action selection, motivation, goal-setting abilities, emotional intelligence, and self-regulation along with communication capability utilizing the cognitive constructs listed earlier [11].

One of the critical factors to help facilitate the implementation of the aforementioned is the selection of an appropriate modeling technique. Current literature suggests that there are two approaches for such modeling. These are a hierarchical and non-hierarchical approach [42], where a hierarchical model treats consciousness as a single reality with different levels of depth and a non-hierarchical model treats consciousness as a self-organizing multiplicity of embodied states (this allows the emergence of intelligence which is greater than the sum of its information).

Non-hierarchical methods can be used for modeling emergent artificial general intelligence [42], while hierarchical methods can be used for modeling a cognitive system comprised of multiple complex subsystems interacting together in synergy to generate conscious behaviors [42]. Both approaches have strengths and weaknesses. Keeping in mind the limitations of both methods, one of the successful methods for modeling is hybrid. The hybrid approach allows the modeling of higher abstraction in a hierarchical fashion. The functional level of these abstractions consists of subsystems that may operate according to the different paradigms. The hybrid approach seems to be the most promising as it ameliorates the deficiencies associated with the other methods.

Apart from bio-inspired modeling discussed above, this study also takes into account quantum inspiration. There are a number of school of thought associated with quantum inspiration explaining the functioning of brain/mind, consciousness, and intelligence. The reason for taking into account quantum inspiration is that the Universe is governed by the laws of nature [43]. The brain, mental processes along with other biological reactions, physical realities from quantum to classical world, computation, are all part of nature. If the Universe is quantum mechanical then mental processes can be described using quantum theories [43] and the mysteries of the brain, mental processes, and emergence of consciousness can be due to quantum processes or quantum computations [14][44]-[46].

Quantum mechanics is the study of subatomic particles that possess features such as superposition and entanglement, and the computation performed on them is referred to as quantum computation. Analysis of interpretations of quantum mechanics suggests that it has the computational/mathematical potential to model cognition/consciousness. There are different schools of thought on this issue, namely: (i) quantum mind/ consciousness, (ii) quantum cognition, (iii) quantum artificial intelligence.

Quantum consciousness assumes that the brain works on the principles of both neural and quantum computations [14][43][44][47]-[50]. Quantum cognition does not explicitly discuss the involvement of quantum mechanics in the function of the brain at the physical level [51]-[53]. Rather this paradigm acknowledges the mathematical and abstraction strength of quantum mechanics to model human memory, knowledge representation issues, perception, decision making and reasoning process. There are a number of useful references that expound this school of thought [15][16][54]-[58] which uses quantum inspired neural networks, quantum Bayes network and other quantum cognition algorithm to model complex human mental facilities. In contrast to quantum consciousness, quantum artificial intelligence is about transforming existing artificial intelligence algorithms to make them work on quantum computers [12][13].

The existence of consciousness in machines can be evaluated using both qualitative and quantitative methods. Qualitative analysis can be performed using Aleksander's axioms of conscious [59]. Qualitative analyses using Aleksander's Axiomatic postulates that an agent having depiction, imagination, attention, volition, and emotion may possess some kind of conscious activity [59]. Moreover, the quantitative analysis includes Quantum Mutual Information (QMI) and ConsScale method [60]-[63]. QMI is a method that was developed to determine the correlation between the subsystems of two quantum states where these states are not pure states [8]. ConsScale is a characterization mechanism for the evaluation of consciousness in an agent [61].

Moreno originally proposed ConsScale [61], a method that was later improved upon [62][63], as the reference method for analysis of the correlation between cognitive and conscious capability. ConsScale mainly evaluates an agent based on its behavior and architecture [62].

Following the legacy of the aforementioned studies, project NiHA (Nature-inspired Humanoid Cognitive Computing Platform for Self-aware and Conscious Agent) was initiated. In this paper, NiHA is introduced as an entity with a limited level of consciousness and general intelligence. The design and implementation strategy are also articulated and the results acquired so far presented. The results are encouraging and suggest that NiHA may possess a certain level of consciousness. This does not imply that NiHA is fully conscious or that it possesses human-level of phenomenology or general intelligence, neither do the authors intend to claim such. Indeed, NiHA is an attempt to explore the possibility of designing and implementing an artifact that falls under the domain of machine consciousness and artificial general intelligence.

In this paper, Section II details NiHA's architecture, Section III deals with its applications and functionality,

Section IV describes the test of consciousness, and Section IV documents the results and discussion.

II. NATURE-INSPIRED HUMANOID COGNITIVE COMPUTING PLATFORM FOR SELF-AWARE AND CONSCIOUS AGENT (NIHA)

NiHA is based on previous work related to the unified theory of the mind, 'Quantum & Bio-inspired Intelligent & Consciousness Architecture (QuBIC)' (see Figure 2) and on the code-base of an agent called Johi [8].

A. *Cognitive Architecture (QuBIC) of NiHA*

The cognitive architecture of NiHA is constructed in layers (see Figure 2). The first layer consists of physical components, while the second layer comprises of mental processes. The physical layer consists of sensors and actuators. The mental regime further consists of unconscious and conscious layers. . The unconscious layer consists of several cognitive units working together in order to regulate the involuntary and pre-programmed tasks that are essential requirements for the agent's self-regulation and optimum performance. The modules of the conscious layer are responsible for awareness, attention, intention and voluntary tasks. The conscious layer serves as the executive control of the mind and the functional description of the whole architecture is discussed in [8].

i. Memory Units

Unconscious components consist of several modules; these include memory systems, circadian clock, implicit behavior center, reflexes, decision action center, deed assessment module, seed knowledge, memory management, drives, and a synchronization unit.

a) Sensory Memory

Sensory Memory is responsible for the storage of sensory inputs coming from external and internal sensors. Sensed contents are collected in the implicit knowledge repository. Sensory processes apply basic filters to the sensory contents. The filters include those responsible for resizing the incoming image stream, encoding the stream as required and applying part-of-speech-tagger on the lingual contents. These sensory contents are then transferred to various unconscious modules as per the connections shown in Figure 2.

b) Perceptual Associative Memory

A copy of processed sensory contents is received by the Perceptual Associative Memory (PAM). PAM is responsible for the formation of an association between objects based on recognition, perception, and classification. Information is encoded for further processing, using structural and semantic analysis and collaboration between Short-Term Memory (STM) and Working Memory (WM). The percepts are then transferred to conscious memory system for further processing.

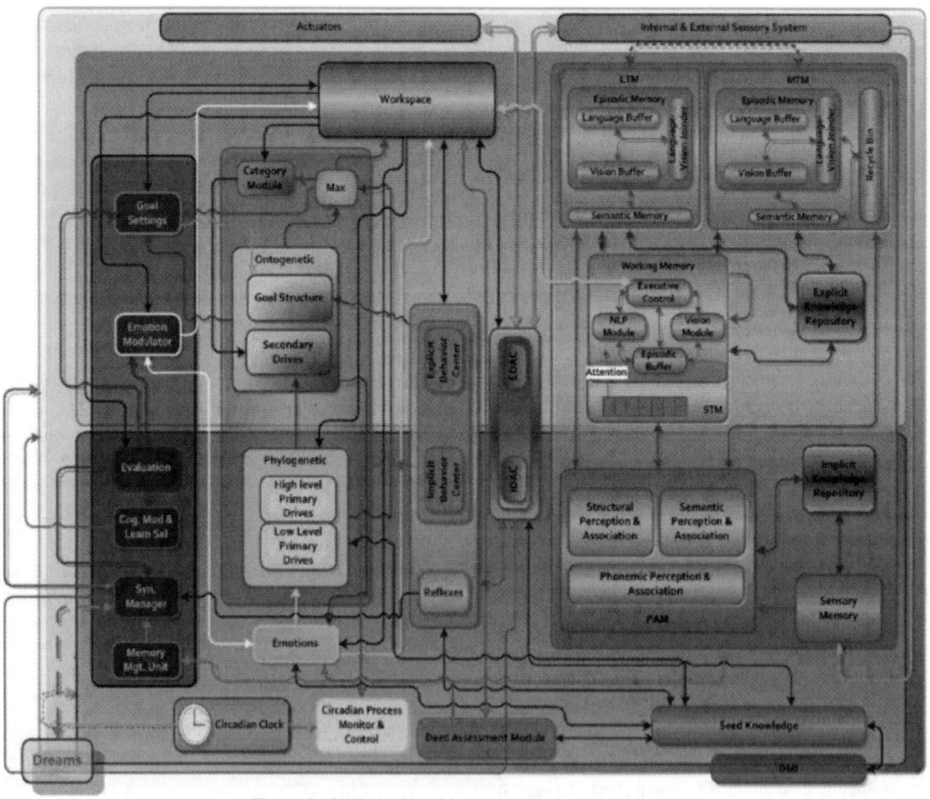

Figure 2 - NiHA's Cognitive Architecture (QuBIC) [8]

c) Decision Execution Center

The Decision Execution Center (DEC) consists of both conscious and unconscious components. It actually acts as a procedural memory. This unit consists of "how to perform a task" information which is needed mainly for motor actions.

d) Short-term Memory

Short-Term Memory (STM) receives and examines contents from PAM to determine what requires attention through a process called 'selective attention'. The content, which does not get attention, is forgotten when short-term memory overflow occurs or content's signal is decayed. This selective attention process acts as a gateway between unconscious and conscious layers, resulting in an awareness of sensory contents.

e) Working Memory

Working Memory (WM) is responsible for the manipulation and processing of information during the course of the cognitive process. WM consists of the central executive that is supported by visual memory (which process visual content) and spatial memory (contains the spatial maps and information about size and location of content).

ii. Long-term Memories

Long-Term Memory (LTM) holds the information for longer periods. LTM is composed of episodic and semantic memories. The episodic memory contains the information related to the agent's experience of particular events, while the semantic memory contains the record of meanings, facts, and knowledge related to objects.

iii. Circadian Clock, Monitoring and Control

The Circadian Clock (CC) triggers several high-level and low-level drives (and ensures the optimal performance of an agent), while the Circadian Monitoring and Control (CMC) units safeguard the activities by maintaining the threshold levels. CMC also protect various conscious and unconscious cognitive modules from malfunctioning.

iv. Seed Knowledge

One of the major challenges when modeling artificial general intelligence is to implement safe artificial intelligence. Seed knowledge acts as apriori knowledge implemented at design time. This provides ethical norms and a set of rules that try to ensure "safe" artificial intelligence. To date, a conceptual knowledge base has been designed but not yet implemented [64]. This knowledge-base contains information relating to ethical values, laws related to daily life, rules regarding social etiquette and an understanding of the difference between right and wrong. Seed knowledge has already been implemented in NiHA [8] [64].

v. Deed Assessment Module

The Deed Assessment Module (DAM) acts as the "inner self" and assesses performance with regard to the guidelines available as seed knowledge. Conscious and unconscious activities are regulated in the DAM based on predefined parameters and evolved knowledge.

vi. Emotions

The Emotion Module regulates and influences the rational decisions based on basic emotions [65]. The emotions are extracted from the facial expression of a human interacting with NiHA. The extracted expressions are then used for the regulation of decisions.

vii. Meta-cognition

Meta-cognition performs a regulatory role of managing several conscious and unconscious modules. These modules perform numerous tasks i.e. memory management, evaluation, emotion modulation, synchronization between conscious and unconscious modules, learning management and goal setting.

viii. Behavioral and Motivational System

The Behavioral System is responsible for generating implicit and explicit behaviors in the agent based on current context and experiences. The Motivational System [67], inspired by the work of Manzotti [66], generates motivations in an agent in the form of goals. These goals are then used to take desired actions, along with what and how the task will be done.

ix. Dreams

Dreams are the most important cognitive unit. It is responsible for memory consolidation, the evolution of ideas, and creativity through the manipulation of known objects. The first stage of Dreams (i.e. memory consolidation) has been implemented in NiHA [68], and is based on Quantum Neural Network and Quantum Genetic Algorithm.

x. Imagination

Imagination is the manifestation of scenarios that are not directly present to the sensors. The first stage of its implementation in NiHA had the goal of emulating the imagination of a young child. Studies suggest that young children only understand simple sentences. Imaginations implemented to date simulate psychological aspects comparable with that of a four-year-old child [69]-[70]. Further exploration in this area is in progress.

B. Design Rationale & Implementation Philosophy

The design and implementation principles that have been utilized are based on ConsScale guidelines [60][62][63]. According to these, every conscious agent must possesses mental processes and a physical or simulated body. The mental processes in NiHA are based on QuBIC. Currently, the mental processes have been interfaced with a simulated iCub robot [71]. The simulated iCub runs on a laptop mounted on an iCreate robot platform along with Microsoft Kinect sensor and is collectively known as NiHA's body. Moreover, the integration of the Allison humanoid robot with NiHA is underway.

The motivation behind this study is to address a number of philosophical and design issues not taken into account previously. These issues are associated with quantum-inspired modeling, synchronization of autonomous functions through the circadian clock, imaginations, dreams, personal semantics, and psychophysiological regulation of drives through the modeling of insulin and glucose interplay, seed knowledge including deed assessments. Further details on these features are documented in [8][70] The quantum inspiration is based on methods from quantum cognition and quantum artificial intelligence.

The aforementioned features are complex systems and depended on one another as shown in Figure 1. Therefore, modeling of such systems requires the implementation of the cognitive architectural framework, together with a set of cognitive processes, cognitive cycles, and representation schemes [72]. The cognitive processes and cycles are inspired from pandemonium theory [1], feature-integration theory [73], unified theory of an artificial mind, global workspace theory [74] and QuBIC architectural model [8]. The neural correlates of the architectural model are summarized in [75]. These features were implemented separately due to computational and design complexity and are yet to be integrated into the architectural framework (moreover, some are still at the conceptual stage). The overall design and implementation was service oriented. These modules are implemented using different programming languages and run on Windows and Ubuntu platforms. Further details are provided in the 'languages and tools' section.

C. *Cognitive Processes and Codelets*

The pandemonium theory suggests the presence of demons (mini-agents) in the mind, working in synergy to perform various cognitive tasks in parallel [1]. These cognitive tasks may range from simple identification of objects to learning and to execution of complex sensory motor controls. Generally, these demons are called codelets in cognitive computing domain [2][76][77]. According to the pandemonium theory, these codelets are an independent set of programs working in parallel to process incoming signals. Therefore, each of these codelets has well-defined responsibility and executes continuously and cyclically. Further details on codelets and their standard implementation and guidelines are available in [2][76][77].

In NiHA, the codelets were implemented as proxies to the actual implementation of the code in QuBIC architectural framework. The actual implementations are either in the form of C#'s tasks from 'Task Parallel Library' (TPL) [78] or services implemented running as nodes on the network. Implementation of these codelets as TPL-tasks or services was determined based on response time and the programming language in which they were coded. Cognitive processes with short running time and programmed using C# were developed as TPL-tasks. Cognitive tasks, which were implemented on different platforms or had large execution time, for example learning codelets, were implemented as services. This division is simply a rule of thumb, and in order to keep cognitive optimization, variations can be made as per requirement and future need. Table 1 summarizes the list of codelets in NiHA.

TABLE I - CODELETS OF NiHA

Codelets	Working
Sensory-Motor	A codelet converts internal planning to motor actions
Learning	A codelet responsible for configuration of learning algorithms for a different type of streams.
Vision	A codelet work in collaboration with detection and recognition codelet to assign meaning to visual streams.
Language & Understanding	Language codelet works with several other codelets for the understanding of text and speech processes.
Perceptual	A codelet train system to assign meanings to sensory signals.
Drives and Motivation	Based on a high level and low drives, codelet formulate motivation for an agent to do specific tasks.
Attention and Awareness	Attention codelet bring sensory contents into the conscious part. A codelet that attempts to train attention on some particular kind of information. Examples: Expectation codelet, intention codelet
Emotions	A codelet that regulate the internal representations based on emotions detected from the external environment.
Dream	A codelet work in synergy with memory consolidation codelet to generate dreams and restructure memory blocks.
Circadian	Circadian is just like clock used to check the mode of NiHA every few minutes.
Memory Consolidation	A codelet accountable for the restructuring of associated memory constructs.
Imaginations	Imagination codelet works on storytelling technique. It makes visualization based on internal representations and current scenarios.
Deed Assessment	Deed assessment codelets evaluate agent on the basis of ethical knowledge stored in seed knowledge.
Signaling and Synchronization	Codelet responsible for the interaction and synchronization of numerous signals of the cognitive stream.

Conceptually, each codelet is a part of the codelet eco-system running on top of a cognitive module. As shown in Figure 3, a set of codelets are working on the contents of workspace module. These codelets are pre-programmed for specific tasks, for example, the conversational codelet generates a potential response after processing the lingual contents from the workspace. In parallel to this, the tagging codelet tags the current mental state with the prevailing positive and negative emotions. Responses from various codelets are compiled together by the underlying modules as chunks. These chunks are then broadcasted to relevant modules for further processing.

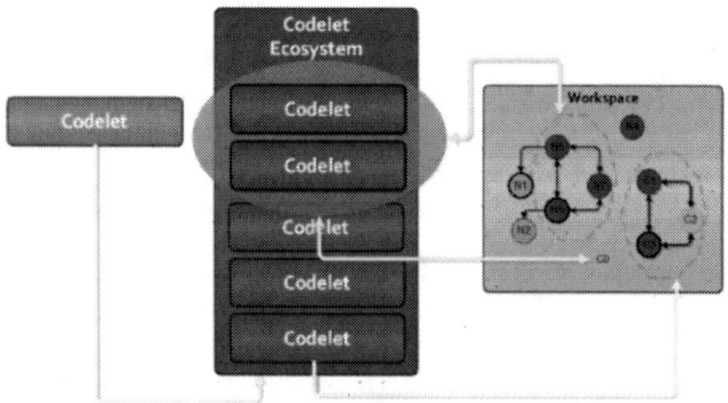

Figure 3 - Codelets in NiHA working in Synergy

D. Tools and Languages used for Implementation

The following programming languages were used: C#, Java, Python, and C++. The high-level abstraction of NiHA's design is shown in Figure 4. The cognitive structure (QuBIC architectural framework) is written in C# using service-oriented programming. The service orientation is done using Apache Thrift, ROS.NET and YARP.NET. Apache thrift was used as the primary tool for implementing network computing between various services in the framework. ROS.NET is used where communication between modules written in C# and Robotic Operating System (ROS) is required.

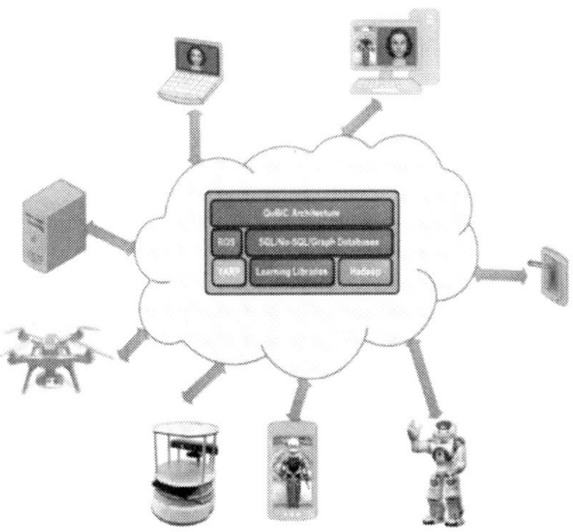

Figure 4 - Proposed NiHA Cloud

The software framework (YARP) for the iCub robot is written in C++ and YARP.NET is a wrapper/binder to interface YARP with C# code, which was acquired after compiling the YARP C++ code using SWIG. Python is used for natural language processing. Accord.NET and EmguCV are used for computer vision support and Accord.NET for audio processing. The conversation module was implemented using the Artificial Intelligence Markup Language (AIML). Weka.NET is used for machine learning support and MaryTTS for text to speech processing. Neo4j is a graph database used for the implementation of episodic and semantic structures. Moreover, quantum computations are performed using an in-house developed quantum computing library written in C# (see download section of the official NiHA website [79]).

E. Application and Functioning of NiHA

The current implementation allows NiHA to have general communication with a human operator. Moreover, it can play the popular paper-scissor-rock game. It can also construct an artistic work through storytelling processing utilizing imagination codelets. Moreover, it can construct short dreams using annotated images placed in the memory system. Details of the implementation of these applications and functioning will be published in the future but related video demonstrations are already available to be reviewed [79].

III. Test for Consciousness

The objective of this paper is to report on progress to date on constructing NiHA, an agent that currently has limited consciousness and general intelligence. The presence of a certain amount of consciousness in an agent can be evaluated using qualitative and quantitative analyses. Qualitative methods include Aleksander's Axioms [59] and the quantitative methods, Quantum Mutual Information (QMI) [8] and ConsScale [63].

A. Aleksander and Dunmall (ADM) Axioms

Aleksander and Dunmall, based on neuroscience studies, articulated the necessary properties for an agent to have indications of its own existence [59]. In this section, NiHA is assessed to determine its level of consciousness.

i. Depiction

Depiction is the mechanism of bringing the perceptual experiences into awareness. NiHA is able to formulate meaning from sensory information. The visual and auditory cues generate selective awareness about the existence and movement of the object(s) in an environment. Similarly, the acoustic cue in NiHA reacts by generating appropriate replies. According to Gamez [23], the integration of various perceptual signals give the sensation of something, that is *out there* and consequently, qualify the possibility of the depiction of an agent. The depiction is achieved in NiHA via the collaborative work of numerous codelets.

ii. Imagination

As mentioned earlier, in NiHA imagination is implemented in the form of the collaborative work of several codelets. So, NiHA can be credited with the existence of imagination in its primary form. Aspects of storytelling have been chosen for its initial development [69][70]. Moreover, NiHA is able to generate sensations and future aspects of known and unknown objects in the absence of any sensory information.

iii. Attention

The bottom-up and top-down attention mechanism is implemented in NiHA. The recall represents the top-down attention when signals are generated in working memory from long-term or medium-term memory, whereas signals coming from perceptual memory represent bottom-up attention.

iv. Volition

NiHA plans and simulates its actions before applying them to the environment and regulates them by means of its emotional state.

v. Emotions

Emotions play a vital role in manipulating the generation of goals and motivations. The Emotional Block, in NiHA, influences the effects of drives, decision-making, and planning. This block consists of six basic emotions [65]. Axiomatic analysis advocates the possibility of consciousness in NiHA. Moreover, the axioms suggest that the consciousness can be measured by evaluation of minimum mutual information exchange between cognitive blocks.

B. Quantum Mutual Information

Quantum Mutual Information (QMI) is used to measure the correlation between several sub-systems where the quantum states are not pure. Cognitive blocks can be represented as quantum states. This correlation represents the level of consciousness. For experimental analysis, the selected states are Working Memory (WM) and Perceptual Associative Memory (PAM).

i. Analysis 1

Signals were transmitted from the Sensory Memory block to the Perceptual Associative Memory block, the NiHA was supposed to get the awareness of conscious stream between various unconscious blocks.

ii. Analysis 2

Signals were transmitted from unconscious block (Perceptual Associative Memory) to conscious clock (Working Memory and Medium-term Memory) where NiHA was expected to get the attention of the memory contents.

iii. Analysis 3

Signals were transmitted from Working Memory to the Workspace and Medium-term Memory, where NiHA was supposed to get aware of the memory contents.

C. ConsScale

ConsScale was proposed by Moreno [61] and later matured [62][63] for the characterization of consciousness in an agent. The correlation between cognitive and conscious skills are being measured on the basis of Cumulative Levels Score (CLS) and ConsScale Quantitative Score (CQS). The levels of consciousness in ConsScales range from 0 to 11, from disembodied to super-human. The evaluation is mainly based on its architectural framework and behavior.

IV. Results & Discussion

The experiments have been performed on NiHA to analyze its conscious activity. In this regard, using signals transmitted from the unconscious region to the conscious region, signal analysis to determine level of consciousness were carried out using Quantum Mutual Information (QMI) sharing. Measuring of mutual information sharing is an established practice [23].

i. Analysis 1

NiHA did not show any conscious activity between unconscious blocks.

ii. Analysis 2

The analysis was performed on the contents being shared between Perceptual Associate Memory (PAM) and Medium-term Memory (MTM), similarly between PAM and Working Memory (WM). This resulted in conscious activity (see Figure 5). These results were recorded for 1,000 circadian clock cycles against 25 sample streams. The level of mutual information sharing shown in Figure 5 represents the level of consciousness recorded at different data sample points. The x-axis represents the sample number and the y-axis represents the level of consciousness in terms of mutual information sharing.

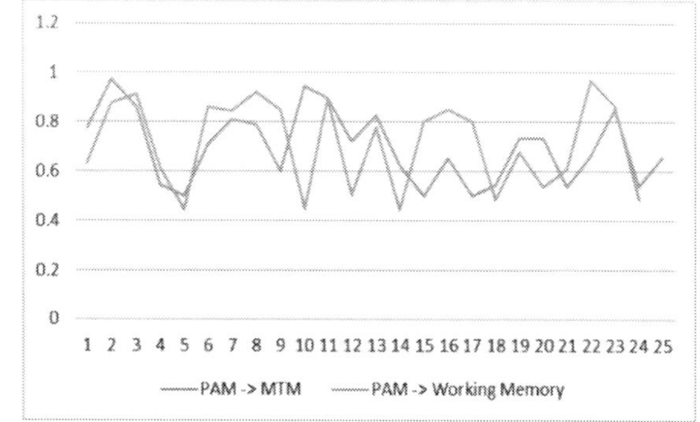

Figure 5 - Conscious activity between Perceptual Associative Memory and Working Memory [8]. The x-axis represents the sample number and Y-axis represents the conscious level in that sample.

iii. Analysis 3

The analysis was performed between conscious modules. These modules were Working Memory, Workspace, and Medium-term Memory. The consciousness level obtained between these modules is shown in Figure 6.

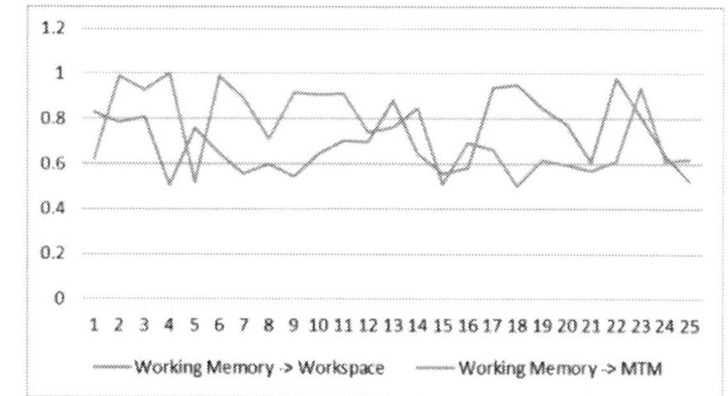

Figure 6 - Conscious activity between Working Memory and Workspace [8]. The x-axis represents the sample number and Y-axis represents the conscious level in that sample.

iv. ConsScale based Evaluation of NiHA

ConsScale was also applied in order to further clarify the class of consciousness which NiHA possess, given the current state of its implementation. A Cumulative Levels Score (CLS) of 1.27 and a ConsScale Quantitative Score (CQS) of 2.94 were obtained.

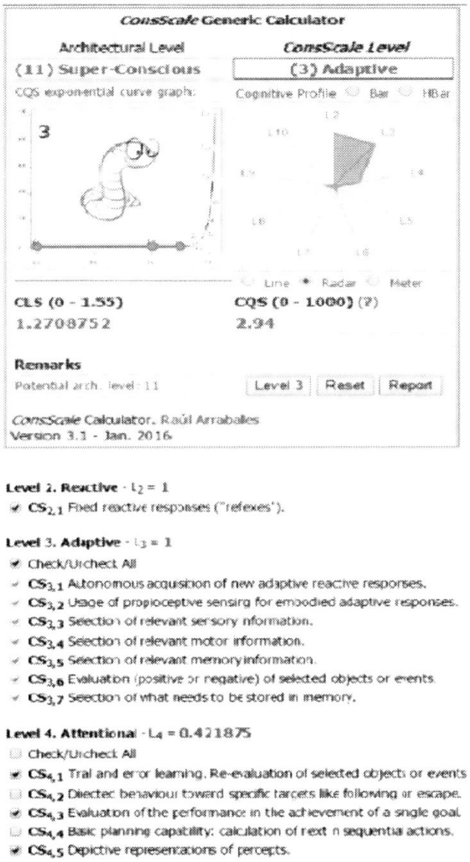

Figure 7 - ConsScale Evaluation Method for NiHA

The ConsScale result is summarized in Figure 7. It suggests that NiHA achieves a 3 on the 11 levels scale. It further proposes that by design NiHA is computationally equivalent to adaptive species, and therefore it still requires a lot of developmental work before anywhere close to achieving human level of consciousness.

V. Conclusion

The study reports an ongoing work in the development of NiHA which is based on the QuBIC architecture. NiHA is composed of several success stories, cognitive memories, dreams, imagination, machine ethics and socio-cognitive capabilities and other blackboard-like projects. Results obtained from various isolated studies imply that NiHA (as the extension of Johi) has a certain degree consciousness. The qualitative analyses suggest that all necessary conceptual and theoretical ingredients required to model a conscious agent are present. The quantitative analyses using quantum mutual information sharing suggests that at certain points in the signal stream, conscious activity was registered. This indeed supports the presence of a minimum level of consciousness. Furthermore, analysis using ConsScale suggested that this presence of consciousness can be classified as computationally equivalent to level 3 species.

Acknowledgement

The authors acknowledge the financial support from the Higher Education Commission of Pakistan, and the sponsorship of EDVON Pakistan to help facilitate the acquisition of the Allison Humanoid Robot.

References

[1] S. Franklin, Artificial Minds, MIT Press, 1995.

[2] S. Franklin, A. Kelemen and L. McCauley, "IDA: A Cognitive Agent Architecture," in IEEE Conference on Systems, Man and Cybernetics, 1998.

[3] R. Manzotti and V. Tagliasco, "Artificial Consciousness: A discipline between technology and theoretical obstacles," Artificial Intelligence in Medicine, vol. 44, pp. 105-117, 2008.

[4] P. O. Haikonen, "The Comparison of Some Cognitive Architectures," Series on Machine Consciousness, vol. 2, pp. 185-202, 2012.

[5] P. Langley, "Progress and Challenges in Research on Cognitive Architectures," in Proceedings of the Thirty-First AAAI Conference on Artificial Intelligence, San Francisco, California USA, 2017.

[6] G. Buttazzo, "Artificial consciousness: Hazardous questions (and answers)," Artificial Intelligence in Medicine, vol. 44, no. 2, pp. 139-146, 2008.

[7] D. J. Chalmers, "The Puzzle of Conscious Experience," Scientific American, vol. 273, pp. 80-86, 1995.

[8] W. M. Qazi, "Modeling cognitive cybernetics from unified theory of mind using quantum neuro-computing for machine consciousness," Lahore, 2011.

[9] S. Franklin, "IDA, a Conscious Artifact?" Journal of Consciousness, vol. 10, pp. 47-66, 2003.

[10] D. Feil-Seifer and M. J. Mataric, "Defining Socially Assistive Robotics," in International Conference on Rehabilitation Robotics, Chicago, IL, USA, 2005.

[11] A. V. Samsonovich, "On a roadmap for the BICA Challenge," vol. 1, pp. 100-107, 2012.

[12] B. Aoun and M. Tarifi, "Quantum Artificial Intelligence," Quantum Information Processing, pp. ArXiv:quant-ph/0401124, 2004.

[13] K. Sgarbas, "The Road to Quantum Artificial Intelligence," Current Trends in Informatics, pp. 469-477, 2007.

[14] S. Hameroff , "The Brain is both Neurocomputer and Quantum Computer," Cognitive Science, vol. 31, no. 6, pp. 1035-45, 2007.

[15] J. Busemeyer and P. Bruza, Quantum Models of Cognition and Decision, Cambridge: Cambridge University Press, 2012.

[16] E. M. Pothos and J. R. Busemeyer, "Can quantum probability provide a new direction for cognitive modeling," Behavioral and Brain Sciences, vol. 36, p. 255–274., 2013.

[17] Z. Wang, J. R. Busemeyer, H. Atmanspacher and E. M. Pothos, "The potential of using quantum theory to build models of cognition," Topics in Cognitive Science, vol. 5, no. 4, pp. 672-688, 2013.

[18] I. Aleksander, How to build a mind : Towards machines with imagination, New York : Columbia University Press, 2001.

[19] D. Friedlander and S. Franklin, "LIDA and a Theory of Mind," in Proceeding of the 2008 Conference on Artificial Genral Intelligence, 2008.

[20] R. Kurzweil, The Singularity Is Near, Viking, 2006.

[21] R. Manzotti and A. Chella, "Physical integration: A causal account for consciousness," Journal of integrative neuroscience, vol. 13, no. 02, pp. 403-427, 2014.

[22] R. Sun, "Motivational Representations within a Computational cognitive Architecture," Cognitive Computation, vol. 1, no. 1, pp. 91-103, 2009.

[23] D. Gamez, "The Development and Analysis of Conscious Machines," 2008.

[24] R. Manzottia and S. Jeschkec, "A causal foundation for consciousness in biological and artificial agents," Cognitive Systems Research, vol. 40, pp. 172-185, 2016.

[25] "The Blue Brain Project - A Swiss Brain Initiative," 2005. [Online]. Available: http://bluebrain.epfl.ch/. [Accessed 15 January 2018].

[26] "Human Brain Project," 2013. [Online]. Available: https://www.humanbrainproject.eu/en/. [Accessed 15 January 2018].

[27] "DARPA and the Brain Initiative," 2013. [Online]. Available: http://www.darpa.mil/program/our-research/darpa-and-the-brain-initiative. [Accessed 15 January 2018].

[28] S. Boixo, V. N. Smelyanskiy, A. Shabani, S. V. Isakov, M. Dykman, V. S. Denchev, M. H. Amin, A. Y. Smirnov, M. Mohseni and H. Neven, "Computational Multiqubit Tunnelling in Programmable Quantum Annealers," Nature Communications, vol. 7, pp. 1-7, 2016.

[29] S. Gu, T. Lillicrap, I. Sutskever and S. Levine, "Continuous Deep Q-Learning with Model-based Acceleration," in Proceedings of the 33 rd International Conference on Machine, New York, NY, USA, 2016.

[30] A. Globerson, N. Lazic, S. Chakrabarti, A. Subramanya, M. Ringgaard and F. Pereira, "Collective Entity Resolution with Multi-Focal Attention," in Proceedings of the 54th Annual Meeting of the Association for Computational Linguistics, Berlin, Germany, 2016.

[31] E. Whitmire, L. Trutoiu, R. Cavin, D. Perek, B. Scally, J. O. Phillips and S. Patel, "EyeContact: Scleral Coil Eye Tracking for Virtual Reality," in The International Symposium on Wearable Computers (ISWC), Heidelberg, Germany, 2016.

[32] Y. LeCun, "Facebook AI Research (FAIR)," Facebook, [Online]. Available: https://research.facebook.com/ai/. [Accessed 26 September 2016].

[33] Y.-W. E. Sung, X. Tie, S. H. Wong and H. Zeng, "Robotron: Top-down Network Management at Facebook Scale," in ACM Special Interest Group on Data Communication (SIGCOMM) , Florianopolis , Brazil, 2016.

[34] N. Zeghidour, G. Synnaeve, N. Usunier and E. Dupoux, "Joint Learning of Speaker and Phonetic Similarities with Siamese Networks," in Interspeech, San Francisco, United States, 2016.

[35] "Watson-IBM," [Online]. Available: http://www.ibm.com/watson/. [Accessed 15 January 2018].

[36] "National Robotics Initiative (NRI)," [Online]. Available: http://www.nsf.gov/pubs/2014/nsf14500/nsf14500.htm. [Accessed 15 January 2018].

[37] K. Korosec, "Saudi Arabia's Newest Citizen Is a Robot," 2017. [Online]. Available: http://fortune.com/2017/10/26/robot-citizen-sophia-saudi-arabia/. [Accessed 30 October 2017].

[38] S. Strain, S. Kugele and S. Franklin, "The Learning Intelligent Distribution Agent (LIDA) and Medical Agent X (MAX)," in IEEE Symposium on Computational Intelligence for Human-like Intelligence , Orlando, Florida, USA, 2014.

[39] M. F. Lynch, R. Sun and N. Wilson, "CLARION as a Cognitive Framework for Intelligent Virtual Agents," in IVA'11 Proceedings of the 10th international conference on Intelligent virtual agents, Reykjavik, Iceland, 2011.

[40] "IOS SIRI," [Online]. Available: http://www.apple.com/ios/siri/. [Accessed 15 January 2018].

[41] "Cortana Microsoft," [Online]. Available: https://www.microsoft.com/en-us/windows/cortana. [Accessed 15 Januray 2018].

[42] R. Bosnak, "Hierarchical and Nonhierarchical Models of Consciousness: Commentary on Paper by Hilary Hoge," Psychoanalytic Dialogues, vol. 18, no. 1, p. 27–41, 2008.

[43] D. Song, "Quantum Theory, Consciousness, and Being," NeuroQuantology , vol. 6, no. 3, pp. 272-277, 2008.

[44] J. Acacio de Barros and P. Suppes, "Quantum Mechanics, interference, and the Brain," Journal of Mathematical Psychology, vol. 53, pp. 306-313, 2009.

[45] S. Hameroff, "Quantum walks in brain microtubules--a biomolecular basis for quantum cognition?," Top Cognitive Science, vol. 6, no. 1, pp. 91-97, 2014.

[46] S. Hameroff, T. Craddock and J. Tuszynski, "Quantum effects in the understanding of consciousness," Journal of Integrative Neuroscience, vol. 13, no. 2, pp. 229-252, 2014.

[47] I. J. Thompson, "Quantum Mechanics and Consciousness: A Causal Correspondence Theory," in The Second Mind and Brain Symposium, London, 1990.

[48] G. Globus, "Quantum Consciousness is Cybernetics," Psyche, vol. 2, no. 12, 1995.

[49] M. K. Samal, "Speculations on a Unified Theory of Matter and Mind," in Science and Metaphysics: A Discussion on Consciousness and Genetics, Bangalore, India, 2001.

[50] R. K. Pradhan, "Subject-Object Duality and States of Consciousness: A Quantum Mechanical Approach," NeuroQuantology, vol. 8, no. 3, p. 262 - 278, 2010.

[51] D. Aerts and S. Sozzo, "Modeling Concept Combinations in a Quantum-Theoretic Framework," in Advances in Cognitive Neurodynamics (IV), 2014, pp. 393-399.

[52] S. Sozzo, "A quantum probability explanation in Fock space for borderline contradictions," Journal of Mathematical Psychology, vol. 58, pp. 1-12, 2014.

[53] D. Aerts and M. Sassoli de Bianchi, "The unreasonable success of quantum probability I: Quantum measurements as uniform fluctuations," Journal of Mathematical Psychology, vol. 67, pp. 51-75, 2015.

[54] A. Khrennikov, "Quantum-like brain: "Interference of minds"," Biosystems, vol. 84, no. 3, pp. 225-241, 2006.

[55] P. Bruza, K. Kitto, D. Nelson and C. McEvoy, "Is there something quantum-like about the human mental lexicon?," Journal of Mathematical Psychology, vol. 53, no. 5, pp. 362-377, 2009.

[56] J. A. de Barros and P. Suppes, "Quantum mechanics, interference, and the brain," Journal of Mathematical Psychology, vol. 53, no. 5, pp. 306-313, 2009.

[57] D. Aerts, J. Broekaert, L. Gabora and S. Sozzo, "Quantum structure and human thought," Behavioral and Brain Sciences, vol. 36, no. 3, pp. 274-276., 2013.

[58] S. Kak, "Biological memories and agents as quantum collectives," NeuroQuantology, vol. 11, pp. 391-398, 2013.

[59] I. Aleksander and B. Dunmall, "Axioms and Tests for the Presence of Minimal Consciousness in Agents," Journal of Consciousness Studies, vol. 10, 2003.

[60] R. A. Moreno, "ConsScale Generic Calculator," ConsScale, January 2016. [Online]. Available: http://www.conscious-robots.com/consscale/calc_30.html. [Accessed 15 January 2018].

[61] R. A. Moreno, A. L. Espino and A. S. d. Miguel, "ConsScale: A Plausible Test for Machine Consciousness?," in Nokia Workshop on Machine Consciousness, 2008.

[62] R. Arrabales, A. I. L. Espino and A. S. d. Miguel, "ConsScale: A Pragmatic Scale for Measuring the Level of Consciousness in Artificial Agents," Journal of Consciousness Studies, vol. 17, no. 3-4, pp. 131-164, 2010.

[63] R. Arrabales, A. Ledezma and A. Sanchis, "ConsScale FPS: Cognitive Integration for Improved Believability in Computer Game Bots," in Believable Bots, Springer, Berlin, Heidelberg, 2012, pp. 193-214.

[64] S. Gull, "Development of Seed Knowledge Representation Technique and Method for the Transformation of Human Explicit Knowledge to Machine's Instinctive Knowledge," Department of Computer Science, Government College University, Lahore, 2014.

[65] P. Ekman, "Basic Emotions," in The Handbook of Cognition, M. Power and T. Dalgleish, Eds., Sussex, John Wiley & Sons, Ltd, 1999, pp. 45-60.

[66] R. Manzotti and V. Tagliasco, "From behaviour-based robots to motivation-based robots," Robotics and Autonomous Systems, vol. 51, no. 2-3, pp. 175-190, 2005.

[67] S. A. Raza, "Ontogenetic & phylogenetic control in conscious Robots," Department of Computer Science, Government College University, Lahore, 2010.

[68] M. Gillani, "Machine Dreams: A Quantum Computational Approach to Model Dreams for QuBIC based Cybernetic Agents.," Lahore, 2011.

[69] S. T. S. Bukhari, "Modeling and Simulation of Emotion-Based Imagination in Cognitive Machines," Lahore, 2014.

[70] S. T. S. Bukhari, A. Kanwal and W. M. Qazi, "Machine Imagination: A Step Towards the Construction of Artistic World Through Storytelling," in 2nd EAI International Conference on Future Intelligent Vehicular Technologies,(2017), Islamabad, 2018, in-press.

[71] "iCub - an open source cognitive humanoid robotic platform," 2004. [Online]. Available: http://www.icub.org/. [Accessed 15 January 2018].

[72] S. Franklin and M. Ferkin, "An Ontology for Comparative Cognition: A Functional Approach," Comparative Cognition & Behavior Reviews, vol. 1, pp. 36-52, 2006.

[73] A. M. Treisman and G. Gelade, "A Feature-Integration Theory of Attention," Cognitive Psychology, vol. 12, pp. 97-136, 1980.

[74] B. J. Baars, "In the Theatre of Consciousness : Global Workspace Theory, A Rigorous Scientific Theory of Consciousness.," Journal of Consciousness Studies, vol. 4, no. 4, pp. 292-309, 1997.

[75] W. M. Qazi, S. T. S. Bukhari, J. A. Ware and A. Athar, "Neural Coorelates," Project NiHA, 2018. [Online]. Available: http://www.projectniha.org/niha-neuralcorrelate/. [Accessed 15 January 2018].

[76] A. L. Paraense, K. Raizer, S. M. Paula, E. Rohmer and R. R. Gudwin, "The cognitive systems toolkit and the CST reference cognitive architecture," Biologically Inspired Cognitive Architectures, vol. 17, pp. 32-48, 2016.

[77] S. Franklin and F. P. Jr., "The Lida Architecture: Adding New Modes of Learning to an Intelligent, Autonomous, Software Agent," in Integrated Design and Process Technology,, Society for Design and Process Science, 2006.

[78] "Task Parallel Library (TPL)," Microsoft, 03 March 2017. [Online]. Available: https://docs.microsoft.com/en-us/dotnet/standard/parallel-programming/task-parallel-library-tpl. [Accessed 15 January 2018].

[79] Project NiHA, 2018. [Online]. Available: http://www.projectniha.org/. [Accessed 15 January 2018].

International Academy, Research, and Industry Association (IARIA)
412 Derby Way
Wilmington, DE 19810

CURRAN ASSOCIATES INC.
proceedings.com

ISBN 978-1-5108-6134-3
9 781510 861343